REVELATION AND THE GOD OF ISRAEL

Revelation and the God of Israel explores the concept of revelation as it emerges from the Hebrew Scriptures and is interpreted in Jewish philosophy and theology. The first part is a study in intellectual history that attempts to answer the question, what is the best possible understanding of revelation? Norbert M. Samuelson draws on his extensive knowledge of western philosophy and explores the conception of the God of revelation as classical or medieval Jewish philosophers such as Maimonides and modern Jewish theologians such as Buber and Rosenzweig subsequently interpreted it. The second part is a study in constructive theology which asks whether it is reasonable to affirm belief in revelation. Here Samuelson focuses on the challenges given from a variety of contemporary academic disciplines, including evolutionary psychology, political ethics, analytic philosophy of religion, and source-critical studies of the Bible. This important book offers a unique approach to theological questions and fresh solutions to them and will appeal to those interested in the history of philosophy, religious thought, and Judaism.

NORBERT M. SAMUELSON is the Harold and Jean Grossman Chair of Jewish Studies and Full Professor of Jewish Philosophy in the Religious Studies Department at Arizona State University. He is an internationally renowned scholar of Jewish philosophy and the author of six books including *Judaism and the Doctrine of Creation* (Cambridge, 1994) and most recently *A User's Guide to Franz Rosenzweig's Star of Redemption* (1999). He has published over 200 articles and is the co-editor of three collected volumes of essays. Professor Samuelson is the founder and secretary of the Academy of Jewish Philosophy.

REVELATION AND THE GOD OF ISRAEL

NORBERT M. SAMUELSON

Arizona State University

CAMBRIDGE
UNIVERSITY PRESS

PUBLISHED BY THE PRESS SYNDICATE OF THE UNIVERSITY OF CAMBRIDGE
The Pitt Building, Trumpington Street, Cambridge, United Kingdom

CAMBRIDGE UNIVERSITY PRESS
The Edinburgh Building, Cambridge CB2 2RU, UK
40 West 20th Street, New York, NY 10011-4211, USA
477 Williamstown Road, Port Melbourne, VIC 3207, Australia
Ruiz de Alarcón 13, 28014 Madrid, Spain
Dock House, The Waterfront, Cape Town 8001, South Africa

http://www.cambridge.org

BM
610
.S28
2002

First published 2002

Printed in the United Kingdom at the University Press, Cambridge

Typeface Baskerville Monotype 11 / 12.5 pt.   *System* LATEX 2$_\varepsilon$ [TB]

A catalogue record for this book is available from the British Library

Library of Congress Cataloguing-in-Publication data
Samuelson, Norbert Max, 1936–
Revelation and the God of Israel / Norbert M. Samuelson.
p.   cm.
Includes bibliographical references and index.
ISBN 0 521 81202 x
1. God (Judaism)   2. Revelation (Jewish theology)   3. Philosophy, Jewish.   I. Title.
BM610 .S28   2002   296.3′115–dc21   2001052957

ISBN 0 521 81202 x hardback

To my beloved Angelica

"There was (a conversation) where he bet I couldn't tell him anything that was absolutely true. So I said to him, 'God is love.'"

"And what did he say?"

"He said, 'What is God? What is love?'"

"Um."

"But God really is love, you know," said Miss Faust, "no matter what Dr. Hoenikker said."

From Cat's Cradle by Kurt Vonnegut

Contents

vii

Acknowledgments

Let me begin by expressing my appreciation to the staff of Cambridge University Press – especially to Kevin Taylor for his willingness to support this kind of serious project in constructive Jewish philosophy, and to Jan Chapman for her detailed and rigorous editing of the manuscript. This book is the product of more than a decade of conversations with a number of academics in a variety of disciplines. Many of them are active members of the Academy for Jewish Philosophy. I would like to single out for mention Jean Cahan (University of Nebraska), Elliot Dorff (University of Judaism), Richard Gale (University of Pittsburgh), Ze'ev Levy (University of Haifa), David Novak (University of Toronto), Peter Ochs (University of Virginia), Heidi Ravven (Hamilton College), and Kenneth Seeskin (Northwestern University).

Equally important to my thinking have been two workshops on Science and Judaism that I sponsored at Arizona State University in 1999 and 2000 with funds provided by the Harold and Jean Grossman chair for Jewish studies and with assistance from the chairs (Joel Gereboff and James Foard) and staff (Patricia Friedman and Melanie Hunyady) of the Religious Studies Department. Dialogue with the contemporary life sciences is a critical part of this study of revelation, and my particular dialogue partners included Carl Feit (Biology, Yeshiva University), Elliot Goldstein (Zoology, Arizona State University), Fred Grinnell (University of Texas Southwestern Medical Center), Kenneth Kendler (Psychiatry, Virginia Commonwealth University), Kenneth Mossman (Microbiology, Arizona State University), Robert Russell (Physics and Christian Theology, Graduate Theological Union), and Solomon Schimmel (Psychology, Boston Hebrew College). Other scholars of Judaica involved in these dialogues and from whom I learned included Kalman Bland (Duke University), Bernard Levinson (University of Minnesota), Elliot Wolfson (New York University), and especially two of my former Temple University graduate students – William Grassie

(Philadelphia Center for Religion and Science) and Julius Simon (University of Texas El Paso).

I am deeply appreciative of the generosity of all of the above friends and scholars for sharing their time, their knowledge, and their intellect with me in my pursuit. However, the single scholar who has been most generous in all of these respects has been my wife, Hava Tirosh Samuelson (History, Arizona State University). I know that the best of what I have to say on almost every topic in this book is a result of our private almost continuous dialogue.

Introduction

This book is a constructive study of the concept of revelation as it emerges from the Hebrew Scriptures and is interpreted in Jewish philosophy. The first part of the book is an attempt to answer the question, what is the best possible understanding of what revelation is? "Best possible" here means most detailed and most coherent in its details. As such, the first part is a study in intellectual history. Special attention is given to the conception of the God of revelation in the Hebrew Scriptures as classical or medieval Jewish theological philosophers, such as Moses Maimonides, and modern Jewish philosophical theologians, such as Martin Buber and Franz Rosenzweig, subsequently interpret it. Its conclusion is the formulation of the concept of revelation that will be the subject for the second part.

The second part of the book is a critical study of the concept of revelation in the light of possible challenges to its affirmation from contemporary academic disciplines. It is an attempt to answer the question, is it reasonable to affirm belief in revelation? What "reasonable belief" means is in itself somewhat complex and will be discussed within the body of the book, especially in the concluding chapter. As such, the second part is a study in the philosophy of religion. For now, suffice it to say that a particular belief is "reasonable" if it is logically coherent and there is no contrary belief whose probability is greater. Just what "probable" means here will also be discussed as well as how on different topics probability is to be determined. With specific reference to the concept of revelation, the discipline that offers contrary beliefs that profess to have greater probability is evolutionary psychology. Attention also has to be paid to issues about the morality of revelation in political ethics, the existence and nature of God in philosophy of religion, and the credibility of the Hebrew Scriptures as an authority for reasonable belief in the source-criticism tradition of contemporary academic biblical studies.

This book is a follow-up study in constructive Jewish philosophy to an earlier work entitled *Judaism and the Doctrine of Creation* (Cambridge: Cambridge University Press, 1994). This study of revelation is independent of the creation work in at least two ways. First, the interpretations and positions argued for in this book on revelation should be intelligible to a reader who has not read the creation book. However, that is not to say that the arguments presented in the revelation book are entirely independent of the arguments presented in the creation book. Much is presupposed that is argued in relation to creation that is taken for granted in the presentation of revelation. Not knowing the creation book should not hamper readers in understanding the claims made here, but it will restrict their ability to understand sufficiently the reasons for making many of the claims about revelation. For example, I argue in the creation book that what it means to say that a book of philosophy is "Jewish" is that it is influenced by and compatible with major works in Jewish philosophy. In this sense the philosophy of Spinoza is Jewish, because it is grounded in earlier works of Jewish philosophy, even though his conclusions are, at least with respect to classical Judaism, entirely heterodox. Because of his conclusions Spinoza cannot be read in any sense as a spokesperson for classical Jewish religious thought, even though his work is entirely Jewish. This understanding of "Jewish" is taken for granted here without argument.

This book on revelation, like the earlier book on creation, does not argue to defend positions I hold where such an argument would require detailed textual analysis that I have presented in earlier articles. A case in point in connection with creation is the close similarity between Maimonides' position in the *Guide of the Perplexed* and Plato's *Timaeus*. In this book on revelation the situation will be the same with my presentation of Maimonides' theory of negative attributes. I will assume without argumentation an interpretation close to the one presented by Hermann Cohen. I do so because the argument for my interpretation requires a close, lengthy, and detailed analysis of texts that I have already published. However, in every case where I am conscious that my interpretation does not reflect a scholarly consensus, I will footnote where I have given the required argument in print.

The second way in which this book on revelation is independent of the earlier work on creation is that there are structural differences between the two books. In this revelation book the source texts in Jewish philosophy that are considered are presented chronologically, from the Hebrew Scriptures to Rosenzweig, without any question about the Jewishness of the works. Furthermore, the number of texts considered here is quite diverse, ranging in commentary form over the entirety of the Hebrew Scriptures. The non-Jewish texts considered are equally diverse, ranging from life sciences like biology and psychology to humanistic disciplines such as ethics and political theory. In contrast, the creation book begins by presenting Rosenzweig's position as a best possible contemporary interpretation of Jewish philosophy and then proceeds to consider his position historically in an entirely non-chronological order. There the controlling questions are whether Rosenzweig's views are Jewish and whether they are true. The question of whether or not a work is "Jewish" rests on whether or not the positions developed, whatever they are, are developed out of Jewish literary sources. In this sense Rosenzweig's theory of creation was judged to be Jewish because it was grounded in Maimonides' doctrine of creation, which itself was grounded in two sources – Plato's *Timaeus* and the opening chapters of the Book of Genesis in the Hebrew Scriptures – where the *Timaeus* provides a reasonable schema for interpreting the mythic narrative of Genesis.

The critical discipline outside the domain of Jewish texts relevant to claims about creation is astrophysics, where there is a reasonable consensus among scientists about the claims that relate most directly to Jewish religious affirmations about the origin and nature of the universe. The second part of the book on creation simply summarized that consensus and compared its conclusions with the conclusions reached from examining what Jewish philosophical commentators have written about the meaning of the Genesis account of creation. The comparison yielded general coherence except on one and only one significant claim – whether the universe is governed by moral purpose or solely by mechanical chance. The universe that emerges from the Jewish conception of creation is a universe governed by purpose and therefore is subject to moral valuation. It is a universe where knowledge is inherently moral in two senses – first, the act of understanding is itself a moral act, and second, an ethical valuation of a state of affairs in the universe is a necessary component of understanding that state. In contrast, the universe that emerges from the conception of its origin in modern physical cosmology is a world in which everything happens by chance, without any inherent purpose whatsoever, and what counts as knowledge, which also is morally neutral, is a statistical determination of a high degree of conjunction between two otherwise unrelated events. What this conclusion called for was a further study of Jewish philosophical topics in the light of ethics, and that is precisely what this book on the

Jewish conception of revelation does. Why that is so requires a word of explanation.

To focus on the God of creation is to focus on an act of God whose product is the universe as a whole. God perceived from this perspective is clearly transcendent – beyond everything and anything that is – and so much so that it is difficult to imagine how such a deity could be immanent, that is, present to and intimate with anything and everything created. This consequence clearly emerged at the conclusion of my book on creation. The problem was no longer how a contemporary, well read, intelligent individual could believe in the God who created the universe. Rather, the problem was how a deity who made the universe the way that it is could possibly care for, let alone love, any creature in the universe, especially something as lowly and clearly insignificant from a universal perspective as a *Homo sapiens*, let alone a Jewish one. The corrective is to focus instead on God from the perspective of revelation in which God reveals himself as a lover of Israel, and through Israel, of all humanity. What then emerges as problematic is how a God who is such an intimate focused-on-particularity lover can be the God of creation. What will emerge at the conclusion of this book, I hope, is that belief in the utterly immanent God of revelation is no less rationally believable than the utterly transcendent God of creation. What will become problematic, however, is how there can be a single deity who underlies both modes of perception. How can a God whose sole act is directed towards the world as a whole in creation be the same God whose sole act is directed towards the single individual in revelation?

I certainly believe that the deity who creates the universe and the deity who loves the individual is the same deity, and I believe that such a belief is reasonable, but I will not deal with this final theological claim in this book. To find the synthesis, so to speak, we must refocus from the deity of creation and revelation on the God of redemption, and that argument requires (God willing) another book. For now it will suffice if I can show that belief in the God of revelation is believable.

Presumably by the final chapter I will have demonstrated this rational belief. At the end, I want to consider more specifically what it means to claim that a religious belief is reasonable, and, finally, what Jewish philosophy in particular contributes to this general topic of contemporary philosophy of religion.

I will concentrate in this general study of the concept of revelation primarily on Jewish texts, just as I did in my general study of creation, and I will do so for the same reasons. The topic of this book, revelation, qualifies as what can be called "a big question," so big in so many ways that its answers lie in principle beyond anything that can be called certainty. In the case of creation, an equally big question, the data (both literary and empirical) about the creator deity, the created universe, and the relationship between them are sufficiently narrow in range (viz., the physical data of the origin of the universe and three chapters of Genesis with their commentaries) and sufficiently limited in range of possible interpretations that it might even be possible to claim knowledge of creation in some sense of the terms "creation" and "knowledge." However, no comparable claim to knowledge can be made in the case of revelation.

First, the texts to study are too diverse even if I limit attention solely to Jewish texts and contemporary science. The relevant texts within the Hebrew Scriptures alone range through the entire corpus. Certainly the descriptive passages in Exodus of God's many appearances to Moses must be privileged, but so must be Ezekiel's single most extensive description at the beginning of the book attributed to him of what it is like to experience God directly. Furthermore, once vision is extended beyond the obviously relevant biblical texts to rabbinic commentaries on them, studies of the commentaries on the Song of Songs are no less important than commentaries on Exodus and Ezekiel, for the Song of Songs as a love poem was understood by the rabbis to be primarily a parable about God's love of Israel and revelation was taken to be an act of love.

In general, creation is discussed in only a relatively small number of texts, none of which compare in length, detail, and importance to the opening chapters of Genesis, whereas revelation is a theme that runs through the entire Hebrew Scriptures and no single text has privileged status in terms of either detail or importance. Hence, epistemic claims about revelation will be structurally weaker than epistemic claims about creation.

Second, whereas the counterpart of biblical creation in modern science is the conception of the origin of the universe in physical cosmology and astrophysics, there is no single science whose subject matter corresponds to revelation. Revelation is a relation between God and individual human beings in which communication takes place. The relevant sciences in this case include both life and communication sciences, all of which have a certain degree of independence from each other and all of which make reasonable but significantly different claims about the same thing. In physics there is a reasonable consensus on how the universe began, but there is no comparable consensus in the life sciences on what a human being is and in the communication sciences on what information is. Hence, choices about what one needs to consider in making reasonable judgments about belief in revelation are far more complex than those in making reasonable judgments about belief in creation.

Third, the difference is no less complicated in terms of epistemic authority than it is in terms of diverse fields of interest. What physics studies is relatively simple. The distances between the objects considered, be they as small as subatomic particles or as large as galaxies, are sufficiently great that the problems of relationship can be translated into fairly simple interactions between two relatively isolated points. No such luxury of simplicity is available in terms of discussing relationships between human beings. Hence, in the life sciences claims of reasonableness are judged by a considerably lower standard than they are in the physical sciences and this necessarily lower standard is in itself a problem for religious belief. If some people object that it is wrong to judge religious belief by the light of scientific claims because the source of religious beliefs is certain (viz., from divine revelation) whereas the source of scientific claims is less than certain (viz., from human discovery), one can (and should) counter that the interpretation of what revelation means is no less a human (and therefore uncertain) activity than is science, and the degree of probability as well as consensus is so high in the case of physics that it is reasonable, even for "persons of faith" to take seriously the claims of physics in determining the nature of their religious beliefs about creation. However, there is no comparable level of epistemic authority of claims in the life sciences, especially those that are most relevant to interpretations of revelation, namely the computational sciences and evolutionary psychology.

Why then, it can be argued, should we take science seriously at all and not rely for our "reasonable" belief on our traditional texts? It is an important question, the answer to which rests on a clearer understanding of what it means to claim that a belief is reasonable. It is one major theme that will be dealt with throughout this book, especially in chapter 7 and in the conclusion.

My decision to focus almost exclusively on Jewish texts was defended in the creation book in terms of general methodological principles. Implicit in that argument was the assumption that there really is no such thing as "religion" in general, but only "religions" in the particular, so that the study of religion should proceed in terms of religions rather than in terms of some abstract entity called religion that has no existence in reality.

If this conclusion is true, results from studying Jewish texts should yield significantly different results than from studying the corresponding texts about revelation in other religious traditions. That there is a significant difference will be in itself an important consequence, since it would entail a strong recommendation about how to study the philosophy of religion, that is, as studies of philosophies of religions. I will return to this methodological issue at the conclusion of the book.

The God of revelation

CHAPTER I

The God of Israel

EQUIVOCALITIES

"Revelation"

Revelation, in its most general theological meaning, is a relationship between God and human beings in which communication takes place. As a form of relationship the word's meaning depends on the terms of the relationship – God and human beings. For Judaism the human beings involved are the Jewish people, the deity is in some significant sense identifiable with what the Hebrew Scriptures describe as "the God of Abraham, Isaac, and Jacob," and the content of communication between what these terms designate is called "Torah." Therefore, Judaism involves essentially an affirmation of the claims that God revealed himself to the Jewish people, and the Torah expresses that relationship. What this sentence means, however, is not in itself clear. Who is this God who reveals himself and who are the Jewish people who receive the communication? On how these two questions are answered depends what claim is being made and whether or not it is reasonable to affirm it. In this chapter I will focus exclusively on the meaning of the term "God."

"God"

When people say "God" they mean many different things, not all of which are coherent. One important reason for the unclarity is that the word, which plays a central role in all expressions of the three Abrahamic religions (Judaism, Christianity, and Islam), has a long history of development, and through this history the meaning of the term has changed. A second reason for the unclarity is that the word "God" is used in every stage of its history with relationship to three kinds of activity – creating, revealing, and redeeming – and these activities are not necessarily consistent. Whatever the view is of God in general, the deity affirmed as the sole deity worthy of worship in these religions is the creator of the world, the revealer of sacred scriptures, and the redeemer of humanity. For Judaism, at least God as the creator is revealed both through the Hebrew Scriptures (especially the opening chapters of Genesis) and through nature (especially physical cosmology and cosmogony). The deity known in this way is a God of natural law whose will, identifiable with that law, is concerned equally with every creature, without differentiation, and primarily with the whole rather than any of its parts, be they animal, mineral, or vegetable. Hence, this is a deity knowable primarily as a God of justice.

In contrast, God as the revealer is known through the words of the Hebrew Scriptures and the tradition of the interpretation of those words in biblical commentaries (midrash). This deity is a God of moral law whose will, identifiable with that law, has special concern for the Jewish people, with whom he has a special love relationship, comparable to that of a loving spouse or parent. Hence, this is a deity knowable primarily as a God of love. Whether or not it is coherent to claim that the same being is both the deity of universal law and the deity of concrete love is not obvious, and much of the discussion of theology in rabbinic texts deals with ways to reconcile these two characterizations of God.

What there is to say about God as the redeemer, who is revealed for the Jewish people primarily (but not exclusively) in the words of communal liturgy, rests on how God the creator and God the revealer are reconciled. In some sense creation must be imperfect, for if it were not there would be no need for redemption. Hence, whatever is the view of God in this tradition, it must make sense of God willing into existence something that needs, and therefore lacks, perfection. Similarly, the divine revelation of the Torah is in some sense a blueprint or program for human behavior whose goal is to bring about a perfection which, in some sense, God cannot bring about without human help. Hence, whatever is the view of God in this tradition, it must make sense of a God who desires something to be that the deity alone cannot bring about.

There are many ways to solve these problems and not all of them are consistent with each other. Which paths of thinking to choose depends on other factors, and it is the "other factors" that have determined the history of change in theology in Judaism, Christianity, and Islam. The sacred scriptures in all three religions say something about God and humanity, but not enough in themselves to answer our questions. The questions themselves are essentially philosophical, and, to be answered, they need to be situated in a broader philosophical context of meaning. God is the creator and redeemer of the world. What that means depends on what the world is. Different ontologies, that is, different judgments about the nature of what is, necessarily will invoke different understandings of what it means for a world to be created or redeemed or both. Hence, the history of theology is inseparable from the history of philosophy, for, as philosophy changes through time, so does theology. The same is true of God the revealer, for changes in what philosophy thinks it means to be human will affect what it means for humanity to receive divine revelation. Hence, ultimately the two reasons given above for the ambiguity of our use of the term "God" are inseparable. The foundation of our views about God and revelation rests on words of claimed sacred texts whose meaning presupposes a philosophical context that undergoes change. As the philosophy changes, so do the determinations by thinking Jews, Christians, and Muslims of what it means to say "God," and "God revealed."

I want now to briefly outline the history of the use of the term "God," but, before I begin, I want to simplify my mode of expression. First, I want to talk only about Judaism and not about the three Abrahamic religions. Much, if not all, of what I have to say about God applies as much to Christianity and Islam as it does to Judaism. However, my perspective in this book comes primarily from rabbinic texts, and it is just shorter to say "Judaism" or "the rabbis," or "the Jewish people" than it is to say always "the Abrahamic religions" or "Jews, Christians, and Muslims." Hence, from this point on I will limit what I say to the deity of Judaism, in recognition that the deity so designated is also the God of the Christians and the Muslims. To be sure, there are theological differences between the three religions, but those have to do more with how God revealed himself to different peoples than how God is to be conceived of. This identity claim needs significant qualification, but that will not be of concern in this book.

Second, I have been avoiding the use of pronouns in referring to God, and to do so is awkward. The avoidance is intended to make at least my initial statements about the God of Judaism gender neutral. The Hebrew Scriptures, as well as all pre-twentieth-century Jewish literature, refer to God as "he," or "him." However, in much of this literature it is clear that God is not conceived of as a male, at least not in any physical sense. (The deity of the Kabbalah is said to have genitals, but clearly the deity of Jewish philosophy does not, and no explicit statement in the Hebrew Scriptures talks about God's genitalia, despite the fact that they say that God has other body parts – hand, face, finger, back, and so forth.)

There are a number of ways to express gender neutrality in English besides avoiding pronouns. One way is to say "she" and "her," but, except for the sake of political balance, I do not see why suggesting that God is female is preferable to suggesting that God is male. Another way is to say "it," but this seems to me worse than using either male or female pronouns, since it suggests that God is not a person. Such language would work in some discussions of God the creator where at least divine will is closely associated with natural law, but it seems totally inappropriate, at least misleading, in discussions of God the revealer as a lover. Even worse is to use the plurals "they" and "them," which suggest that there are multiple deities. (I will not even do so when the Hebrew term used is *elohim*, whose form is plural, but clearly whose meaning has never been understood, in rabbinic literature at least, to express a plural.) Another way would be to alternate between "he/him" and "she/her," which I find confusing, for it is often not clear that the intended referent in successive sentences is the same entity. I see no other options available. Hence, from now on I will use "he" and "him" in speaking about God, especially when I am describing Hebrew texts where the terms used to identify God (notably, *el* and the Tetragrammaton) are masculine. However, there will be some occasions when I will use the feminine singular, in cases in which the intended Hebrew term is feminine (notably *shechinah*, which I will translate as "divine presence").

A HISTORY OF "GOD"

With both of these qualifications in mind, I will now give a brief history of the use of the term "God" in rabbinic Judaism. I do so to isolate different meanings of the term which will influence different understandings of the term "revelation."

The deity of the Hebrew Scriptures

The foundational text for discussing what Judaism has to say about the God of revelation is the Hebrew Scriptures. However, it is not a single text, even by traditional standards. It is an edition formed from many different works written at different times by different authors. The ancient rabbis assumed that everything included in this work is in some sense the word of God even if God is not their author. Some of the books are records of unstated authorship of Israel's history (for example, the books of Joshua, Judges, first and second Samuel, first and second

Kings, and first and second Chronicles). Other non-historical books are attributed to ancient heroes (for example, Solomon is said to be the author of the Song of Songs, Proverbs, and Ecclesiastes; David is said to have authored many of the Psalms). Others are said to be the word of prophets who claim to be repeating what God communicated to them directly. However, among them the Torah proper, namely the five books attributed to the prophet Moses, stands out as paradigmatic in authority. The Torah is both historical and non-historical in content, containing a history of the universe from its creation up to the time when the Israelites are mobilized to conquer the land of Canaan, as well as a constitution for the nascent nation. Authorship in this case is attributed to God himself, revealed to the Israelites through the mediation of the most esteemed of all prophets, Moses.

Modern scholars go well beyond the rabbis in questioning the unity of the Hebrew Scriptures. While the rabbis attributed different authorship to different books, modern scholars question the unity of the sources in each book. The words of the prophets are not seen to be the words of single prophets, but the words of many inspired individuals collected together as if they had a single authorship. This is especially true in the case of the five books of Moses. Hence, there is no reason to think that the views reflected in these works reflect the thought of a single mind. The rabbis also, despite the fact that they attributed greater unity to these Scriptures, isolated and discussed at least apparently conflicting views within these foundational texts. Still, because they believed that all of them express the mind and will of the God of Israel, they thought that the content given was coherent and consistent, and they interpreted the words of the texts on the assumption that with appropriate care in reading they would yield a single true meaning. There is no need to decide this question here. Whatever their origins, most of the books in the final edited version of the Hebrew Scriptures[1] do seem to yield a consistent view of God, and it is that view that I will look at here.

God first appears in the Hebrew Scriptures with a definite description but not with a proper name. The general description is *ha-elohim*, which literally means "the deity." The term *elohim* is a masculine plural form whose meaning is sometimes "judges" but usually means a god. The God of the Scriptures first appears as a member of the class of gods, but

---

[1] Most but not necessarily all. The Book of Proverbs, which seems to identify God with "Wisdom," stands out as a likely exception to the way that I will talk about the deity of the Hebrew Scriptures below.

is identified as the only (proper) member of the class. There may be in theory other gods, but this one and this one alone is the only real one.

What he is doing at his first appearance is creating the world. The details of that creation are not of concern here.[2] What is important is that he creates by uttering commandments. Like the ideal ruler that he is, he speaks, and what he says is taken by his subjects to be a command that they are obligated to fulfill. His first subjects are space (which becomes divided into regions of light and dark), and earth and water (which become separated into distinct regions, separated by a sky [*raki'a*] into earth and sky, and, on earth, seas and dry land). He himself wills lights into existence, which he sets in the sky, which he commands the sun to govern as his designate. He also commands the earth to generate life forms upon it, and he tells one of the forms, the human, to govern the earth as the sun governs the sky. At the end of this process he calls the whole product "good," which seems to mean well ordered and structured into clearly differentiated domains. In general, God prefers order over disorder, and he associates separation with order and transcending separations with disorder.

The God of creation who has a definite description ("the God," *ha-elohim*) has, primarily in his activity as a revealer, a proper name, which we do not know how to speak. The consonants of the name are four letters (the Tetragrammaton) – *yod*, *he*, *waw*, *he* – but we do not know what vowels go with it. By tradition this was a secret passed on from Moses and Aaron through the line of high priests of the Temple, but knowledge of that pronunciation disappeared after the Romans destroyed the second Temple. It is traditional to say in Hebrew "my lord" (*adonai*), as in "my lord and master," as if it were a proper name, and I will follow that tradition here. Hence, "*adonai*" will be used as a proper name for the deity of the Hebrew Scriptures.

The usage is not consistent, but generally it can be said that it is the impersonal deity, identified through a definite description, *ha-elohim*, who acts in relationship to the world as its creator, and it is the personal deity, identified with a proper name, *adonai*, who relates to his creatures by revelation. What is revealed are commandments. God speaks, sometimes in imperatives (as in "Be fruitful and multiply") and sometimes in cohortatives (as in "Let us make the human in our image"), and his statements function as commandments to those addressed. Generally, what God commands is that things be separate from each other. At creation earth

² See N. Samuelson, *Judaism and the Doctrine of Creation* (Cambridge: Cambridge University Press, 1994).

and sky, dry land and the seas, and the week days and the Sabbath day are made separate. Next God separates a garden in Eden from the rest of the earth, as well as two trees (one of the knowledge of good and evil and another of immortality) from the other trees in the garden. The first sin, which here means violation of what God says, occurs when the human female leads the human male to cross over the line separating the two trees in the garden from the others. The human offspring in later generations will commit another major separation prohibition when they attempt to form a bridge between the earth and sky by building a tower at Babel.

This *adonai* who is *ha-elohim* will make more separations through the course of the narrative of the Torah. At creation he separates the earth from the sky, and on the earth he separates the human from the other animals. We are not told why of all the life forms that the earth generates (following God's command) the human is special except that he is made in God's image. Somehow the human is more like God than any other creature, but we are not told what this means. In any case, he does seem to be special in the number of commandments he is given by God. The human, like the sun, is given a domain to govern. Every life form from the earth, including the human, is commanded to procreate, presumably without limitation, so that the more offspring produced the better in the eyes of God.

Procreation seems to be all that other animate entities are obligated to do. However, human responsibility to God does not end here. There are, for example, implied obligations – such as not killing brothers, as the first human's son Cain did to his brother Abel. These special human responsibilities to the creator are revealed to Noah, the true first man (since all subsequent humans are generated solely through his line, the others dying out in the flood), as a set of laws that by tradition are seven in number. One of these duties, the commandment to procreate, human beings share in common with all living things. It is, as it were, their unity. But the remaining six duties are distinctly applicable to humans. They are, as it were, their difference. In general the biblical narrative distinguishes species not by biology but by political ethics or, more precisely, by commandments that define the purpose of the species in the politically understood domain of God's universe.

Before the first of the five books of Moses is completed God will also separate Semites from the rest of humanity. Semites are different from other people as people are different from animals. People have six divine commandments not shared by animals. Semites have an eighth commandment, uttered by God through Abraham. Semites, unlike other people, are to circumcise their male children.

Subsequently, in the remaining books of the Pentateuch, further separations will be introduced. After Sinai the people Israel will be rendered different from all other peoples of the earth by a law code to which they and they alone are obligated. Rabbinic tradition will list these laws, not so numbered within the Bible itself, as 613, of which eight are shared in common with fellow Semites. Furthermore, subsets of people will be separated through divine command within the nation Israel as well. Most importantly, the tribe of Levites will be separate from all other tribes to administer the government of the nation Israel as well as to administer the Temple, and among the Levites the priests (*cohanim*) will become further differentiated.

Nor is it just people whom God separates. We have already noted that at creation light is separated from dark as are sky and earth. On earth the land of Israel will be separated from all other lands; within Israel Jerusalem will be separated; within Jerusalem Mount Zion will be separated; on the Mount the site of God's Temple will be separated; and within the Temple the Holy of Holies will be separated.

Each separation constitutes a distinction between holy and profane that is associated with good and evil. There is holy time – it is the seventh day. There is holy space – it is the Holy of Holies in the Temple on Mt. Zion in Jerusalem in the land of Israel. There is a holy language (at least according to subsequent rabbinic tradition) – it is Hebrew. And there is a holy people – Israel. Whether or not these distinctions are based on any objective criteria is not revealed in the Scriptures themselves. We are not told what makes either the people or the land of Israel better than other peoples and lands. (These are questions to be considered later when I turn to the concept of the human.) They clearly are not objectively better by any recognizable moral criteria. In fact they may be worse. All that is clear is that they are "better," in the sense that they are uniquely holy, where "holy" means something to be kept separate in the distinct service of God.

Note that so far in discussing who God is I have focused solely on what he says, which in his case seems to be all that there is to say about him. What he does seems to be identical with what he says, since, once again on the model of the perfect ruler, he acts by commands that others, his subjects, carry out. We are told nothing else. The text of the Scriptures read by and large as the work of someone who is blind, for the images are almost exclusively auditory. The references to vision in description are relatively few, and, in the case of God, almost entirely non-existent. We are told that God has physical parts – a hand, a face, a back, a nose, a mouth, eyes, and so forth.

The closest thing to an actual description of God occurs in the opening chapter of the Book of Ezekiel. There we are given what is the most graphic visual description in all of the Bible. Ezekiel, sitting in exile on the banks of the Euphrates, sees a storm cloud approaching which takes on in his eyes the shape of the tabernacle of the recently destroyed first Temple. He sees four winged creatures that move by means of unattached wheels filled with eyes. Above the creatures, studded everywhere with the colors of lightning, there is a throne, above which is the image of a man. But none of this is, we are told, God. In fact none of it is definitely anything at all. It is an image of a likeness of something that seems to be a chariot, upon which is a throne, upon which sits a man. And even this image of a likeness is not of God. Rather it is only a focus, like the burning bush from which Moses first encountered God, from which emerges a divine commanding voice. It is the voice and only the voice that is God – a voice that is located in time and located in space, but is not itself anything spatial. Clearly he is nothing visual. Possibly (but not clearly) he is nothing temporal either.

Is the God of the Bible believable?

Can we believe in the deity described above? The word "believe" here is unclear. It can mean that we affirm that he did or does still exist. However, what does it mean to say that a "voice" exists? Does it mean that the children of Israel heard it? Yes, if the story is to be believed. What does it mean to believe the story? Does it mean that the story is history, that it recounts events that in fact took place in the places and at the times stipulated in the story? That, I think, is a question for historians of the Bible. I suspect there is no clear answer to be found. The tendency today is for historians to answer this question in the negative, and that judgment is important when I return later to ask in what sense the Hebrew Scriptures, as a testament of divine revelation, are authoritative. But it is not important here.

The question is not (at least yet), is the Bible believable? Rather, the question is, is the God described in the Bible believable? In a word, the answer is no, if we read the Bible literally. However, neither we nor the ancient rabbis have ever read it that way. I will explain what I mean.

If the modern scholars of the Bible are to be believed, the Hebrew Scriptures are not just a single edited collection, but an edited collection of previous edited collections of previous edited collections. No one is sure where the process begins, but at some early stage we have the edition that becomes our Book of Deuteronomy and that serves as the basis, positive or negative, of what becomes the Pentateuch. These books of Moses form a unity with other books of the Bible some time after the destruction of the first Temple and the first Jewish polity, which in turn form a core for a further edition some time around the destruction of the second Temple and the second Jewish state.

To a large extent these scholarly views stand in direct opposition to the claims of traditional rabbinic Judaism, but the conflict lies in the historical particulars, not in the conclusion. For both the traditional rabbis and the scholars the final edition, whenever it was formed, reflects a Jewish world that is faced with the reality of national and spiritual destruction. One Temple and one state had already been destroyed. At the time of the final editing, a second destruction is either about to occur or already has occurred. No more Temple and no more state. However, taken literally, the biblical narrative suggests that that state and that Temple lie at the core of the *raison d'être* for the existence of the universe.

If we read the Hebrew Scriptures literally, the universe was created so that God could have a Temple in which a nation of priests would daily offer sacrifices to him. Why he should want such sacrifices is for now at least an open question. Why he should need such an elaborate device as an entire universe for the sole purpose of providing him with meals is even more problematic, but that is not an issue here. More important is that if this is in fact the purpose of the existence of the universe, then, with the final destruction of the Temple and its priesthood, there is no longer any reason for the universe to continue to exist. But it does. In fact, the disappearance of the Temple cult seems to have little if any impact on the ordinary, daily operation of the laws of nature, which presumably were set in operation by divine fiat to support the Temple cult.

There is perhaps no clearer example in all of religious history of a religious document subject to the standards of empirical verification, and clearly the Hebrew Scriptures, read literally, fail the test. Again, if the true meaning of the Bible is its literal meaning, then the world exists for the sake of the Temple, so that, if the Temple ceases to exist, there is no reason for the world to continue to exist. Since it does, either the story of the Bible is false or its correct meaning is not literally what it says.

Both rabbinic Judaism and Christianity are consequences of seizing the second option. Both, in very different ways, continued to believe in the Hebrew Scriptures as divine revelation, an affirmation that was credible only because they ceased (if they ever did otherwise) to read those Scriptures literally.

If the Bible does not mean literally what it says, what then does it mean? In a sense, all the texts of rabbinic Judaism are an attempt to construct an answer to this question. My concern here is not with its reading of all of the Bible, but exclusively with how it interpreted what the Scriptures say about God. That is the next topic, as I look at the history of the concept of the God of revelation.

CHAPTER 2

The God of the philosophers

If what the Bible says is not literally what it means, how are we to decide what it means? For the rabbis the parameters of interpretation were set by the following affirmations. First, what it says is true. Hence, any interpretation that is not true is not a correct interpretation. Second, what it says makes intelligible the presumed facts that (a) the deity who revealed himself to the nation Israel's ancient patriarchs – Abraham, Isaac, and Jacob – is the creator of the world, and (b) the world he created is intended by him to become redeemed by means of the religio-political system revealed in the words of the Torah, which (c) he gave to the nation Israel by means of his prophet, Moses. Third, the words of all the other prophets in the Bible are also the words of the same God who revealed the Torah to Moses. Hence, what they say is consistent with what the Torah says.

THE RABBINIC TURN TO PHILOSOPHICAL COMMENTARY

Any interpretation of the Bible that does not contradict the above limits on meaning may be what the Torah in truth says. However, more than one set of interpretations, some of which are not consistent with others, are possible. Hence, logic (which enables us to distinguish what is possible from what is impossible) alone is not enough to determine what God's words mean. Additional help is needed, since it is incumbent upon Israel, in order to fulfill its mission to aid God in redeeming the world, to know precisely what are the truths embedded in the Torah's language. Much assistance is provided by an orally transmitted chain of interpretation that extends unbroken back to the time of the biblical prophets. The rabbis affirmed the truth of this oral rabbinic law no less than they affirmed the truth of the written law of Moses, and this chain further limits the range of possible interpretation, especially in practical matters, in questions about what people ought to do. However, even the oral tradition is in itself insufficient to determine with precision what the Torah means, especially in theoretical matters, in questions about what the world in fact was, is, and will be.

The critical judgments here are that the domain of what is possible is larger than the domain of what is true, that logic alone can only determine what is possible, and that the oral tradition is not by itself completely determinate of the truth. Something else is needed, namely, a discipline that can determine truth in the concrete. By at least the tenth century CE, and probably much earlier,[1] the rabbis turned for aid to what they identified out of Greek and Roman culture as the wisdom (*sophia*) of a professional class of nascent natural scientists who aspired to the "love of wisdom" (*filosofia*).

Available to the rabbis out of the culture of Judea's Greek and Roman conquerors were different philosophies, some of which were not compatible with others. However, among them the most respected were the philosophic traditions rooted in the written words of Plato and his student Aristotle. Their judgments also were not in perfect agreement, but the rabbis assumed that they were, for a good student like Aristotle would not contradict a good teacher like Plato. Furthermore, they believed that Moses was the teacher of Plato. Hence, as the correct interpretation of the words of Plato and Aristotle must agree, so the correct interpretation of the words of the Hebrew Scriptures must agree with Plato and Aristotle. These rules of textual interpretation gave the rabbis who shared in this love of wisdom – in other words, the Jewish philosophers – confidence that they could determine what precisely, in truth, the words and sentences of the divinely revealed Bible mean, at least at first, that is, in the tenth and the eleventh centuries CE.

As these rabbis read the Scriptures, the Bible informs us about everything. However, "everything" extends far beyond the field of vision of this book. The present concern is solely with how these philosopher-rabbis used a mixture of Platonic and Aristotelian philosophy to interpret what the Bible says about God the creator, revealer, and redeemer.

In answering this question I will focus primarily on the words of Maimonides (Moses ben Maimon, also called Rambam),[2] especially in

---

[1] The biblical Book of Proverbs has already been identified as such a work. Even if it is not, the use of philosophy to interpret the Bible begins with Philo (Alexandria, Egypt, about 20 BCE to about 50 CE), and there is no reason to believe that he was the only such interpreter of his times from the mere fact that no other writings of this kind have survived.

[2] 1135–1204, born in Cordova and died in Cairo.

his *Guide of the Perplexed*.[3] I will do so for the following reasons: first, with the sole exception of Gersonides (Levi ben Gershon),[4] no other Jewish philosopher tells us more about who God is than Maimonides, and everything that Gersonides says presupposes Maimonides' words, especially in the *Guide*; second, no other Jewish theologian compares with Maimonides in influence, including Gersonides, both with Jews and non-Jews.

THE THEOLOGY OF MAIMONIDES[5]

GOD THE CREATOR

"The first mover"

Maimonides' central focus is to explain what it means to say that God is the creator, which he interprets on the model of Aristotle's account of a first mover. For Aristotle anything that undergoes change, which he calls "motion,"[6] must have a "mover," something that is the immediate or proximate cause of the motion. The mover is either the thing moving or something else. If it is something else, there must also be a cause of the mover's motion, which again is either itself or something else, and so forth. If this chain of causes is not to be endless, there must be a

---

[3] *Dalalah al-chairin*. Hebrew translation by Joseph Bahir David Kapach (Jerusalem: Mosad ha-rav kook, 1072). English translation by Shlomo Pines (Chicago: University of Chicago Press, 1963). Henceforth referred to as *Guide*.

[4] 1288–1344, born in Languedoc.

[5] The interpretation of Maimonides' theology presented here draws heavily on more detailed discussions of Maimonides' words in my earlier articles. The most relevant of them is "Divine Attributes as Moral Ideals in Maimonides' Theology," in Ira Robinson, Lawrence Kaplan, and Julien Bauer (eds.), *The Theology of Maimonides: Philosophical and Legal Studies* (Studies in the History of Philosophy 17; Lewiston, Queenston and Lampeter: Edwin Mellen Press, 1991), pp. 69–76. Other relevant essays are: "God: The Present Status of the Discussion," in Steven T. Katz (ed.), *Frontiers of Jewish Thought* (Jerusalem, London, Paris, Buenos Aires and East Sydney: B'nai B'rith Books, 1992), pp. 43–59; "Maimonides' Doctrine of Creation," *Harvard Theological Review* 84,3 (1991), 249–271; and "A Case Study in Jewish Ethics – Three Jewish Strategies for Solving Theodicy," *Journal of Jewish Thought and Philosophy* 5 (1996), 177–190. This interpretation is compatible with other more recent interpretations of Maimonides' theology by Steven Schwarzschild and Kenneth Seeskin, in line with earlier interpretations by Zvi Diesendruck and Samuel Atlas, all of whom agree that Maimonides understands the content of divine attributes to be moral. This interpretation rejects the earlier, more ontological interpretations of Maimonides' theory of divine attributes in Julius Guttman's *Philosophies of Judaism*, English translation by David W. Silverman (Philadelphia: Jewish Publication Society of America, 1964).

[6] Aristotelian terminology will be at first confusing because the words look like words in conventional language but they are not – they are related but not identical. For Aristotle "motion" is any kind of change. Change of place, which is how we use the term in conventional language, is only one kind of motion, namely, "locomotion."

first mover whose motion is self-caused. Such a mover is called a "first mover."

For Aristotle every motion must have a first mover as its cause, for nothing actual in the world can go on for ever. However, there is no obvious reason why it cannot. Behind this claim is another, in this case hidden, assumption, which is that nothing actual, including a temporal chain of events, can be infinite. This presupposition is critical to Aristotelian physics, and, for that reason, it is critical for the way Maimonides interpreted what it means to say that God is the creator.

Infinity

To say that something is "infinite" is not to say that it is very large. Anything merely large is determinate, and, as such, can be attributed to something actual. However, to say that something is infinite is to say that it never comes to an end. For example, the number of natural numbers is infinite, because for every number of which you can think, n, there is always a larger number, n + 1. If the number of these numbers were not infinite, then it would be possible to count all of them, from the lowest (1) to the largest. However, if the number of these numbers is infinite, then there is no largest number. The counting of them would just go on forever.

Anything that is said to be infinite, Aristotle concludes, must be a process that extends indefinitely into the future. However, it cannot be a process that extends indefinitely into the past, because anything in the past is determinate, which means finite. Hence, no causal chain can be infinite with respect to the past. Therefore, every actual thing has a finite chain of causes, which means it has a first mover.

The universe

There is an important exception to Aristotle's belief that nothing in the past can be infinite. It is the universe itself. This judgment is based on his definition of time as the measure of before and after. Time is not something that exists. Rather, it is a way of measuring relative movement of objects such that some are said to be before others (notably their causes), and some are said to be after others (notably their effects). Hence, anything that moves in time necessarily has something before it, for if it did not it would not be in time. Now, the universe is the setting for all temporal events. Therefore, since time has no beginning, the universe has no beginning.

Maimonides sensed that Aristotle's judgments about the infinity of the universe and the necessary finitude of all causal chains seemed inconsistent, which it is. The resolution of this "apparent" incoherence led many interpreters of Aristotle to suggest many explanations. One notable example is to distinguish between horizontal and vertical causal chains.[7] A horizontal chain is a chain of mechanical or efficient causes, such that a pushes b which pushes c, and so on. There is no reason why, they argued, this kind of causation cannot be infinite even into the past, since there is no temporal beginning to the universe. Conversely, a vertical chain is a chain of formal or teleological accounts, such that a happens because of b which happens because of c, and so on. This kind of causation, they argued, must be determinate, for otherwise the causal chain would have no real purpose (because its end could not be realized). This is the sense, they argued, in which Aristotle intended the term "first mover" to be understood. In his physics everything happens for a purpose, and that purpose, more than its immediate or mechanical push, is what we must understand as the cause of the event or thing.

This notion of a first mover as something that is self-caused, where a cause is understood to be the ultimate goal of the motion, is the critical notion in explaining what it means for Maimonides and his fellow Jewish Aristotelians to call God the "creator." God causes everything in the universe, but he does so in a unique way. He does nothing about the things he causes; rather, he thinks about himself, and that self-thinking activity causes the universe.

Simplicity

The universe of Aristotelian physics has at least one first mover. That mover is the end or purpose towards which all motion is directed. As such it must be absolutely simple. I will explain what this means.

The first mover must have a motion of its own, for if it did not it would be no different from anything dead; anything dead is inferior to anything alive, and hence could not be the purpose towards which all living things are directed. However, the motion of a first mover can only have a single motion that never begins nor ends. If it had more than one motion, each motion would have to have different causes, and, because they are different, all but one of them would have to be something other than the first mover, in which case the first mover would not be first. Similarly, that single motion must be invariable, for if it changed, there

---

7 Or, what William L. Rowe calls chains of causes that are "temporally prior" and "causally or perhaps metaphysically prior" to their effects (W. L. Rowe, *The Cosmological Argument* [New York: Fortress Press, 1998], p. 30). Cf. F. C. Copleston, *Aquinas* (Baltimore: Penguin Books, 1955), and Anthony Kenny, *The Five Ways* (New York: Schocken Books, 1969).

would have to be a cause of the change that, again, would have to be something other than the first mover. That there is no change in the motion means that it can have neither a beginning nor an end, for in either case the first mover would have to have changed, in which case, for the same reasons, it would not be first. Hence, whatever it is that a first mover does, it always does it.

The claim for simplicity is even more radical. Not only does a first mover do a single thing, but the thing it does is identical with what it is. If the mover had a motion that was not identical with it, the mover would be complex, for there would be some sense in which it moves and another sense, namely what makes it distinct from its motion, in which it does not move. However, if there is this difference in the first mover, there must be some causes to account for this difference, and, again by the same line of reasoning, the causes would not be the first mover.

Therefore, a first mover is what it does and what it does is a single thing. What then is that "thing"? Whatever it is, it must be the best thing, a kind of activity that is better than any other kind of activity. For Aristotle that action must be thought. Why it should be thought is not self-evident, but, to my knowledge, no one until modern times questioned this assumption. In any case, what the first mover does is think, and what it thinks it thinks invariably all the time, without beginning or end.

What does a first mover think about? It must think about a single object of thought, for if it thought about many things it would have many thoughts. What is this object? Well, it must be something most perfect, for if it thought about anything less perfect, then there could be something else that thinks about something better, and it instead would be the first mover. Hence, the only thing a first mover can think about is itself.

In sum, the universe of Aristotelian physics is a universe in which everything is in motion, and all motion is directed towards an end, the highest or ultimate cause of which is an entity who eternally, without variation, thinks itself. This timeless act of self-thought is the first cause of the universe and everything in it.

It is this notion of a first mover, from the best physics of his day, that provides Maimonides with the conceptual framework to explain what the Bible means when it says that God created the universe. It is a model for explanation. However, it is not the explanation itself. Maimonides uses the concept of a first mover to discuss who God is, but that is not to say that he believed that God is literally the first mover of the universe.

To say so would ignore, in Maimonides' judgment, just how radical is the divine unity entailed by calling God "the creator."

"The One"

Maimonides draws two conclusions from Aristotle's discussion of the notion of a first mover that entail a far more radical interpretation of the uniqueness of God than anything ever intended by Aristotle or his followers when they identified the first mover of physics with the God of theology. The first conclusion is that the difference between a creator and his creatures is so fundamental that there can be no analogy between them. The second is that no intelligible statement can be uttered about God that is informative. Maimonides reasoned as follows.

Analogy

Maimonides tells us, on the authority of Aristotle's logic, that analogies can be made only between things that belong to the same species. A species states what a thing is in terms of two factors – a genus that identifies how the thing defined is like other things, and a specific difference that says how the thing defined is unique, that is, how it is not like the things it is like. Hence, for example, there is no analogy between the proverbial "apples and oranges," because, while they share a common genus (both are fruit and share all the characteristics of fruit as fruit), they are not members of the same species (for some are apples while others are oranges).

Individual oranges are analogous to other oranges, and individual apples are analogous to other apples, but there is no analogy between an orange and an apple. They are only comparable insofar as they are all fruit. Still, being fruit is something, so there is some comparison. However, the more general the difference between things, the less possible is any comparison. Fruits as fruits, for example, cannot be compared with trees as trees, but they can be compared, for example, as vegetative life forms. Similarly, vegetation and animals are comparable as living things, as living things and minerals are comparable as creatures. However, creatures cannot be compared with creators, because there is no more general species to which they both belong. To be a creator is to exist in a certain way, as something whose being is independent of anything other than itself (so that it has necessary being), and to be a creature is to exist in a very different way, as something whose being is dependent on something other than itself (so that it is either necessary solely in virtue of a cause or is a contingent being). Hence, creators and creatures do not share a common genus, for no genus is more general than being. Hence, there is no way to form a valid analogy between the creator deity and his creations, and since there is no analogy, no inferences can be made from one to another.

We do have direct access to information about creatures. In the case of the physical ones, we have sense experiences of them, which our intellects structure as something knowable. Similarly, in the case of non-physical creations – for example, concepts, numbers, and less-than-three-dimensional objects such as geometric figures – we have sense experiences of objects that, according to Aristotelian physics, are unities of being material and being intelligible, the first associated with the principle of matter and the second with the principle of form. From these objects our intellect separates the formal constituents from its material constituents. These isolated forms, according to Aristotelian epistemology (or cognitive science, i.e., according to the Aristotelian theory of knowledge), are the non-physical creations, called "intelligibles," that are the content for all abstract human thought. However, there are no sense experiences of God, for God is not the form of anything.

It might be objected that God is the form of the universe and we have experience of the universe. Why, then, can we not abstract this form from our experience and use it to inform us about God? Because, Maimonides insists (uniquely, I think), we have no experience of the universe as such, but only of what is within the universe, that is, its parts, and no valid analogy can be drawn from the parts of a thing to the whole. Hence, since there is no experience of the universe, even if we could say that God is its form (which Maimonides would deny), we have no knowledge whatsoever of God.

A critical step in this argument for agnosticism is that necessarily God is not physical. I will explain why this claim is made, because it is controversial. The Hebrew Scriptures, as we have seen, made explicit statements about at least parts of what seems to constitute a divine body – his hand, his face, and so forth. Furthermore, actions are ascribed to God which are intelligible to us only as activities of something physical. For example, God ascends and descends. Earlier rabbinic commentators, the authors of the Midrash, raised doubts about these physical attributions to God. However, they did not exclude physical descriptions altogether. God may not literally have a hand, for example, but he does have a hand "so to speak" (*kivyakhol*). Of course it is not clear just what a so-to-speak hand is. It is not a hand, but neither is it not a hand. It is something like a hand. However, Maimonides, as we have seen, rules out the legitimacy of any analogies whatsoever between God and his creations, including human beings, despite the fact that the Hebrew Scriptures tell us that the human was created in his image (Gen. 1:26–27).

In fact some rabbinic commentators before Maimonides (viz., the authors of the *shiur qomah* [the book of the dimensions of the divine body]) went so far as to provide a detailed description of the dimensions and proportions of all of the parts of God's presumed body, and these physical descriptions provided a foundation for centuries of a tradition of theology after Maimonides (viz., the authors of the different texts of the Kabbalah, especially of the *sefer ha-zohar* [the book of enlightenment]) that found in God's physicality the conceptual basis for understanding God, the people Israel, the world, and the relationship between the three.[8]

The reasons for Maimonides' radical departure from the earlier tradition of Midrash have already been stated above. It is a consequence of his understanding of what it means to say that God is the creator and everything else is a creature. The creator is no less than a first cause, and a first cause can be in no sense complex, because anything complex is dependent for its being on the simpler elements from which the complexity is composed. To be physical is to be situated in space, which entails in turn occupying three dimensions – that is, having height, width, and depth – and each of these dimensions, no matter how small, can be divided into different segments. Each dimension is measurable as a line is measurable, and any line segment is divisible into other line segments. Hence, in principle, anything physical is complex, which means that its existence depends on something other than itself. Therefore, nothing physical can be a first mover.

Semantics

The association of prime causation with simplicity accounts for Maimonides' agnosticism in yet another way, one that depends on Maimonides' assumption of the theory of semantics in Aristotle's logic. Aristotle assumed, as did Plato, a reference theory of meaning and a correspondence theory of truth. Words refer to something other than themselves, sentences express relations between words, words mean what they refer to, and sentences are true if the relationship expressed between

---

[8] See Elliot R. Wolfson, "Jewish Mysticism: A Philosophical Overview," in Daniel H. Frank and Oliver Leaman (eds.), *History of Jewish Philosophy* (Routledge History of World Philosophies 2; London and New York: Routledge, 1997), pp. 450–498.

the words in a sentence agrees with the relation that holds between the named referents. Aristotle's model informative mode of speech was the declarative sentence. Grammatically, this kind of expression consists of a subject term (S) connected to a predicate term (P) by a copula ("is"). Hence, the well-formed sentence "S is P" means that something called "S" is related to something different called "P," and the sentence is true if and only if the S-referent and the P-referent are so related.

Aristotle called S referents "substances" and P referents "attributes." Substances exist in and of themselves, while attributes exist in substances as their modifications. Furthermore, substances are concrete or individual, while attributes are abstract or general. Hence, a physical substance (for example, a specific tree) can be located at one and only one space at a time, whereas any of its attributes (for example, brown, woody, green, and leafy) can exist at many places at the same time. Furthermore, the attributes of a substance are the forms which render the substance intelligible (i.e., which in-form it), whereas the substance itself is its forms materialized (and therefore concretized) in space and time.

Plato had claimed that attributes name forms which are single things that exist outside both time and space, and that the connection between them and the substances that exemplify them is an external relationship of imitation, that is, substances are (necessarily) defective imitations in space and time (which is why they must be defective) of the eternal and spiritual (i.e., non-material) forms. Aristotle, primarily for logical reasons,[9] rejected this account, and asserted that the true relationship between substances and forms is not imitation but inherence. Aristotle posits an inherence theory of predication in which predicates name abstract entities (attributes) that actually exist in all of the substances of which the attributes are modifications.

It is Maimonides' acceptance of Aristotle's inherence theory of meaning that makes it impossible for him to admit the possibility of informative statements about God. Such a statement would have the form "God is P," where "P" is a predication of the sort found in earlier rabbinic literature, the prayer book, or (most importantly) the Hebrew Scriptures, such as God is great, good, powerful, and so forth, including God is the creator of the world, the revealer of the Torah, and the redeemer of humanity.

[9] These reasons are not important here. They grow out of Plato's critique in the *Parmenides* of his earlier theory of forms as stated in works such as the *Republic*. Cf. three articles in R. E. Allen (ed.), *Studies in Plato's Metaphysics* (New York: The Humanities Press, 1965): "The Third Man Argument in the Parmenides," by Gregory Vlastos, pp. 231–265; "The Third Man Again," by P. T. Geach, pp. 265–278; and "Postscript to the Third Man: A Reply to Mr. Geach," by G. Vlastos, pp. 279–292.

Given Aristotle's theory of semantics, any such affirmation, taken in its literal sense, would claim that something other than God, namely an attribute, exists in God, and this abstract entity, which is not the substance God, defines him. If true, God would necessarily be complex, because he would be constituted by the attribute in question and whatever else there is that enables the attribute to inhere in the divine substance. Hence, if informative statements can be said of God, no matter what they are, God would be complex, therefore not a first cause, and therefore not the creator of the universe.

The conclusion of these two arguments, from his analysis of both analogy and semantics, means that literally nothing can be said of God that is in any sense informative, including the statements that God exists and is the creator of the universe. However, these denials are based on the presupposition that God does in fact exist as the creator. Hence, there must be some way to talk about God, even if we in principle cannot utter affirmative, declarative sentences whose literal meaning is true. In brief, what we do in these cases is tell stories. Story telling is as close as we can come to using language in an admissible way to communicate information about God. It is really the only way we have to understand what it means to say that God is the creator, the redeemer, and, what is most important for our purposes in this book, the revealer.

GOD THE REVEALER

Maimonides' God is not only identified as the creator of the universe. He is no less a deity who reveals himself. When the biblical Moses first encounters God at the burning bush, God does not say that he is the creator of the world; he says that he is the god of Abraham, Isaac, and Jacob (e.g., Exod. 3:16), which is to say that he is the deity who appeared and spoke (which means, the deity who revealed himself) to the patriarchs of the Jewish people. After the theophany at Sinai this same deity will also have the primary identity as the God who gave (which is to say, revealed) the Torah to Israel.

However, if what it means to say that God created the universe is what Maimonides says it means, how can God also be the God of revelation – to the patriarchs and to the Jewish nation by means of the prophet Moses? There is only one God who must be both. If the explanation of what it means to say God is the creator is not compatible with what it means to say God is the revealer, then the explanation that Maimonides gives cannot be correct.

Yet, clearly, if Maimonides' account of statements about God is cor-rect, we human beings cannot truly understand in principle what it means to say that God revealed the Torah or anything else to Moses or to any other human being. The emphasis here is on the word "truly" as it modifies understanding. There are many ways to understand things, some better than others, and when it is not possible to understand some-thing in the best way – which is to say as something known with certainty and clarity to be the case, as in sound science – it may still be possible to understand it with less certainty and less clarity. One way is to tell a story. This is the way that Maimonides adopts here to explain what it means to call God the revealer. Its justification is rooted in Plato's account of God as the creator.

Telling stories to know the unknowable

Plato's Timaeus – *the story of space*
Plato tells us in the *Timaeus* that Socrates faced such a problem when he tried to explain what space is (ch. 18).[10] Socrates still assumed the theory of knowledge that he spelled out in the *Republic*.[11] There are two ways to understand something – one is by reason and the other is by sense experience. Through reason we can grasp the forms. They can be perceived with precision by the intellect, and what is true of them can be seen to be true with certainty. Conversely, through the five senses we can grasp material entities. They can be perceived vaguely by the imagination through images, and what is true of them can be seen to be true, but not with clarity and not with certainty. Rather, we form beliefs about them which may or may not be true, with varying degrees of uncertainty. Hence, for the Socrates of the *Republic* the universe consists of intelligible forms and sense objects, the former being the subject of knowledge through the rational intellect and the latter being the subject of belief through the imagination. However, the Socrates of the *Timaeus* comes to realize that there is a third kind of entity – space – which is neither a form nor an object, which cannot be known by reason (because it is concrete and not a universal) and cannot be imagined (because it is not something positive that can be directly experienced through

---

[10] For a more detailed account of Plato's use of myth in the *Timaeus* with specific reference to its association with Jewish philosophical cosmology and cosmogony see N. Samuelson, *Judaism and the Doctrine of Creation* (Cambridge: Cambridge University Press, 1994), ch. 6, and Samuelson, "Maimonides' Doctrine of Creation," 249–271.
[11] *The Republic of Plato*. English translation by F. M. Cornford (New York: Oxford University Press, 1945), ch. xxiv, vi, 509d–511b; pp. 221–226 in the Cornford translation.

the senses). What Plato tells us is that, concerning things such as space, we tell stories instead of forming concepts that can be known or images that can be believed to be true. We know that they are not true in any literal sense. However, they are believable as the best way available to us as human beings, given our mental limitations, to grasp what we know exists but is in principle beyond anything of which we can conceive. Plato calls this kind of thinking *"mythos,"* which literally means bastard (i.e., illegitimate) thinking. The cosmogony of the *Timaeus* is itself an example of myth, which tells a story about how the world of space and time came about, because the subject matter of the story, space, is in principle unknowable.

This is not the only instance in which Plato resorts to story telling as a form of explanation. The myth of the cave in the *Republic* is another important example, because this story, more than anything else that Socrates says in this dialogue, is the key to understanding Plato's vision of the nature of the universe and the role of humanity within it.

Maimonides' Guide – two myths of the Torah
Maimonides in the *Guide* follows the example of Plato by resorting to myths, stories, to exhibit the believability of critical doctrines in his Jewish philosophy. This is especially true of his explanation of why the Torah was given and how it can guide human beings toward redemption. The first story is called the myth of the Sabians,[12] and the second is the myth of the Palace.[13]

According to his story, *adam*, the original human, was created as a perfect human. What that means is controversial because what Maimonides says here does not agree completely with what he says in his interpretation of the Bible's garden of Eden story.[14] There, in the garden story, at first *adam* has perfect theoretical knowledge, which deteriorates into mere practical knowledge – knowledge of good and evil – as a result of the fall. Here, in the Sabian story, perfect knowledge is practical wisdom. To my knowledge, scholars of Maimonides have not discussed this apparent contradiction, but it does not seem to me to be difficult to reconcile the two accounts. Perfect theoretical knowledge would involve knowledge of God and the nature of the universe in general – cosmology, cosmogony,

[12] *Guide* III:29–30. See the discussions of the myth in Samuelson, "A Case Study in Jewish Ethics," 177–190, as well as in Howard Kreisel, *Maimonides' Political Thought: Studies in Ethics, Law, and the Human Ideal* (Albany: State University of New York Press, 1999).
[13] *Guide* III:51. See the discussions of this myth in Kreisel, *Maimonides' Political Thought*, and Menachem Marc Kellner, *Maimonides on Human Perfection* (Atlanta: Scholars Press, 1990).
[14] See *Guide* II:30.

and theology – which, as we have seen, transcends human capability. Hence, if *adam* at first had perfect theoretical knowledge, then *adam* was more than a human being. As a human the most perfect knowledge would be perfect practical wisdom, which is what the Sabian story attributes to him. Perhaps, putting the two together, at first *adam* was more than human, and his punishment was that he was reduced to a mere human, albeit a perfect one. Be that as it may, the descendants of the first human, namely a nation of people identified as the Sabians, sought to become more angelic, even divine, by pursuing theoretical wisdom, and that pursuit led to their further fall from perfection. As perfectly human, they sought to become perfect. Instead they became imperfectly human, as are all of their descendants.

Human beings are not deities – neither gods nor angels – who alone have the natural capacity to know God and the universe as a whole. Consequently, the first humans, being perfectly human, never thought about such questions. In their perfection they only thought about what they could know – how to do things within the empirical world – and whatever they thought about, being perfectly human, they thought about correctly. Hence, error had not yet entered the world. They never asked questions like how the world came about, how it will end, and who created it – all of which exceed humanity's natural ability to answer correctly.

As long as humans were perfectly human, they did nothing unnatural. However, human beings, uniquely among God's creatures, have the natural ability to do unnatural things. The most notable example is making tools in order to extend their powers beyond their nature. The most important use of humanity's tool-making capacity is the invention of agriculture. Farming enables people to make land produce more humanly beneficial plants (food) and fewer humanly useless plants (weeds) than the land would produce on its own. Hence, in this respect, farming is unnatural.

The first farmers were Sabians, who therefore were the first of God's creatures to act unnaturally. The Sabians used the model of agriculture to extend their capacities into other areas. They now could ask questions which, as created, they never thought of before – questions such as how the world was created and who created it. In answer to how the world was created, they drew an analogy between the gardens they could create as farmers and the world itself. They reasoned: "Just as this plot of land that we cultivated exhibits an order that points to us as its creator, so the world of nature itself exhibits an order which equally points to a creator." In other words, they correctly inferred that the world, no less than a garden, must have been created by someone. However, this answer raises another, more difficult question, namely, who is the gardener of the world? The question itself is divine and, as such, shows that the Sabians had extended the boundaries of human nature. But it was not extended enough, at least yet, to give a correct answer to the question.

The Sabians looked around the universe that they could perceive to decide what in it was sufficiently majestic to qualify as the creator. The problem was that their search was limited solely to what they could experience with their senses, an approach adequate to solving practical problems but insufficient for finding correct answers to ultimate theoretical questions. Consequently, their answer was false. Having reasonably concluded that nothing in the universe was superior to the stars, they concluded that the stars must be the creator deities, which is wrong.

The answer is more than wrong. It is dangerous, because this mistaken belief is the foundation of idolatry. The Sabians correctly decided, based on their perfect practical wisdom, that the creator of the universe is deserving of worship. However, having misjudged who the creator is, they began to worship not the true creator, but a group of mere creatures, the stars, who in themselves are not worthy of worship. Religion was born, but it was the wrong religion.

The Sabians' set of theoretical beliefs were dangerous, because they led to false religion, and religion spawns morality, collective and individual. Morality rooted in nature (as it had been before the Sabians) or rooted in the dictates of a true religion (one that worships who is truly God) leads to true morality, but morality divorced from nature and rooted in a false religion leads to sin. The original mistake in identifying God produces a false religion (idolatry), which in turn produces a moral code which is not moral but evil. Hence, evil and error enter the created world through the Sabians, a nation of humans whose extension of their nature beyond their humanity makes them, and the rest of the human race who are their descendants, less than human, for they lose the perfection in practical wisdom that they possessed when they left the garden of Eden.

Sin and error spread throughout the human race, which in turn threatens the survival of the earth, because humanity was made its governor at creation. God, therefore, in order to save his creation, the earth, from destruction must intervene into nature to correct his error. What he does at first is produce a flood that destroys all existing life on earth except for a single copy of each species, so that he can begin creation again with generations of species freed from the self-induced unnatural error and sin. He chooses as the sole survivor of humanity a man, Noah, who lacks any accomplishment in thinking. However, his descendants quickly recapture, through their practice of agriculture, their ability to give wrong answers to theoretical questions, which in turn produces idolatry and sin, once again threatening the survival of creation in general.

All living things strive to become better, which in the case of humanity means to strive to become something divine, something angelic. To act in this way is not only natural, it is something good; for, in an Aristotelian universe, to say that something is good means that it approximates perfection, the highest form of which is to become God oneself. Hence, the post-Noah human pursuit of divine wisdom is inherently good. However, there are many ways to be misled in this pursuit.

It is by nature easier for a human being to make a mistake about theoretical wisdom than it is for him to be correct, and false judgments about theoretical wisdom generate false judgments about practical wisdom, which initiate paths to walk upon that lead the person further away rather than closer to God. What humanity must have is a road map that will point people in the right direction. That map is the Torah. What it does is provide a model for a polity, a set of imaginative beliefs, and a code of personal morality that together maximize the possibility of success in collectively actualizing the kind of knowledge necessary to know more correctly. In the end, through the political and moral guidance outlined in the Torah, those humans subject to the discipline of the laws of the Torah will become more than human. They will achieve the level of knowledge of the angels, and in so doing they will redeem themselves and their world. In the end, armed with the discipline of the Torah, humanity will regain the perfection it first had when it was created, and, through that learned wisdom, humanity will lead the universe itself back to the state of perfection it enjoyed when the world was the garden of Eden.

It is the Myth of the Palace that spells out a picture of what the path to perfection through the Torah is like. This story tells us of a walled city that contains a palace in which there is an inner sanctuary in which the king resides. There are people outside as well as within the city, some moving away from the palace and others towards it. Similarly, there are people who enter the palace who either can or cannot find the inner sanctuary of the king's quarters, and there are people within the sanctuary who are and who are not in the presence of the king. Those who have entered the city but not the palace are humanity, whose distinguishing mark is the ability to reason. Those humans outside the city are more like animals, Maimonides tells us, precisely because they do not reason. The city is the domain of intellect. However, not everyone who uses intellect can enter the palace. More than reason is needed. The palace is the world of Torah, the world of the Jewish people. This nation alone, guided by the Torah, can move beyond what human reason can teach towards the ultimate perfection of becoming divine.

The Torah as the guide to perfection

How does the Torah teach us moral perfection? In part it does so by giving explicit laws, obedience to which provides us with the ability to perfect our thinking. Some of the laws deal with the establishment of a just society, which is a society that most values the pursuit of wisdom over all other pursuits. Other laws are directives towards character development, which involve physical, emotional, and intellectual states of the body – excellences such as prudence, patience, temperance, courage, and so on. Without them the mind cannot focus with sufficient concentration to increase its wisdom.

Still other laws express in imaginative language true beliefs. These function as guideposts to lead the thinking mind in fruitful directions. For example, it is not unreasonable to think, given the definition of time, that the universe is eternal and therefore uncreated. It is the doctrine of creation that saves human beings from this mistaken direction in thought. The doctrine as expressed in the Bible in no way constitutes knowledge of creation, for it is, after all, only a story. But as human beings improve in their wisdom, they become increasingly skilled at interpreting the story in ways that yield truth about the origin of the universe.

For example, the use of the term "day" when adequately understood, expresses something about the ordering of space and not something about time, which leads the reader to understand that the creation or origin of the universe is not a temporal event, which further means that the activity of its creator as creator is itself atemporal. Creating is not something God does at one time and then ceases. Rather, it is a single, continuous action, without beginning or end, that expresses both God's nature and God's relationship to the world, since in God, as a consequence of his oneness, every action is identical both with every other action and with both the agent, God, and its product, the world.

Divine attributes as moral imperatives

The same kind of reasoning applies to all explicit statements about God in the Torah. Although they seem to say who or what God is, in truth, when properly understood, they too are moral guideposts towards perfection. I will explain what Maimonides means by this judgment, because it is the heart of his solution to the problem of theological agnosticism that follows from his analysis of God as the creator.

According to Maimonides, no affirmative declarative sentence about God can be true if the sense of the sentence is literally what it says. The Bible, however, presents many such statements which, because they are presumed to be divinely revealed, must be true. Hence, their correct meaning cannot be their literal sense. How then are we to interpret them? Maimonides gives us the following instructions.[15] In every sentence whose logical form is "God is f," the "f" expresses a moral virtue for human beings. All such statements, therefore, are to be interpreted as follows: each of us should strive to become like God, for becoming like God is the ideal end of a process that results in human perfection beyond being human; consequently, what it means to say that God is f is that we should pursue f, so grammatically declarative sentences in the Bible with God as the subject are really neither declaratives nor statements about God. Rather, they are imperatives directed to human beings; therefore, "God is f" really means, "You, oh human being, strive to become f!"

Maimonides distinguished two kinds of Jews (Jews being defined here as those who have accepted upon themselves the teachings of the Torah as authoritative in their lives). Some follow the Torah blindly, without understanding what it means. These are, in the Myth of the Palace, those within the palace who have not yet entered the inner chamber. In itself there is nothing wrong with what they are doing. With or without knowledge it is good to obey the Torah. Those who do so will at least become better persons than they would have been otherwise. However, there is no comparison in level between those Jews who know, or at least strive to know, what the Torah means in all of its statements (both those that express laws of behavior and those that state correct belief) and those who do not. Only those who seek wisdom as well as right practice can enter into the presence of God the king.

Hence, the end of the myth affirms that there can be, at least in principle, positive knowledge of God. However, that knowledge is more

---

[15] See *Guide* 1:52–60, with special emphasis on 1:56–59.

than can be achieved exclusively through reason and exclusively through obedience to the Torah. The former only brings you into the city. It is the key to discovering the palace but it cannot bring you into the inner sanctuary where God resides. The latter brings you into the inner chamber, but it will not in itself enable you to face the king. To know God, which is the highest perfection that any creature can achieve, requires a wedding of revealed and reasoned wisdom that moves the knower beyond the distinction of practical and theoretical wisdom into the form of wisdom to which we may point but not know, for it is the wisdom of those who have transcended their humanity and become one with God, the king.

IS THE GOD OF MAIMONIDES BELIEVABLE?

In the end Maimonides does seem to reconcile the apparently irreconcilable visions of the one and absolutely simple creator deity with the loving and caring revealer deity. The creator is the God whom we know through natural revelation, that is, through his manifestation in the laws of the natural world. However, this is not God as he is. It is only the best that we can discover armed with the tools of human reason. They can point beyond the world of sense perception that provides reason with its sole data, but they cannot by themselves transcend the data to make even one positive and clear statement about God. Unaided reason can tell us nothing about the revealer of the Torah.

The Torah also cannot tell us who God is. Literally it cannot give us, at least on its own, any knowledge at all, since nothing that it says has a clear or precise (what Maimonides calls "univocal") meaning. Rather, the Torah is a moral guide that directs us to a perfection whose end is a knowledge of God that is possible only when we transcend our humanity. It is the revealed Torah that provides us with the beliefs necessary to follow this moral path.

The Torah is not a book of science; it is a work of human ethics. The God of revelation is not an object for scientific inquiry. He is rather a moral ideal. The primary principles to guide reading of the Torah are that human beings are created in the image of God and human beings should be holy as God is holy. The holiness is what human beings, as moral agents, and God, as the revealer of the Torah, share in common.

Not every Jewish philosopher agreed with Maimonides' theology. Especially problematic was his radical disavowal of any positive human knowledge of God. For Maimonides all we know at this level about God is that whatever it is that we know is not God. Gersonides in particular thought that Maimonides' judgments were too extreme. He argued instead for an interpretation of statements about God where what the predicate terms express is an ideal, a perfection, that God exemplifies and humans strive to realize.[16] To be sure, this is not literal knowledge of God, but it is still a form of knowledge, not only of human ethics but of God's nature as well. How different Gersonides' interpretation is from what Maimonides in fact intended to say is an unsettled question. Personally I do not think it is as radically different as Gersonides himself thought it was. Be that as it may, subsequent generations of Jewish philosophical theologians – notably Hermann Cohen, Martin Buber, and Franz Rosenzweig – will affirm what Maimonides says about God and interpret what that means in ways that are consistent with Gersonides' theology. It is to their understanding of the God of revelation that I now turn.

---

[16] I have labeled this interpretation of equivocal God-talk "*pros hen* equivocation." See N. Samuelson, *Gersonides on God's Knowledge of Particulars* (Toronto: Pontifical Institute of Mediaeval Studies, 1977), ch. IV, with specific reference to pp. 28–29.

CHAPTER 3

The God of the theologians

THE DISCREDITATION OF RATIONALIST THEOLOGY

The primary goal of this book is analysis and critique of the concept of revelation, as a philosophic concept, out of the sources of rabbinic Judaism. Revelation is to be understood at its most general level as a relationship between humans, as the recipients, and God, as the transmitter, of revealed information. In the case of Judaism, where the humans involved are the Jewish people, the term applied to the information is "Torah." Hence, the concept of revelation in Judaism builds on four other concepts – God, the human, the Jewish people, and the Torah. Of the four, my focus so far has been on the concept of God. The discussion has included the other three concepts as well, because they are all conceptually interrelated in Jewish belief, but the focus, at least for now, has been on the purported entity from which the revealed information originates. This kind of historically grounded, philosophic thinking about God is called "theology."

MAIMONIDES AS THE BENCHMARK OF JEWISH THEOLOGY

Classical Jewish, rabbinic, philosophical theology does not end with Maimonides. On the contrary, the tradition continues, without disruption, to the present day, without any indication of an end. However, for present purposes, where the focus is on the notion of God as it relates to revelation, Jewish philosophy (perhaps even philosophy in general) reached its highest development with Maimonides. Others, such as Gersonides, will modify Maimonides' views. Still others, from Crescas[1] through Spinoza,[2] will offer major philosophical critiques of

---

[1] Chasdai ben Judah Crescas, born in Barcelona around 1340, lived much of his life in Saragossa. Died 1410/11.

[2] Baruch Spinoza, 1632–1677, lived most of his life in Amsterdam.

Maimonides' view. Yet, what Maimonides said about the God of Torah remains the benchmark for all Jewish thinking about God – be it late medieval, early modern, modern, and postmodern. Some advocate his enterprise and others critique it, but the origin of all their own theology is Maimonides' writings about God.

POST-RAMBAM CRITIQUES OF MAIMONIDES

Kabbalah

Imagination versus intellect

The major critique of Jewish philosophy after Maimonides comes not from the philosophers but from the Jewish mystics, the Kabbalists. Many of the best and most inquisitive Jewish intellectuals in the centuries following Maimonides turn to Kabbalah rather than to philosophy for their investigation of the meaning of the Hebrew Scriptures, and they do so in a way that is entirely alien to Maimonides' philosophical quest – they use their imaginations in order to picture in visual terms God's nature, the nature of the world, the nature of humanity, and the relationship between them. Of these works the most influential is the *Zohar*, which, either intentionally or unintentionally, stands in direct opposition to practically everything Maimonides says. From a philosophical perspective, the most critical challenge from Kabbalah is its affirmation of the epistemic value of imagination over intellect.

Undergirding Maimonides' entire enterprise was the first conviction, rooted in the success of the Aristotelian natural philosophy or science of his day, that thinking about the truth of what our religion commands us to believe must be based on rational speculation rather than creative imagination. Through imagination we can become aware of all that is possible, but the realm of the possible far exceeds the domain of the actual, and imagination in itself provides us with no guidelines to distinguish the possible from the actual. As such, reason alone cannot lead us to the truth assumed to be embedded in the Torah. Reason and only reason provides the only natural tool available to human beings to understand divine revelation.

The philosophical critique of Aristotelian reason

The confidence that Maimonides had in reason, which he shared with Muslim intellectuals of his time (notably Ibn Sina [Avicenna] and Ibn Rushd [Averroes]) undergoes sharp, critical attack in subsequent generations – especially from Al-Ghazali (1058–1111) against Ibn Sina near Maimonides' own time and from Crescas against Maimonides and Gersonides in later generations (1340–1411). The details of their arguments are not important here. I will only briefly summarize certain relevant conclusions.

The Aristotelians affirmed reality, at least within the sublunar world, as a complex of entities, called "substances," which themselves were concrete individuals, locatable in and moving through space and time. What constituted these substances as real was their individuality, identifiable by their singular spatial-temporal location. This physical identity was attributable to a principle called "matter." Matter made substances material, that is, it accounted for their materialization in reality, but it did not address what they are. What they are consisted not in what made them unique but in what made them like other substances. To know what an individual is is to define it, and definition consists in noting formal characteristics that the individual shares in common with other substances (the genus) as well as formal characteristics that distinguish the individual from the other members of its genus (the specific difference). However, the definition in general deals only with formal characteristics, with forms, and forms are in principle general, because what defines any form (as well as any complex of forms) is that it can exist in many places at the same time. Hence, forms, which render substances intelligible, are always universal, and, as such, are not real. Consequently, through reason we can know what something is, for we can grasp its formal nature, that is, we can grasp the constituent forms of a thing. However, we cannot in this way grasp the reality of the thing as something materialized in space and time as a distinct individual. Reality is material and individual, while philosophical-scientific-logical thought (reason) is always immaterial (or, formal) and general (or, abstract). Therefore, what we can know through reason is never real, and, given the Aristotelian commitment to a correspondence theory of truth, never true. Truth is in principle unknowable, at least through reason.

Maimonides' argument against relying on imagination and the senses to probe the meaning of the revealed word of God in the Hebrew Scriptures was that it could not yield truth, whereas through reason truth was (at least in part) discoverable. However, it turns out that the confidence (however qualified) of these philosophers in reason has rationally, that is, on its own terms, no foundation. To trust reason turns out not to be reasonable. Why not then, it can be argued, return to the use of imagination, which at least has the virtue of enabling us to think in ways broader than those our senses suggest from lived experience, which we know to be at best an inadequate picture of reality?

This is precisely what those Kabbalists did who asked the same kinds of theoretical questions that the philosophers asked (notably about God, the human, the world, and how the three are related). Whereas Maimonides took statements about the divine body to be non-material metaphors, the Kabbalists extended and radicalized these statements in order to picture in detail what God's body looked like, including his/her genitals,[3] and how both the universe and the human were images of the corporeal divine being.

Modern science

While the growth of Kabbalah itself took the inadequacies of the Mai-monidean presuppositions in one new direction, early European science took it in another direction. The notion of what is rational thinking itself began, in the late medieval and early modern period in western Europe, to break out of the restraints of the ancient Greek and Roman natural philosophy, as it evolved into the philosophic presuppositions about re-ality that are taken for granted in modern science. The development of the philosophical system presupposed in the modern scientific method reached its classic form in the seventeenth- and eighteenth-century writ-ings of the natural philosophers René Descartes (1596–1650), Baruch Spinoza (1632–1677), Gottlob Leibniz (1646–1716), Isaac Newton (1642–1727), and, most notably, the French Positivists.[4] There are important dif-ferences between all of these thinkers, but for present purposes what they share in common is more important, because that common philosophical position, accepted as it stands, undercuts everything that Maimonides, and therefore Jewish philosophy, had to say about the philosophical God of the Hebrew Scriptures. It has to do with what they shared in their understanding of mathematics, logic, linguistics, and ontology.

New philosophic presuppositions: positivism and the ideal of mathematical precision
In a few words, whereas Aristotelian natural philosophy affirmed the reality of the negative and the vague as well as the positive and the precise,

---

[3] See Elliot Wolfson, *Through A Speculum That Shines: Vision and Imagination in Medieval Jewish Mysticism* (Princeton: Princeton University Press, 1994).
[4] Such as Auguste Comte (1798–1857).

increasingly the new science affirmed that only what is positive and only what is precise can be real. With respect to ontology, the definitions of Aristotelian substances had (in modern terms) "fuzzy borders." In part, that is because the terms for the definitions were taken from ordinary language, which, as a reflection of ordinary usage, is unavoidably vague. But the vagueness was deeper than just language, for the imprecision of the language was seen to reflect the imprecision of reality, imprecision whose source was the notion of matter. Mathematical entities, such as numbers or geometric shapes, can have precise definitions, because they are no more than their definitions, which, as such, exist in logical thought but not in material reality. Once materialized, the precision vanishes, because matter itself is undefinable. In contrast, the modern positivist philosophers insisted that what is real exists at any precise moment in a precise place, and that all these individuals – the moments, the places, and the things that occupy them – can be expressed clearly and distinctly, because each exists as something discrete.

The same is true of logic. The scientific language of Aristotelian logic was ordinary language that, as such, contained all the vagaries that arise from being "ordinary." The new scientific language (as it was finally formalized in written symbols at the beginning of the twentieth century), however, reflected a form and logic more in common with algebra than with literature. It assumed two kinds of terms, non-capitalized letters to name concrete individuals, and capitalized letters to express their general properties. Copulas were abandoned. Instead you had sentences in which the individuals and their properties were next to but not incorporated into each other. This language was seen to reflect a reality in which individuals are real and their properties are not, so that the relationship between them is external and purely conceptual. Names of individuals had references but not meanings, and meanings were concepts that had no proper material existence. Furthermore, the ultimate conceptual expressions about these existent, material, discrete individuals were algebraic statements, which were viewed to be the sole bearers of meaning and the only things that have truth value. Sentences have meaning and can be true or false; names for things only have reference, and the things referred to have neither meaning nor value.

Calculus and infinity
What is perhaps most important about the new scientific thinking is that its model was mathematical, or, more precisely, algebraic. What is most

important about it, for present purposes, is that the new language of logic with its entailed new philosophy solved the riddle of infinity. It provided us with a formalism – calculus – to make sense out of real infinities. First, it discovered many different kinds of infinity. (In part the problem of medieval discussions of infinity was that it assumed that all infinities are of the same kind.) Second, it used one fairly simple kind of infinity (viz., infinite series with a finite limit) to make sense out of locomotion, which, in contrast to alteration, is continuous, which seems to mean change through an infinite number of real points on a finite spatially conceived line.

THE PROBLEMS WITH MAIMONIDES' THEOLOGY

All of these changes in scientific thinking played a critical role in undermining the authority of Jewish philosophy, especially its theology. I have already alluded to the most important challenges. Two in particular need to be emphasized. First, in terms of mathematics, Maimonides' analysis assumes that because infinity names an endless process nothing actual can be infinite. However, all motion between two points in space is an infinite transition towards a finite limit and the limit, which is both rational and intelligible, expresses the real actuality of the infinite process. In fact all interesting applications of physical mechanics involving measurements of real things, such as areas or volumes of actual physical bodies, are instances of infinite change in the direction of finite limits, where the infinitely distant limits are the expression of the measurable reality of the things studied. Hence, the presumed fact that God is infinite in every respect does not mean that God is unknowable. On the contrary, he is humanly knowable through a logic, modeled on calculus, of ideal limits.

Second, logical expressions of the sort that can be judged true and false state, as they did for Aristotle, relations between subjects and predicates, but the predicate expressions are the sole conveyers of meaning that stand in an external relationship of predication to individual subjects that, in and of themselves, have reference but no meaning. Hence, relations between predicates and subjects do not entail complexity in the subjects, because the relations are external. However, all of Maimonides' arguments against literally affirming properties of God presupposed internal predication, where the term predicated of the subject God is understood to assert that God contains within his nature some attribute with which he is not identical. Given this new and improved logic, there is no apparent reason to restrict language about God to mere story telling.

HERMANN COHEN

The philosopher of Judaism who first dealt seriously with the impact of modern science and philosophy on understanding the theology of the rabbinic literature, including the writings of Maimonides, was Hermann Cohen. His initial distinction was as interpreter of the philosophy of Immanuel Kant.

THE PHILOSOPHY OF IMMANUEL KANT

Kant had written three major critiques – a first of what he called "pure reason" (reinen Vernunft), a second of practical reason, and a third of aesthetics. In subject matter Kant's pure reason is close to what I have identified in Aristotle as theoretical reason. It is that rational activity that formulates conceptual knowledge from sense experience whose principles are what we human beings understand as physics and the other physical sciences. However, the two are not identical. For the Aristotelians these principles are ultimate principles of the universe; not so for Kant. He followed in a tradition of philosophy and science that had both absorbed the Muslim and Jewish critiques of Aristotelian science and moved beyond them to new, more mechanical rational philosophies, such as Descartes', and new more mathematical positivist sciences such as that of Newton. Kant no longer could make the same general claims for the epistemic authority of theoretical/pure reason that the Aristotelians had made. Like his ancient and medieval predecessors, Kant believed that this kind of reason yields certain objective knowledge, but it is not knowledge of reality. Kant therefore made a distinction between what is objective – views shared in common by all right-thinking human beings – and what is real. Pure reason, being dependent on the data of sense experience, can only tell us what is universally true of the world of empirical experience, but this world, although it is objective, is not reality. To understand reality requires a different kind of thinking, which he called "practical," as did the ancients, but we call "moral." This change is the most notable break with the epistemology of the Aristotelians, and it is a change that reflects the changes in thought about thinking that Maimonides and those who followed him expressed in terms of ethics.

I have already noted that the ambiguity of the Aristotelians on the question of whether human happiness has more to do with theoretical or with practical reason expresses itself in Jewish philosophy as an ambiguity over the nature of prophecy and human happiness.[5] All of the Jewish thinkers identify happiness as the moral end of human existence, associate its achievement with the attainment of happiness, and affirm, in line with Plato, that wisdom is of two sorts – theoretical (viz., the highest and most general truths of science) and practical (viz., judgments about how to live well [ethics] and how to guide others to live well [politics]). The question is, which is higher? In general, at the highest levels of wisdom, where humans become prophets and seem to be able to realize at least the horizon of the line that separates humanity from divinity, the distinction between the two kinds of wisdom disappears. In other words, the ultimate end towards which the human tends is to become, at least ideally, what Plato called a "philosopher king" and the Jewish Aristotelians called "prophets," whose practical thinking flows directly from their theoretical knowledge. In this sense, ethics – the study of what ought to be – transcends science – the study of what is, because at its highest level science becomes ethics.

It is in the spirit of this tradition of western thinking that Kant saw practical reason to be beyond pure reason. The domain of pure reason is scientific thinking, which gives us knowledge of, but only of, the world of sense experience, which Kant calls "phenomena." Beyond it is reality, which Kant calls "noumena." The realm of the noumena is the domain of God and his kingdom, which are both to be grasped, not with the discursive logic of science, but with a new, imperative logic of ethics. If this move is successful, Kant has brought philosophy and religion beyond the story-telling, myth-making stage of the rabbis. They rightly told stories, because they knew that their logic and their sense data were insufficient to inform them of the ultimate truths of God and his kingdom.

COHEN'S JEWISH PHILOSOPHY

The question is whether Kant succeeded. The major, intuitive problem for most of us is his seemingly peculiar claim that in knowing what ought to be true we know what really is true. Most people tend to think that ethics may tell us what is right and wrong, but it is powerless to inform us about what is and is not true. Hermann Cohen thought that Kant was right, and first wrote commentaries on Kant's three critiques and then

5 See Howard Kreisel, *Maimonides' Political Thought: Studies in Ethics, Law, and the Human Ideal* (Albany: State University of New York Press, 1999), and Kenneth Seeskin, *Searching for a Distant God: The Legacy of Maimonides* (New York and Oxford: Oxford University Press, 2000).

constructive philosophical works of his own – on philosophy of science, on ethics, and on aesthetics – to demonstrate what he thought to be Kant's correct and conceptually revolutionary insights. Finally, he applied his philosophical discoveries to the study of religion in general and to rabbinic Judaism in particular, for he believed that rabbinic Judaism was already, especially on Maimonides' reading of it, the embodiment of Kantian philosophy. In other words, Cohen used Kant to reconstruct the Jewish philosophy of the Maimonideans as they had used Aristotle to reconstruct the Judaism of the Hebrew Scriptures and the early rabbis of the Midrash.

Cohen used the mathematical notion of the finite limited infinite series as a model for picturing reality. The phenomena are the series, and the noumena are the limit, where the series expresses actuality and the limit is the ideal that is identical with reality. God is presented primarily as the ideal end, analogous numerically to the number one, towards which the lived world, whose origin as creation is analogous numerically to the number zero, tends. History, human as well as natural, is a movement of integration from the nothing of creation towards the single something that is the unity of God with the world. Both the Torah and the classical rabbinic literature express this fundamental insight about the nature of reality in language guided practically to lead ordinary human beings towards their own understanding of this ultimate truth.

The theology of Cohen was a theology of a liberal progressive Judaism that affirmed the values of both Judaism and western European modernism and sought to synthesize the two into a coherent whole. Cohen provided such a synthesis. There is no question that, from the perspective of intellectual history, Cohen is one of the great philosophers, certainly one of the great Jewish philosophers. However, his appeal is limited solely to those who initially accept the values of both Judaism and modernism. Few outside the camp of progressive Judaism did. Non-Jews as well as assimilated Jews rejected the asserted values of rabbinic Judaism, and other Jews rejected the asserted values of modernism. The rejection of many of the values of modernism – rationality and individual autonomy being most critical among them – became strong, at least among European intellectuals, after the First World War. They tended, rightly or wrongly, to take the senselessness and brutality of that war as a *reductio ad absurdum* of the values, most apparent at least for Jews in the philosophy of Spinoza, that produced the modern, secular nationalist, capitalist, democratic nation state. These intellectuals were attracted more to forms of socialism – fascism, anarchism, and communism – than they were to the verbalized political ideals of the French and American revolutions;

their Jewish counterparts were drawn more to a search for a new kind of Jewish religious spiritualism, even traditionalism, than they were attracted to forms of liberal Judaism.

BEYOND COHEN

I will focus attention on two of these postmodern Jewish theologians, both of whom were deeply influenced by Cohen's thought in almost every respect except one – his modernist, rationalist liberalism. They are Martin Buber and Franz Rosenzweig. Buber and Rosenzweig were not disciples in the sense that they actually studied with Cohen. One did (Rosenzweig), but not the other (Buber). Nor were they Cohen's disciples in that they were his spokesmen. Rosenzweig had a political theory, but he did not advocate any form of political ideal for the world. Rather, he saw human salvation in religious communities, Jewish and Christian, instead of in secular politics. Buber, in contrast, remained his entire life a believer in the political process and a sort of utopian, but his political idealism was closer to the anarchist-agrarian vision of Tolstoy than to the mercantile-republican ideal of Locke and Jefferson. Buber was an active Zionist his entire life, first in Germany and then in Israel. Rosenzweig, in contrast, used his practical wisdom to create a small Jewish worshiping and studying community in Frankfurt.

The focus in this part of the book is on Buber's and Rosenzweig's conception of the God of revelation. In stating it I will have to speak of more than just their views of God, because what both say about the deity is inseparable from what they say in general about the world, the human, and the relationship between the three. Their view on the God of revelation is not cleanly separable from their views of revelation. However, again, my focus in this part is on their views of God. I will expand on their views of the human (the second term of the relationship that defines revelation) and revelation later.

MARTIN BUBER

The three most important philosophical influences informing Buber's conception of God were Maimonides, Cohen, and (by means of Cohen) Immanuel Kant. The influences are both positive and negative. Buber accepts much that Maimonides said, but what he rejected in Maimonides is no less important. The same applies to the influence of Kant and Cohen. Those influences constitute the presuppositions of Buber's theology.

From Maimonides

In agreement with Maimonides, the God of revelation is no less the God of creation, so that what we believe about the revealer must be consistent with what we believe about the creator. Clearly the creator is radically different from anything created, and God creates everything that exists in any way. Hence, there can be no human knowledge of God in any literal sense. Human knowledge consists of conceptual objects inferred from sense experience, and there can be no objective experience of anything that has not been created by God. However, this negative component of theology cannot be understood in the radical way that Maimonides presented it, for such a view of God the creator is incompatible with a deity who also reveals himself to human beings. There must be some way that God can be known even though that way cannot be literally through grasping conceptual objects.

From Kant

In agreement with Kant, the universe can be divided into phenomenal and noumenal realms. We are knowing subjects who experience a world of objects and relations whose source lies in an interaction between our minds and something else. The domain of scientific knowledge is limited to phenomena. Phenomena are the world that our experience and logical reasoning inform. However, logical reasoning cannot tell us about the something else beyond phenomena, except that there is more to reality than phenomena. That something else – what Kant called "noumena" – is somehow knowable, for otherwise we would not be aware that there is something else, but it is not knowable in the same way that we know phenomena. It must be knowable in some other way.

Kant believed that the "other way" is moral reasoning. He developed a logic of practical wisdom (to use the terminology of classical Jewish philosophy) which in many respects paralleled the logic of theoretical wisdom. Both logics express universal value claims. The theoretical claims are expressed as declarative sentences whose values are either true or false; the practical claims are expressed as imperatives whose values are either good or bad. Both kinds of claims are "universal" in the sense that they are rules that apply to everything within their domain, but the domains are different. The values of theoretical logic range over all states of affairs involving objects in the world, while the values of practical logic range with equal unqualified universality over acts of will by knowing subjects. Buber presupposed all of this philosophy, except for two claims – Kant's judgment that ethics are about a noumenal reality divorced from the empirical world of lived life, and Kant's claim of universality for moral judgments.

Ethics applies to the lived life of individual conscious entities – human beings – in their lived relations with other individual conscious entities in the phenomenal world. An ethics such as the one that Kant proposes could have no practical application in such real life. Moral judgments are not universal rules derived from another, albeit more pure, world. On the contrary, they arise in concrete life in the realm of phenomena. Whatever value such rules may have in making moral judgments, in lived life the same rules are not always applicable. No moral judgments are without qualification applicable to all human beings. On the contrary, moral judgments, like the life contexts to which these judgments apply, are always concrete. Abstract laws cannot capture what is right or wrong in any particular context. Good and bad are values that apply to concrete relations between particular conscious subjects, and it is these concrete relations, not abstract rules, that determine the values.

Still, it is not the case that Kant's moral rules are irrelevant. In short, Kant's general rules for moral judgment amount to the following assertion: do not treat others as mere objects; treat them rather as ends in themselves. In knowing an object we know something that we can use. However, it is never right to treat an other – that which is not us – as an object. Hence, even the act of knowing an other is not moral. In general, "not moral" here means morally neutral, non-moral. However, if the other is something like us, that is, another conscious subject, then to reduce the other to an object of our knowledge, even an object of our consciousness, is more than non-moral. With such others there is a duty to treat them as non-objective, as something that is not a thing, as someone whose demands upon us are equal in moral value to our demands upon ourselves, as (in Kant's words) "ends in themselves."

What Buber accepts from this Kantian picture of the domain of the ethical is that morality deals with the domain of will rather than objects, and that others must be treated not as a means to an end but as ends in themselves. He does not accept, however, that these "facts" of morality constitute rules for moral judgments. Rather, there are two ways in which an other can be treated. One way is as a means to an end, as an object or (in Buber's words) as an "it" (Es). Another way is as an end in itself, as another subject like ourselves, as a loved-one, or (in Buber's words) as a "you" in the intimate sense of the term (Du) and not in its impersonal sense (Sie), that is, as a (in now archaic English) "thou."

Hence, contrary to Kant, the domain of the moral is not separable from the domain of the phenomenal. All objects are given to us in experience as something other than ourselves. Whether the object is an object is itself not objective. When the other is experienced as an object, as something that can be differentiated from us as an instrument to serve our will, then it is an it, a thing, and our relationship to it is an "Ich–Es" relationship. Such relationships are the domain of theoretical wisdom, which, as such, are scientific and morally neutral. However, when the same other is experienced as another subject, indistinguishable from ourselves as subjects in no respect other than being other, that is, not being us, then it is a thou, a person, and our relationship to it is an "Ich–Du" relationship. Note that these two relations do not distinguish two kinds of reality. They distinguish two ways in which we as conscious subjects experience reality itself.

From Cohen

Buber's rejection of Kant's radical separation of reality into noumenal and phenomenal realms in itself reflects the influence of the philosophy of Hermann Cohen. A critical separation must be made between the domains of the scientific and the moral. Contrary to the dominant trends in Anglo-American naturalist philosophy, there is and can be no science of ethics. The domain of science is the positivist world of sense objects and their relations. However, the domain of ethics is a radically different world of conscious subjects and the relations between them. In this case the appropriate discipline is religion. Buber accepted that it is religion, not science, to which you look to understand ethics, and the primary subjects of religion – God and his relations to human beings – are intimately tied to ethics.

Kant's God was a noumenal object whose existence was deduced by means of moral arguments. The strategy underlying those arguments was one that said that while we cannot know whether or not God exists, we can know that God ought to exist. As such, God functioned as something ideal rather than actual. Cohen used his model of philosophic thinking based on science's employment of infinite series with finite ends or limits to make Kant's claim intelligible. The phenomenal world is analyzable into sets of processes that are expressible as infinite series directed towards asymptotes, definite limits. These limits are ideals that are more real than the (merely actual) processes that endlessly approximate them. The actual universe itself is also to be understood as such a process, and in this case the end or ideal of all of the universe is God.

However, as Cohen himself recognized,[6] while natural philosophy may be sufficient to know that this deity is real, it is not sufficient to know anything else about him. Most importantly, it is not enough to know what this God wants from his human creatures. For that knowledge, God must reveal himself to them, and the record of that revelation is the content of religion. It is a content that is totally concrete in its nature. It expresses a moral code that can and should guide the life of individual human beings in all of their inter-human relations. It is a code by which we learn values such as compassion (Mitleid) for others, values that are unattainable through philosophy and science alone.[7]

Buber takes over all of these judgments from Cohen about the inter-relationship of natural philosophy/science, religion, and ethics, and develops them further into a dialectic of how to think about all human institutions, not just religion. In doing so, he distinguishes between "religion" as a way of conscious living in interpersonal relationships and "religion" as an institution. As an institution it is no different than any other institution. In all of them there is interpersonal life as well as non-personal existence, and here the institution of religion has no special status. Buber spells out this judgment in his major work in philosophy, *I and Thou*. All institutions reflect God's presence and all of them express alienation from it. As such, all of them are domains for the moral, the immoral, and/or the non-moral. However, it is also true, as both Kant and Cohen assert in their significantly different ways, that theology, religion, and ethics are intimately interconnected and unavoidably associated.

---

[6] Or, at least came to recognize by the end of his career as a philosopher.

[7] In speaking of the kind of (limited) ethics of which philosophy is capable, Cohen argued in *Religion der Vernunft aus den Quellen des Judentums* (English translation, *The Religion of Reason out of the Sources of Judaism*, referred to below as "RV") that (quoting Andrea Poma in *The Critical Philosophy of Hermann Cohen* [English translation by John Denton. Albany: SUNY Press, 1997]) ethics "cannot understand the other man as 'You,' but only as 'He,' not as a *Mitmensch*, but only as a *Nebenmensch* and, being unable to reach the full meaning of the interpersonal relationship, turns out to be unsatisfactory for us as a task . . . (cf. RV 17f.; Eng. trans. 14f.) . . . Religion discovers the other man as *Mitmensch* in suffering."

THEOLOGY

These claims, then, are Buber's intellectual inheritance, which are presumed, either affirmatively or negatively, in Buber's theology. I will turn now directly to what he says.

The eternal thou

For Buber everything, with only one exception, can be expressed as either I–You (Ich–Du) or I–It (Ich–Es). This is not a statement about the way that something is substantially. There are no substances in Buber's philosophy. Things are not independent entities that enter into relationships with other independent entities. Rather, there are only relationships, where substances or things are constructs out of these relations. Everything, again with one exception, is given in both of these relationships. Neither is primary. Everything is both an object for other knowers and a knower who grasps others as objects. Similarly, everything stands in concrete moral relations to others through which they experience and are experienced by others in compassion as lovers as well as loved ones. Knowing is the purest example of an I–It relationship; loving is the purest example of an I–Thou relationship. However, these are only examples.

The exception to this rule is God. God is always experienced in an I–Thou relationship. Hence, contrary to the claims of the philosophers, God knows nothing and is totally unknowable. What God does, exclusively, is love and be loved, and loving is not a cognitive activity. In this sense, at least, Buber follows the rabbinic traditions that, when discussing the God of revelation, tell stories that speak of him on the model of the Song of Songs, which is the central text that they used for commentary in order to express an understanding of revelation. That God reveals himself to Israel means that God loves Israel, and the rabbinic story of the relationship between God and Israel is understood as a love story.

How does Buber interpret this story? He does so as part of a general dialectic of movement through history between these two primary forms of relationship – I–Thou and I–It.

The dialectic of the two ways of being

Buber's most important work in philosophical theology is *I and Thou*.[8] It begins with a discussion of language. Here he presents the basic concepts

---

[8] *Ich und Du* (Heidelberg: Lambert Schneider, 1958). English translation by Walter Kaufmann, *I and Thou* (New York: Scribner, 1970).

of I–Thou and I–It summarized above. What is critical in this format is that it locates Buber clearly within the tradition of modern, western philosophy, where, in direct contrast to both ancient and medieval philosophy, including Jewish philosophy, thinking about the traditional topics of philosophy – God, the world, and the human, that is, the subject matter of metaphysics, physics, psychology and ethics – roots itself in linguistics. Buber begins by saying that the forms of verbs in western languages are hierarchically related such that some forms are logically and linguistically prior to others. The singular is prior to the plural, and the first person is prior to both the second and third. Plurals are constructed from singulars, and the second and third persons as subject forms are derivative from the two ways that objects are related to subjects – personally and impersonally. Personal and impersonal objects are expressed as subjects respectively in the second and third persons. Hence, the central theme of Buber's analysis of language is that through language we experience the world in two forms of relation – I–Thou and I–It.

Buber uses this understanding of language to discuss how we function in social relationships, that is, in relationship to other human beings. The prime example is love between two people, which he characterizes as a three-stage movement – from a pure I–Thou relationship, to a complex relationship where the I–Thou is associated with an I–It (I–Thou/It relation), to a pure I–It relationship.

Associated with the I–Thou is vivacity as well as instability. When the relationship is purely I–Thou, it is intimate and alive. Both the I and the thou give themselves to each other in a way that only living persons can. It is also an ultimate manifestation of love, because each is totally present to the other without any thought of exploitation for the advantage of a self. However, the relation is unstable, because there is no way to guarantee from moment to moment that the relationship will continue.

On Buber's view it is primarily this need for stability, to find ways for the relationship to continue, that initiates the movement of the I–Thou in the direction of becoming I–It. After the initial stage of the relationship, the unknown other becomes associated with identifying marks – a name, a description, a temporal-spatial location, and so on – simply to be able to find the other and to know that the other whom I meet today (i.e., in the present) is the same other whom I met yesterday (i.e., in the past) and will be the same person I can meet tomorrow (i.e., in the future). At this stage the "its" of identity are only tools to meet the person, but in time, as the number of its increases, progressively (or, retrogressively) these identities become who the other is. Then, when the relationship has become pure I–It and the I–Thou is lost, the relationship is held together primarily by usefulness and/or a memory of what was, in the hope that perhaps it can be regained. Sometimes it is regained, which is to say, there is renewal. However, more often it dies, and each person seeks separately for new relationships to replace the one that has died, so that they may regain the life whose loss they mourn. However, once found and life is regained, the need for stability reasserts itself, and the process of deterioration begins anew.

In this way, Buber tells us, social institutions are born and die – from marriages, to businesses, to nation-states, to religions. Marriages end in divorce and often lead to new marriages; businesses go bankrupt and others are reborn; nations corrupt and are rebelled against to form new nations; and religions decay into idolatry, to give way to new religions formed either through schism or through renewal.

Religions decay into idolatry, because those prophets who encounter the pure God who is eternally Thou respond to that encounter by formalizing it in memory as a code of law, a Torah. That code, which is a memorial to the encounter, a way to recapture the encounter, decays into a dogmatic assertion of the will or word of God. At first that written word is associated with the living God, but in time it replaces it. Dogmas – either in the form of statements of purported true beliefs (especially in the case of Christianity) or in the form of imperatives of correct behavior (especially in the case of Judaism) – at first are used as ways to reexperience the initial (prophetic) experiences with God, as a way to be sure that the deity encountered today is the deity who encountered our ancestors in the past as well as a way to secure the continuance of the relationship into the future. However, inevitably the dogmatic form of identity becomes the identity itself.

Buber uses this structure to present a history of Judaism, from its origins in prophecy through multiple schisms that produced Christianity and rabbinic Judaism out of the decay of prophetic religion – Protestantism out of Roman Catholic Christianity, and Hasidism out of a stagnant rabbinic Judaism.[9] For decadent Christianity, God/Christ becomes nothing more than a set of assertions about his nature, so that worship of God/Christ decays into a worship of dogmatic beliefs called catechisms.

---

[9] Buber does not consider progressive Judaism to be a form of renewal. He does not say explicitly why he does not. I assume it is because of its rationalist faith in the value of human reason as a way to reform belief as well as the rigid formalist structure of its liturgical changes. Far more in keeping with Buber's understanding of revelation would be contemporary Jewish renewal institutions such as P'nai Or.

Similarly, for decadent Judaism, God becomes nothing more than a set of rules that express his will, so that worship of God decays into a worship of dogmatic laws called Torah.

The source of the idolatry is the inescapable need that human beings have for stability, which expresses itself as a wish for certainty, which manifests itself as a desire for knowledge. This need-become-wish-become-desire reaches the level of idolatry when, as in the case of classical Jewish philosophy, the pursuit of knowledge becomes identified with the imitation of God, the attainment of wisdom (theoretical or practical) becomes the highest moral human end (called "happiness"), and this rationalist happiness is identified with God.

However, Buber's God cannot in any sense be grasped. That is his nature. Revelation properly understood is a contentless appearance of God, as nothing more than presence, in the present. It cannot be understood; it has no content other than the awareness that the other who is radically other appeared to you in the concrete, and that you love the other as the other loves you – for you yourself alone and for no purpose whatsoever.

If I–Thou describes what "good" is, as it did for Kant, the love of God is the ultimate expression of love, and the love of any other human being, any neighbor, is its imitation. However, knowledge is not love. Hence, the classical Jewish philosophers, like their counterparts in Christianity and Islam, were deeply mistaken and seriously misleading to others, when they identified knowledge with revelation and wisdom with God. In truth, revelation yields no knowledge and God has nothing to do with at least this kind of wisdom.

IS THE GOD OF BUBER BELIEVABLE?

In my judgment no philosophy is better suited to make intelligible what western liberal religions such as Judaism claim about revelation than Martin Buber's analysis of encounter with God. On this analysis the Hebrew Scriptures are a record of the initial encounter in prophecy of the God whom Israel professes to worship. As such, it testifies to the truth of revelation. However, it is a truth which entails no commitment to dogma of any form, be it belief or practice. To be sure, the Torah states imperatives of behavior that entail dogmas of belief. However, these in themselves are not what God said. In fact God said nothing. Rather, they are honest expressions of what the prophets believed (mistakenly) that they heard God say. They were misled by their hope to transform an essentially transient experience of God's presence into a stable, ongoing, secure relationship. What they said is worthy of our concern, because it is the word of our ancestors who had the supreme good fortune to have encountered God. Those words might even be valuable for at least some of us as we seek to relate to God as well. However, they are more likely to hinder us in our pursuit.

The experience of God is an experience of pure love. Because of its purity there is no way for it to be invoked at will. To be loved by God is to be chosen by God, and God will choose whom he will choose when he chooses them. Hence, there is no way to guarantee divine presence. All we can do is prepare ourselves to receive it if and when it comes. We do that by loving our fellow human beings, our neighbors. We can identify a neighbor, because neighbors are not only I–Thou. In this sense they are easier to love than God, because they are more like us than God. However, they are not God. They are only a "glimpse" of God. To love them is not the same as loving God; still, it does sensitize us to God and it does prepare us to accept God's love, which otherwise we might pass by without notice. Hence, the closest thing to a dogma that Buber will affirm is that man is created in the image of God (for both enter into I–Thou relations), and his only commandment is to love one's neighbor (for the love of neighbor is both a preparation for and a consequence of the love of God).

All that being said (about how well suited Buber's theology is to liberal religions), it may not be the case that Buber's religious thought is best suited for a theology of Judaism as such. Most critically, it is significant that while Buber speaks about the God of revelation, he says nothing about the God of creation. He cannot, in part because the tendency in the religious philosophy of his time was to divorce religious thought from questions that deal with physical reality, to leave the latter exclusively to the domain of science, and to grant that questions about the origin of the universe are questions about physical reality. Buber is a phenomenologist, which is to say a thinker who limits the domain of his speculation to what can be deduced about reality from what we as human beings can experience, and the origin of the universe in general does not fall within this domain.

It may also be the case that he, following the dominant trends of the science of his day, believed that the universe is eternal and therefore uncreated. In doing so, he was not unusual. Whereas discussions of God in classical Jewish philosophy rooted themselves in thought about God as the creator, and only then extended to thought about God the revealer and the redeemer, almost no Jewish philosopher, from at least the time of Spinoza to the present, dealt with creation. However, if this is the case, Buber's (hypothetical) rejection of the dogma of creation will undermine the very foundations of his theology, for Buber, no less than earlier Jewish theologians, must ground his account of revelation in a theory of creation.

As we saw at the beginning of this discussion of Buber's religious thought, his primary notion that God is an eternal I–Thou – meaning that God is radically unlike anything else that exists in that he can in no way be subject to objectification, especially as an object of knowledge – is drawn from Maimonides' negative theology, but the basis of that theology is Maimonides' analysis of what it means to say that God is the creator and everything else is a creature. If there is no creation, God cannot be a creator, and if God is not a creator, there is no radical separation between God and everything else in the way that Buber claims there to be.

The absence of any association of the God of revelation with the God of creation in Buber's theology is unacceptable for yet another reason. A revealer deity who is not the creator is inadequate as the God of Judaism even if he be affirmed to be the revealer of the Torah, for creation is no less (possibly more) a root-principle (*'iqqar*) of Judaism than is revelation. Furthermore, even if it were the case that the universe is temporally eternal (which is not obviously the case on the authority of physics alone; at least our universe is considered by almost all scientists today to have a definite point of origin in time), that would not mean that it was not created by God, since almost without exception the classical Jewish philosophers considered creation to express a non-temporal activity. Hence, on at least these grounds – that Buber's God of revelation is not the God of creation – Buber's theology is unsatisfactory for present purposes.

However, this is not its only weakness. It is more critical that while Buber makes intelligible the notion of a God who can reveal himself to human beings, including Moses, what this view of revelation says about the Torah is problematic. While Buber does not reject the Torah as such, his radically antinomian interpretation of it does mean that any claim that the Torah makes proper demands upon us, both for belief and practice, is worse than wrong – it is inherently idolatrous. The liberal Judaism that follows, therefore, from Buber's theology is a Judaism in which all that matters is personal relations between people. Nothing else can be required or even sanctioned. This liberal Judaism is a viable form of Jewish religion, but on Buber's terms such a religion is inherently imperialist, because it entails the illegitimacy of every other form of Judaism – especially Orthodoxy. For most religiously affirmative Jews, the Torah and rabbinic tradition are not idolatrous. That tradition makes legitimate claims on both our beliefs and our practices, and the authority for that legitimacy is that the Torah at least is in some significant sense revealed. If this account is correct, Buber's conception of the God of revelation and his revelation cannot be true.

Where, then, can we turn to find a theology of revelation and the revealer that both affirms the authoritative legitimacy of the Torah and rabbinic tradition and leaves room for individual judgment about what in it is compelling, that is, true and right? It is with this question in mind that I turn to the theology of Buber's close colleague and friend, Franz Rosenzweig.

CHAPTER 4

Franz Rosenzweig

Rosenzweig's systematic statement of what he believes about God is to be found in his *The Star of Redemption*.[1] There he presents what may be characterized as a complex verbal picture of reality.[2] That picture is constructed from three layers, each laid on top of the other. The three layers are the elements of reality (in part I), the dynamic relations[3] between the elements (in part II), and the structuring[4] of these relations into a single, ideal reality (in part III). The term "God" plays a critical, although different, role in each of the three constructions. The interrelationship of these three uses of the term "God" constitutes Rosenzweig's conception of God.

---

[1] *Der Stern der Erlösung*, in *Franz Rosenzweig: Der Mensch und sein Werk, Gesammelte Schriften* (Haag: Martinus Nijhoff, 1976), vol. II; henceforth referred to as *The Star*. Also see N. Samuelson, *A User's Guide to Franz Rosenzweig's Star of Redemption* (Richmond: Curzon Press, 1999).

[2] Literally it is a picture of "truth" (*The Star*, part III, ch. 3). As we shall see, each part of *The Star* uses a different language to construct his picture, and each part builds on top of the part before it. (This claim may [but need not] contradict at least one understanding of what Leora Batnitzky argues in *Idolatry and Representation: The Philosophy of Franz Rosenzweig Reconsidered* [Princeton: Princeton University Press, 2000]. As I argued in *An Introduction to Modern Jewish Philosophy* [Albany: State University of New York, 1989, chapter 11, p. 216] the structure of the content of *The Star* is more like a picture than a book in that it can be viewed coherently in almost any direction, including backwards, as Batnitzky maintains.) Part III, the final part, uses the language of Jewish liturgy, and there it is said that "God is truth." The "is" here is an is of identity. God and truth are one and the same thing. However, this is not what they are now. Part III is not what is, but what is the end of what is. In the end, as a functioning ideal, the world, the human, and God will become one and the same. In this aimed-for unity of everything in a single thing, God is truth. "Truth" here refers to truth's correspondence theory, in which what is meant by saying that an idea in the mind of a human is true is that the idea corresponds to reality. In the end there is only one reality, hence God (as well as the world and the human) is (are) truth, viz. a single reality.

[3] Literally these are paths or directions ("Bahnen" in the original) that Hallo translates as "courses" (*The Star of Redemption* [Notre Dame, IN: Notre Dame Press, 1985]). Rosenzweig's conception here in fact is mathematical. The idea is that of a vector, a pure, directed motion from a point of origin towards an end point.

[4] "Gestalt" in the original. Hallo translated the term as "configuration." The idea here again is mathematical. It is the asymptote, i.e., the point towards which a directed function (a "Bahn") tends, in a motion that is infinite.

Rosenzweig's universe is a world, not of things but of motions. All these motions are asymptotic, that is, they are best described as directed vectors from a point of origin towards an end point. Both points, the origin and the end, are infinitely distant from any present actuality of the vectors themselves. In this context, "reality" (or "truth") expresses the complex relationship between all of these movements and their infinitely distant origins and ends. The points of origin are the "elements," and the ideal ends towards which the vectors are directed are the final "structure" of everything. The final "structure" is singular and not plural, because in the end everything will become one in every significant theological sense of the term. In contrast, the "origins" are plural, because the dynamic, constantly in motion, universe is to be understood as a movement from plurality towards unity, rather than (as it is for Idealists) a movement from unity (viz., in the one, absolute deity) to plurality (viz., in the many particulars in what Rosenzweig calls "the plastic world," i.e., the world that appears to us through our senses).

Part I of *The Star* is about the elements; part II about the paths between the elements; and part III about the end to which the paths point. Throughout all three parts Rosenzweig uses a single methodology, which is to do what we might call "close readings" of texts.[5]

What distinguishes the three parts, besides their subject matter, is the texts that Rosenzweig submits to analysis. In part I the texts are what Rosenzweig accepted as the canon of philosophy, beginning with Plato and ending with Hegel. In part II the texts are the rabbinic canon of the Hebrew Scriptures. And in part III the texts are the authorized statements of liturgy in orthodox Judaism, the Roman Catholic Church, and the German Evangelical Lutheran Church. Rosenzweig identifies the canon of philosophy with "Idealism," and calls reading Idealism

---

[5] This is my interpretation of what Rosenzweig is doing. It is not precisely what he says, which is that his methodology in part I is philosophical (or, more accurately "meta"-philosophical), in part II, theological (or, again, more accurately "meta"-theological), and in part III sociological. As I read *The Star* the difference between Rosenzweig's philosophy, theology, and sociology has to do with the texts that he is looking at, but not at the way he looks at them. In part I the texts are a standard canon of works in philosophy, from Plato to Hegel. In part II the texts are the Hebrew Scriptures, notably Genesis, the Song of Songs, and Psalms. In part III the texts are Jewish and Christian liturgy. In all three cases the way he reads these texts is what I would call "philosophical," viz. using the tools of logic to dissect (analyze) the words and sentences in the text in order to critique them, and then to reconstruct them into a new, constructive conceptual whole. Hence, from what I can see in the actual text of *The Star*, what Rosenzweig means by "philosophy" is critical and constructive reasoning whose data ultimately come from human sense experience; "theology" is the same kind of reasoning applied to revealed texts. In the same way "sociology," the so-called "discipline" of part III, is the same kind of reasoning, but now applied to communal religious liturgies, especially in the German Orthodox Jewish, Evangelical Christian, and Roman Catholic liturgies.

critically in order to construct a new way of seeing everything beyond Idealism "the new thinking."

This practice of philosophy and metaphilosophy involves what Rosenzweig calls "silent speech." It is what we would call symbolic thinking, constructing interdependent declarative sentences (the kind that can be valued as true or false) where the key terms are abstract variables connected by abstract relational expressions. In my own words, Rosenzweig's silent speech is thinking modeled on algebra.

According to Rosenzweig this kind of thinking has a limited range. In mathematical terms, it can be applied to points through which vectors pass, for they mark definite things or states-of-affairs. However, it cannot be applied to the vectors, which are nothing in themselves (because they are not things) and are always indeterminate (because they are motions, which is to say, constantly changing in every respect except direction). Knowledge of such movement requires a source beyond what we, as human beings, can know on our own. It requires revelation from another, some one other (in fact, radically other) than ourselves. Reason can point, in its analysis of the elements, to a need for an external source of information, but it cannot provide the information on its own. The Hebrew Scriptures are such a source of a revealed word.[6]

Similarly, according to Rosenzweig, as philosophic (i.e., algebraic) reasoning has limits that can only be transcended through the revelation of an other, so revelation itself is limited in that it may point to an end but it cannot understand the end. This limitation is transcended solely through liturgy. Liturgy differs from both philosophy and theology in two critical ways. First, it is a communal rather than an individual product. Second, it invokes reality rather than merely discovering it. In both of these ways, Rosenzweig's "sociology" manifests the highest possible

---

[6] Rosenzweig limits his discussion to the Hebrew Scriptures as a revealed text, but he does not explicitly deny that there can be others. He considers Indian and Chinese religious texts, but he does not treat them as revealed scriptures. Similarly, he says that the Quran appears to be revealed but is not. However, there is no reason to deny that he considers the New Testament to be revealed scriptures, even though he does not discuss it explicitly. The basis for this inference is, of course, that Rosenzweig grants to Christianity the same legitimacy that he grants to Judaism as a religion of revelation, i.e., as a religion rooted in revealed texts. I suppose this claim could be made for Christianity solely on the basis of its adoption of the Hebrew Scriptures as foundational. On this interpretation, the New Testament is to be treated like rabbinic Midrash, which is very important but not revelation. However, I think that this interpretation is somewhat far-fetched, motivated more by wanting to distance Rosenzweig from affirming Christianity than by wanting to provide an accurate reading of his theology. On Rosenzweig's view, Christianity is not for Jews, but that does not mean that he did not affirm it as a true revelation. Again, he did not deny the truth of Christianity as such; what he denied is that it has any religious relevance to Jews living the Jewish life that they ought to live.

human epistemic state, where the line between thinking and being collapses into a single activity.

God is known first through reason as an element of reality, who becomes the other from whom the relations between the elements is revealed, which point to him as the single end towards which all the movements of reality point. I shall now briefly consider God in all three respects – the originating element, the idealized end, and, in between, the radical other who reveals the way or path of reality from origin to end.

THE GOD OF THE ELEMENTS

God is one of the three elements of reality that we know, as elements, from the history of philosophy. The other two are the human and the world. The justification for these claims is the history of western philosophy with which *The Star* begins. That is its primary purpose, namely, to tell us that human conception sees three topics of rational thought that are not reducible to each other. Anything of which we can think is either God, human or part of the human, or the world or part of the world of sensible objects. In each case rational thought ("silent speech" or algebraic reasoning) gives us enough knowledge to know that we do not know anything about what we grasp. In each case there is a critical philosopher whose thinking produces the absolute doubt about its subject matter that can only be transcended through a source other than the isolated thinking individual philosopher or scientist.

In the case of the world, Descartes provides this function. As Rosenzweig reads him, Descartes demonstrated that the physical and mental worlds are radically different worlds, so different that we have good reason to doubt that we can with any rational certainty move beyond the world of our ideas about physical reality to that suspected reality itself.

In the case of the human, the key philosopher is Kant. Kant, as Rosenzweig read him (à la Cohen), demonstrated that human consciousness is reducible to acts of will that are radically different from all objects in the world of consciousness, so different that we have good reason to doubt that we can with any rational certainty move beyond our mere consciousness of being conscious to an understanding of conscious will itself.

Finally, in the case of God, the key philosopher is Maimonides. As we have already seen, Maimonides' negative theology demonstrates that God as the creator of everything else is so radically different from everything that is that this difference constitutes for human reason the definition of God. I will say some more about this definition in relationship to general western philosophy, because the point will play a central role when I later consider general proofs of God's existence as part of this investigation into whether or not the God of the theologians is believable.

Medieval Christian philosophers, such as Anselm, defined God as "a being no greater than which can be conceived."[7] In the light of Maimonides' critique it is important to understand this definition in strict negative terms. God is not, as Descartes interpreted Anselm, a most perfect being. Such a definition means that we can have some kind of positive understanding of what God is, namely, as something perfect. However, God, as Maimonides rightly determined, is so radically different from anything else, that it is literally not correct to say that God is "something" or that he is "perfect," both words having a range of meanings which apply to all creatures, but not to the creator. Rather, the definition of God is that God is uniquely such that anything of which we can think, including something perfect, is not God.

Note, however, that this conclusion of the history of philosophy, that in principle we know nothing about God, does not entail either atheism or even agnosticism. We are not justified in saying that we *know* anything about God. Here the emphasis is on the word "know." That does not mean that we are not justified in *believing* anything about God. Philosophy has no room for belief. Its goal is certainty, but where there is certainty there is no need for belief. Belief is what we have, justified or not, when we affirm something that we cannot know. Hence, philosophy can show us that there is no knowledge of God, but it can say little (if anything) about justified belief in God.

Belief is dependent on a source of information other than us. Whether or not that belief is justifiable depends, not on logical demonstration, but on the reliability of the sources. For Jews at least and probably Christians as well, the source is revelation. Belief in God does not rest on logical inferences from empirical data. There is in this sense no "science" of God. Rather, it comes through a report from a source beyond the human, which, for believing Jews and Christians, is the Hebrew Scriptures. Hence, ultimately, belief in God, at least as the revealer, is dependent on the authority of the words of the Hebrew Scriptures, and that authority in turn rests ultimately on determining their epistemic legitimacy.

---

[7] See *St. Anselm's Proslogion.* English translation by M. J. Charlesworth (Notre Dame, IN: Notre Dame University Press, 1979).

How, then, can philosophy – here meaning human reason – contribute to judging the epistemic legitimacy of a text claimed to be revealed? Clearly Rosenzweig does not accept all claims to revelation as legitimate and therefore authoritative.[8] This question will have to be answered later,[9] but for now I am concerned solely with how Rosenzweig answers it. His answer is that the concept of creation provides a bridge from philosophy to theology.

CREATION AS A BRIDGE FROM PHILOSOPHY TO THEOLOGY

Rosenzweig points out that every complete philosophical or scientific picture of the universe has a cosmogony, a theory of its origin. Through such theories we know something about its origin, but not much. We know that the universe as a whole has an origin, but, whatever that is, it is more than we can fathom. Certainly that is true of most theories of cosmogony advocated by most physical cosmologists at the beginning of the twenty-first century. The universe is seen to be expanding everywhere in such a way the vectors point to a fixed origin in time. However, that origin is such that the universe would have had to be a single object infinitely small with infinite density and infinite temperature. The word "infinite," as it is thrice used in the preceding sentence, is something inconceivable, for nothing actual can be actually infinitely anything, and whatever was in the past in time must have been something actual. Scientists seem convinced that there is a point in time of at least our universe's origin, but the state of the universe at that point is a "singularity." "Singularity" here means that the laws of the universe as we, physicists, know them do not apply, perhaps not even in principle. In other words, astrophysicists claim to know that the universe has an origin, and that all that we know about it is that we know nothing about it. Rosenzweig would read this description[10] as a confirmation of his thesis that of all the relations between the elements, the one that we know the most about scientifically and philosophically is creation, but what we know about it is that we cannot, limited to this tool, know anything about it. What neither philosophy nor science can demonstrate is that

[8] The most notable example is Rosenzweig's discussion of Islam and the Quran (*The Star*, part II, ch. 1, "Islam: The Religion of Necessity"; ch. 2, "Islam: The Religion of Action"; and ch. 3, "Islam: The Religion of Duty," "Islam: The Religion of Progress").

[9] In the concluding section of this chapter that asks whether the God of the theologians is believable.

[10] In his life time most physicists still affirmed a steady-state theory of an eternal universe.

there is more to knowing than knowing; there is also believing; and belief falls not within the domain of philosophy (reasoning from empirically informed premises) but in theology (reasoning from premises derived from the words of revealed texts).

THE GOD OF THE WAYS

There are three kinds of relational movements between the elements God, world, and the human. There is creation, whose origin is in God the creator and whose end is the created world. There is revelation, whose origin is in God the revealer and whose end is the informed human.[11] And finally, there is redemption. Its origin is in the informed human who, through revelation, enters into relation with God. Its end is in the world that becomes transformed through human action into a kingdom of God. Hence, to speak about the "God" of Rosenzweig's thought involves four phases – God as an isolated element (together with the elements the world and the human), God as the creator of the world, God as the revealer of the Torah, and finally God as an idealized kingdom that constitutes human and world redemption.

Belief in the God of creation is informed by the first three chapters of Genesis. I will not deal with them at any length here, since I have already written two books about God in this relationship.[12] Nor will I say much here about belief in Rosenzweig's God of redemption. First, redemption is primarily about the relationship between human beings and the world, and not about God. Second, the primary texts for this discussion are liturgical, neither philosophical nor biblical, and an adequate philosophical/theological analysis of Jewish liturgy would require a separate book. Here I will limit myself only to pointing out that the concept of redemption functions as a bridge from theology to sociology in the same way that creation bridges philosophy and theology. The Scriptures tell us something about the end of days, just as philosophy tells us something

---

[11] More literally, for Rosenzweig, who identifies revelation with the act of love, God is described as the lover and the human as the beloved. I choose this way of speaking here so that I can put off until later the question of just what kind of relation revelation is, viz., does it involve content or just presence? That Rosenzweig, following Buber, identifies it with the act of love, in itself indicates that for him revelation is contentless presence. I agree with this judgment, but it is too soon to affirm it. That affirmation will be held off until later when it can be presented as a reasoned conclusion, and not made here where it can only be an unjustified premise. Besides, Rosenzweig's conception of revelation as contentless is not entirely identical with Buber's, since the former's conception entails a legitimacy to the Torah that the latter did not grant.

[12] *Judaism and the Doctrine of Creation* (Cambridge: Cambridge University Press, 1994) and *The First Seven Days: A Philosophical Commentary on the Creation of Genesis* (Atlanta: Scholars Press, 1993).

about creation, but what it tells us, other than the fact that a kingdom of God is promised and therefore predicted for the end of days, is that we know nothing about it. It is only in the liturgy of the community of worshipers that we gain more information about redemption and the end, but there the information is not even belief, let alone knowledge. Rather, it is only a hope or expectation to which we gesture in communal prayer. However, that gesture is not merely less than belief. On the contrary, it does something that mere belief cannot do – it in itself brings about the hoped-for reality. Hope here is not just a way of believing; it is a way of doing. It generates what neither knowledge nor belief can do; it creates "truth."

What this means, however, is independent of belief in God the creator and the revealer in the sense that while belief in redemption depends logically on the existence of God, the existence and nature of God is independent of redemption. Hence, I will set aside the question of redemption now in hope of returning to it in another book and turn instead to say what, on Rosenzweig's understanding, the Scriptures tell us about revelation between God and the human.

THE GOD OF REVELATION

The God of philosophy is at most the God of creation, about whom we know that we know nothing. This not-knowing is a kind of knowledge. God is uniquely defined as that being, such that whatever is is not God. Hence, everything that was, is, or comes to be in the world defines God by not being him. In this sense, creation is itself a form of revelation, for what is created gives content, albeit negative, to the God of creation.

CREATION AS REVELATION

Creation is revelation in yet another sense – the natural laws of the universe are understood to be manifestations of the will of God. Hence, in knowing science or natural philosophy, we know, albeit imperfectly, the will of God. However, our knowledge that the laws of nature are the will of God is not literally "knowledge." Rather, it is a belief whose source is the text of Genesis that says that God creates the universe by speaking. This speech defines God in yet another way. What God says is his word, his word is expressed as a commandment, and imperatives entail acts of will. Hence, God, like human beings and unlike other kinds of physical objects, has a will through which he utters commands. In this sense there is, so to speak, a common genus for the human and the divine, that is, both will and express what they will. However, here also is the critical difference between the human and the divine. In our case to will to do and to do are different. What we will does not happen just because we will it. Often it does not happen at all. However, in God's case there is no such separation. What God says, so to speak, is.

The "so to speak" here is a necessary qualification. To literally utter speech entails a distinction between the act of will and the physical act. However, as we have seen, in God every act is the same act that is in itself indistinguishable from God. This is how the classical Jewish philosophers interpreted Genesis, and at least in this case their interpretation seems to be the literal meaning of the texts where we are told that "God says" followed by "and it was so" without an intervening "God did" or "God made" or "God caused."

Hence, creation is itself the first revelation, and, as a revelation, it is timeless, for the act of creation is identical with God, so that it must be continuous, without beginning or end. As with creation, so with all subsequent revelation. It is something continuous that, while operative through time and in space, stands outside time and space. The verb "stands" here refers to its origin in God the revealer. While God's act of will/speech is continuous in time and space, God himself is neither temporal nor spatial. In biblical terms, he is neither on earth nor in the heavens, for he precedes both as their creator. Presumably whatever else we may conclude from the Hebrew Scriptures about God the revealer cannot contradict this claim. However else God reveals himself, that revealer as the revealer is non-temporal and non-spatial, even if his revelation can be given a spatial-temporal location.

The reason why every revelation of God must be consistent with God's act of creation is that every act of divine revelation, including creation, is an expression of God's will and God's will is God. Hence, what is primarily revealed in every biblical instance of revelation is God himself, even when what is said says nothing about God.

In general the Hebrew Scriptures say nothing about God even though God appears constantly in them. When he appears it is almost always to an individual human being, and what the text tells us about that appearance is, again, not who or what God is but what God says, and what he says is almost always an explicit or an implicit imperative. Hence, what the Scriptures tell us, beyond what philosophy or science can inform, is the will of God, expressed as the word of God, which is what we can believe about God. In this sense, those Kabbalists who identified the Torah with God[13] understand correctly the literal meaning of the Scriptures. In this sense, then, the Torah is God, that is, God the revealer.

REVELATION AS LOVE

The initial summary I have given so far of what Rosenzweig says about the God of revelation is not explicitly what he says,[14] but it does, I believe, capture the logic underlying his written word. More literally, what Rosenzweig says is the following. Revelation is a movement from an infinitely distant point of origin in the element, God, towards an equally infinitely remote end point in the element, the human. As defining or limit points of this infinite movement, both are transformed. God, who as an element is concealed from everything else, becomes manifest in creation and becomes loving in revelation. Simultaneously, the world – the object of God's act of creation – is transformed from something "enchanted" into something created, and the human – the object of God's act of revelation – is transformed from something secluded into something disclosed. Prior to creation the world is enchanted in the simple sense that whatever is simply is. It is for no reason or for no cause; it is by sheer chance, which is the same as saying, in more poetic language, its existence is magical, "enchanted." Similarly, prior to revelation the human stands alone, isolated from everything except their[15] own act of will. The human wills, but there is no point to the willing, since, unlike God, the human so isolated cannot affect anything by their will.

As long as the human is closed to anything but their own acts of will, they can do nothing. To become effective in the world – to redeem it – the will must become open to a will, a voice, other than their own. That is

---

[13] See two articles in Daniel H. Frank and Oliver Leaman (eds.), *History of Jewish Philosophy* (Routledge History of World Philosophies 2; London and New York: Routledge, 1997): "Jewish Mysticism: A Philosophical Overview," by Elliot R. Wolfson, pp. 450–498, and "Jewish Philosophy on the Eve of Modernity," by Hava Tirosh-Rothschild, pp. 499–573.

[14] For a more literal summary, see Samuelson, *Introduction to Modern Jewish Philosophy*, "Franz Rosenzweig," pp. 212–266, and *A User's Guide to Franz Rosenzweig's Star of Redemption*.

[15] The grammatical inconsistency of using the plural pronoun "their" to refer to the singular expression "the human" is intentional. The human who is the receiver of revelation is necessarily singular, because, as we shall see below, the terms of the relationship of revelation are necessarily individual. Hence, it will not be correct in this case to substitute for the singular "human" the plural "human beings." This judgment would seem to force me to decide, English being limited in the way that it is, between calling the human either masculine or feminine, which is not appropriate – primarily because there are no valid grounds in Rosenzweig's conception of revelation, let alone in the Bible, for saying that males rather than females or females rather than males are the human recipients of divine revelation. Hence, I prefer to be ungrammatical in these cases and use a plural pronoun.

what the word of God does. It opens the willing human to the will of another whose will is not their own. In this openness, the human overcomes their seclusion and becomes, in Rosenzweig's words, "disclosed," for this act of divine self-revelation, self-exposure, also reveals and exposes the other, the human, with whom God so relates. Rosenzweig characterizes this mutual nakedness as "love."

Rosenzweig defines revelation primarily as a relationship between an acting lover, God, and a receiving beloved, the human. In so understanding revelation, Rosenzweig reflects both Kabbalah and early rabbinic interpretations in the Midrash of the accounts of revelation in the writings of the prophets, who also described the relationship between God and Israel as a love affair. More specifically, they characterized it as a troubled love affair, in which God, the husband, loves Israel, the wife, who loves other less deserving deities, to her own shame and guilt.

The early rabbis seized on the Song of Songs as the model of this love relationship, and raised its status in their commentaries as the critical book in the Scriptures, as Genesis is for creation, for understanding divine revelation. Hence, as Rosenzweig caps his discussion of creation with a commentary on Genesis, so he caps his discussion of revelation with a commentary on the Song of Songs. In this commentary, Song of Songs 8:6 – especially the clause "for love is as strong as death" – stands out as the single most important text, in much the same way that the opening verses of the Book of Genesis are singled out for attention in Rosenzweig's discussion of creation. In fact Rosenzweig opens his chapter on the God of revelation (*The Star*, part II, ch. 2) with an explanation of this clause.[16] The way that Rosenzweig sees death and love to be comparable in itself illuminates his understanding of revelation.

No human act is more isolating than the act of dying. It is totally individual in at least the material sense that no one can participate in your death even if they can cause it or aid it. No human may be able to live alone, but every one, in this sense, dies alone.

Death also brings an individual life to its conclusion, both in the sense that with it life ends and in the sense that whatever it is that you can become you have become it at the moment of death. From that point on, you simply are who you are, for the time to change is past. Love also is a conclusion, for in love you cease to be a secluded individual and become, in Rosenzweig's terms, a "soul," which he interprets to mean someone who has opened themselves to an other. In love you become disclosed.

---

[16] See Samuelson, *A User's Guide*, pp. 144–146.

You can no longer hide yourself. You are who you are, but now who you are is not for yourself, but for a specific, totally concretized other, the lover. In love your isolated life comes to an end, for who you were then is no longer who you are now. You come to life, but that life is a life for another, which entails an end, a death, to your life for yourself. In other words, contrary to Buber, the I and the you have been transcended by the we. Now, again as in death, this act is radically particular. You cannot love an abstraction, and you cannot love in general. You may love often, but each love is a love of a single individual. That individual remains other than you. The lover and the beloved do not become absorbed into each other. Rather, they cease to be two people; instead they become, again in Rosenzweig's words, "besouled," which is to say, each becomes a soul, a being who is a being by being open and receptive to the other.

God loves everything he creates, for everything he creates makes him who he is by not being him. However, he does not love the world, because that is a mere abstraction. What he does is love each and every thing or person in it, one at a time, all of the time. When we become open to that love, which is always available, we too become, like God (or, in the image of God), a living soul. When so opened to God's presence, we hear God's word, but that word is not literally words; it is God's presence, grasped intimately and lovingly as a pure presence without any cover whatsoever, which is to say – as it was for Buber – without definition, conception, spoken or unspoken language or speech (Sprache). However, and here again is a major difference between God and us, the love we experience as a pure, undefined act of will must be expressed by us as speech. It is we, the beloved, who speak words, not God, because we must make real what we desire, and that requires action, not mere thought, for it is the essential limitation of our humanity that what we wish and what we do are not the same thing.

It is in this way, according to Rosenzweig, that the revelation of God becomes expressed in human language as imperatives, and it is this response that is recorded through the actual words of the Hebrew Scriptures. Still, although they are products of human action, they are nonetheless divinely revealed, because they are our necessary response, "necessary" because of our inherent limitations as (albeit willing and speaking) creatures, to God's presence as our lover, which is to say, as the God of revelation.

The verbal form of the responses to God's presence is not exclusively, but overwhelmingly, expressions of law. Buber saw these expressions as the first step of religious communities in the direction of idolatry.

Rosenzweig reads them differently, and that difference is why Rosenzweig is more successful than Buber in providing a philosophical theology that can make sense out of the fundamental claim of any form of rabbinic Judaism that God gave the Torah to Israel through Moses at Sinai.

THE DIALECTIC OF REVELATION

Buber described revelation as a three-stage movement from encountering God as an eternal I–Thou, to an I–Thou associated with an I–It, to an idolatrous misidentity of the living God with some It. In the case of rabbinic Judaism, the "It" is Torah, here understood as *halakhah*, the entire legal system of Jewish communal life. For Buber, the history of revelation is a history of disintegration from a living, albeit unstable, relation at the beginning to a dead, albeit stable, lack of relationship at the end.

Rosenzweig's description of the history of revelation is more complicated and more constructive. It may be characterized in five steps: monologue, question, call, hearing and command, and revelation proper.

Monologue

Every individual human being comes into existence like every other living creature, uttering the word "I." "Uttering" here is not, of course, literally an expression of speech. It is, rather, a way of being in the world. We all begin as nothing seeking to become something. Each act we, and all life, take by nature in the world is to make something of ourselves, to be something, in full recognition that just as we are created out of nothing so what we are when first created is nothing. This is the human being whom the life sciences – biology, anthropology, sociology, paleoanthropology, and so on – study. It is who we are by nature. In the terms of the Hebrew Scriptures, human beings, like all created life forms, have one and only one divine commandment that is programmed into our created natures – "be fruitful and multiply" (Gen. 1:22, 28) – which simply means that each of us in our singularity, our "I," strives to become something, to "matter."

If God were only a God of creation and the human were only a creature, there would be nothing more to say about being human than what the human sciences, at least potentially, say. However, in fact there is much more to being human than this, and the "more" lies beyond the domain of scientific knowledge. More is manifest to us about the will of God than self-promotion. There is also selfless love for the other that God manifests to us through revelation.

Question

God's uncovering of himself to the human begins with the question, "Where are you?" What Rosenzweig has in mind here is Genesis 3:9. It is the first time that God speaks directly to the first human in the created world, that is, after the entire process of creation – including the separation of the female and the male from the generic human – reaches its conclusion (at the end of Gen. 2). That process ends with the words "And they, the male and the female, were both naked and were not ashamed" (Gen. 2:25). Maimonides (*Guide* II:30) interpreted this story to mean that the man (at least) had perfect theoretical wisdom, but as of yet had no practical, that is, ethical, wisdom, because he had, in his perfection, no need for it. On Rosenzweig's interpretation, the perfection involved here is that of a natural creature, someone who is a living animal much the same as other animals, which is why his perfection involves no consciousness of ethics, and therefore not as yet someone who is fully human, because he has not as yet a soul. Ethical consciousness begins with the question, "Where are you?" (Gen. 3:9).

The call

Rosenzweig characterizes the initial response to the question that God's presence raises as not an answer *per se* but a call. The initial call is "I am." "I am" says more than just the "I" of the originating monologue. In "I" there is consciousness of nothing but self. "I am" is no less self-centered and self-serving, but it involves recognition that there is more, at least in principle, than yourself. If I can say "I am," I can recognize that I need not be, and that I need not be means that I am not all that is.

These realizations from God's initial presence provoke fear, or, as Adam says in answer to God's first question, "I heard your voice in the garden and I was afraid, because I was naked, and I hid myself." A "voice" is not speech. In fact it is in itself nothing at all. Here all that it means is that Adam was aware of God, and his response to that awareness was fear.

His quoted answer to the non-question question is an explanation of the fear. It is not something he says; it is something he becomes. First, he becomes self-conscious of being naked, of being who he is without any concealment. Second, that consciousness produces shame. He knows who he is, namely, he is not God, and that knowledge makes him ashamed. Third, his response to his shame is concealment. God's self-revelation makes the human aware of his mere humanity, and that awareness produces a shame-of-being-one's-self, that the human responds to with concealment. He makes clothes to cover himself so that no one – neither God nor himself – can see or hear who he really is. He is really someone alone, and it is the loneliness, despite the presence of his other "side" (his "Eve"), the isolation, that is shameful.

Clothing, hiding, will not solve his problem. What he needs is to be loved. So his unspoken, lived call to God, in response to the question of the divine presence, is (in Rosenzweig's words) "Love me now." However, it is a call that God does not answer, at least not until the time of Abraham.

Abraham is the first human to whom God appears after he recreates the world with the descendants of Noah. God does not question. He simply addresses Abraham by his proper name, as a definite individual. He says "Abraham," but Abraham answers as if the utterance of his name were the question addressed to Adam. Abraham says, as if he were asked where he is, "Here I am" (Gen. 22:1).

Abraham's call is different from Adam's call. Pre-revelation the human only knows "I." With revelation he at least knows that he is, but he has no sense of who or what he is. He is still, as he was born, a nothing, only now he is a nothing that can become something. Abraham, on the other hand, is something, because he is somewhere – he is and he is "here." Being here means he has location in the world, so that at least to some extent his identity is broader than himself. Now God appears to him, and from that appearance he learns that his context in space and time is not really his, for God asks him to give up everything that he so far is.

When God first appeared to Abraham (in Gen. 12:1 ff.) he told him to give up all that he was, namely, being a man with a country and a family, to become something else. Abraham had become something else – a founder of a nation of his own, that God has promised to make great and mighty (Gen. 17:8), and that this greatness would be achieved through a line of biological descendants beginning with Isaac, his "only son" (Gen. 22:2). Still, God calls on him at least to be willing to give up that son before God's promise has been fulfilled. Abraham was something who again saw himself as nothing in the presence of God, only to become something again, which God, through his presence, again commands Abraham to give up. In his call to God Abraham is something, but

the call entails a response from God that will change what he was into
something new.

The hearing and the command

God's response is to command, as he commands Abraham to sacrifice
his son. However, this is not the highest level of revelation. As the description of Abraham's encounter with God represents a higher level
than that of Adam, so beyond the level of Abraham's prophecy is the
prophecy of Moses. In Moses' case the call is first to "hear" before being commanded. "Hear" (*shema'* in the imperative form) means here to
obey. Israel, through the presence of its leader Moses, agrees to obey the
word of God even before they hear the word (Exod. 24:7). This is, on
Rosenzweig's reading, the proper transition into a relationship of love.
Here relation is no longer dependent on self-service. Here there is total
openness to the presence of the other. Israel with Moses does not say
"love me now" – love me because I need your love. It says instead that it
is ready, without thought of self, to love God – to hear what God desires
and (at least try) to obey.

What God says in response to Israel's hearing is to command love.
His words are the so-called "love command" (Liebesgebot) which con-
flates two otherwise separate divine commandments – "you shall love the
Lord your God . . . " (Deut. 6:5; 11:1) and "you shall love your neighbor
as yourself" (Lev. 19:18). The proper response to recognizing the total
openness, that is, love, of another to you is to respond in kind to them.
However, there can be no direct response to God as God, because of his
perfection. Hence, the response, namely, to love, is directed not to God
the revealer who is the creator, but to his creation. However, "creation" as
such cannot be loved, because it is an abstraction while love is inherently
particular. Hence, you are commanded, so to speak, to love not creation
as such but that particular creature, whoever he or she is, who happens
to be nigh to you, that is, your "neighbor." In loving the neighbor, you
love God.

Revelation and beyond

It is this commandment to love a particular person who simply happens
to be near to you that is revelation proper. Its expression in the Scriptures,
according to Rosenzweig, is "Thus says the Lord." Of course, that does
not mean that God in fact says what he says. Rather, God's love, given

as a pure divine presence, calls for a response from you, the beloved, that can only be fulfilled by doing to another what God has done for you, namely, loving them. However, that love command can be no more general than the object of love can be general. As the lover and the beloved must be concrete, so must the obligation to love, which is expressed as an imperative (as commandments), be specific. Hence, it is Torah, the system of law, that is a concrete instantiation of the love of neighbor that is, in turn, a specific manifestation of the love between God and the human, which is, finally, simply nothing more than the pure (Buber-like) mutual presence, without content or even form, of God and the human.

The reception of and response to the specific expressions of love of neighbor call for shame as well as atonement. "Shame" because in being commanded you are aware that you have not done what you ought to do, and "atonement" because in accepting the obligation to do what is right you atone for not having done it yet. However, shame and atonement are only an initial response in relationship to the neighbor. Beyond and through that relationship is the relationship with God the revealer himself. With God there is the acknowledgment by the human that "I am yours," and in God there is the recognition that "You are mine."

What Rosenzweig has in mind by this last biblical quotation is Isaiah 43:1. The full verse reads as follows: "And now, thus said the Lord, your creator O Jacob and your former O Israel. Do not be afraid, because I redeemed you. I called you by your name; you are mine." As Rosenzweig reads this text it is an expression of revelation, of the word of God, that goes beyond the prophecy of Moses in the sense that it points beyond the revelation at Sinai, whose command was to form the Jewish people into the theocratic nation described in the Torah as Pentateuch, to the reformation of the Jewish people after the destruction of the first Jewish polity into a land-transcendent nation who, through their obedience to the Torah, now in the sense of *halakhah*, will be a light beacon to humanity as it redeems the world.

The "now" with which the verse opens says that revelation is always in the present, never in the past or the future. Hence, in this sense, revelation is no less atemporal than is creation.

"Jacob" and "Israel" identify the beloved of God's love as the Jewish people who are here identified as a singular, as an individual, over and against individual Jews. It is important to note, as I will discuss below, that for Rosenzweig the element that stands in relationship to the world and God, the human, is a singular. It is not a generalized reference to the plurality of human beings. That single entity becomes, through its relationship with God in revelation, two. It becomes the Jewish people and the rest of humanity who are designated either as pagans (i.e., those who have not, at least from birth, experienced the love of God) and those individual pagans who, as Christians, have experienced divinely revealed love by other Christians, as they join together on the way to redeeming the world.

"I have called you by your name" says that revelation is intimate and non-conceptual, because a proper name has reference but not meaning, and it is completely definite in that it has only a single referent. Finally, "you are mine" expresses the nature of the relationship as one of love between a divine lover and a human beloved. That love is the founding act for the redemption of the world, as the rest of the Isaiah passage goes on to describe. In other words, the love-command described in the first verse of chapter 43 initiates a process through history of lovers transforming through love those unloved into beloveds who in turn love others until "all the nations are gathered together and the peoples are assembled" (Isa. 43:9) to acknowledge the "truth" (Isa. 43:9) of an ultimate, finally universal redemption.

What the Jewish people do to contribute towards that redemption is the final stage of revelation. They pray. It is critical to Rosenzweig's understanding of the universe that the Jewish people, as a people, are a single individual who collectively exists, and that the essential function of this people in history is to pray collectively to God in accordance with Jewish law.

There is much in this claim about prayer and redemption that is controversial and requires critical investigation. However, it is a topic that lies beyond the scope of this book. For present purposes it is sufficient to say, and is sufficiently problematic on its own terms, that the revelation that Rosenzweig describes has as its lowest manifestation creation and as its highest expression redemption. Hence, ultimately the God of creation, who is accessible at least (no matter how inadequately) through human reason and science, becomes the God of redemption, who is barely accessible through revelation but becomes as manifest as he can become through what Jewish (and Christian) liturgy express in gesture about the vision of a realized kingdom of God. These claims are sufficient for now to entertain the same question that I raised with the Hebrew Scriptures, Maimonides, and Buber – is this conception of revelation believable?

IS THE GOD OF ROSENZWEIG BELIEVABLE?

REVIEW

The discussion of the God of revelation from the perspective of Judaism concluded with the theology of Rosenzweig. I began by focusing on the centrality of the concept of revelation for the Abrahamic religions – Judaism, Christianity, and Islam. None of these religions can survive if as religions their practice is not compelling on individual members, and it cannot be compelling if it is not believable. Hence, no Abrahamic religion can be simply a system of spiritual practice; such practice must be motivated by a system of beliefs that means that the practice has moral value, and the practice cannot have moral value if its underlying beliefs are not true. Hence, at its heart, the problem of religious identity in the modern world is a philosophic problem – what beliefs are foundational for the religious practice, and are those beliefs true? The answer given to the first part of the question – what beliefs are foundational? – is a belief in revelation, which is only believable if it is true that there is a God who is not only a creator but also a revealer, which, in the case of Judaism, means a God who is revealed in the Torah to the people Israel. However, before I can deal directly with this question – why can some but not most people believe in such a deity? – I have to clarify just what is involved, at least for Jews, in such a belief, and that is why I have been surveying what the resources of Jewish philosophy, both classical and modern, have to say about God the revealer. That survey brought me – by way of Maimonides and from him to Cohen and Buber – to the theology of Franz Rosenzweig.

CHALLENGES

From ethics

The sources of Rosenzweig's theology include at least those isolated in discussing Buber's description of an eternal thou – Maimonides' negative theology, Kant's metaphysics, and Cohen's infinitesimal method of philosophical analysis – but there are other texts as well that are distinctively part of Rosenzweig's analysis. These other texts are both Jewish and German.

Most importantly, in terms of Jewish texts, Rosenzweig's reading of Maimonides is tempered by his understanding of, and commitment to, the religious philosophy of Judah Halevi (*c.* 1075–1141). Halevi believed, as did Rosenzweig, that being Jewish is different than being, for example, Christian, primarily because Christians become Christian solely because they affirm the faith claims of Christianity, but Jews are Jews by birth. Hence, there is something like (but not identical with) a racial dimension to Rosenzweig's theology that is not operative in any Jewish philosophy considered so far.

Furthermore, Halevi, even more than Maimonides, believed that the range of what can be known by empirically informed reasoning on an algebraic model is limited, and that almost every critical or fundamental religious belief transcends that range. Similarly, Rosenzweig absorbed the critical perspective on reason of German thinkers, such as Friedrich Nietzsche (1844–1900), who sowed the seeds in early twentieth-century Europe for a revival of a new conservatism that opposed – both intellectually and politically – the modernist synthesis that had won wide acceptance (at least among intellectuals) at the dawn of the twentieth century. That synthesis included an affirmation of the moral value of the rational life, the veridical value of the empirical method of the natural sciences, and the political virtue of individual human autonomy, which in turn entailed the moral values of democracy and human rights.

Rosenzweig does not discuss any of these values, and the omission itself is problematic, especially because it suggests the kind of German intellectualism current at the time that influenced his religious beliefs. That intellectualism played no minor role in forming the most insidious aspects of the Nazism that swept the German-speaking world in the generation after Rosenzweig died. In part what draws us to Rosenzweig is that his religious thought, in many ways like Buber's, seems to make sense out of Jewish religious tradition in a way that Buber's thought cannot. To slightly oversimplify, Buber was too committed to modern liberalism to see any viability in Jewish traditionalism. In this respect at least, Rosenzweig is more satisfactory. However, Rosenzweig may not be liberal enough to save us from affirming a kind of Jewish fascism – one that sees the world in terms of race and that has no place in its system of values for individual rights.

The question is, are these accidental or essential features of the religious thought of Buber and Rosenzweig? Is valuing traditional religious observance, especially in Judaism and Christianity, intellectually incompatible with valuing modernist politics, especially in western republics and democratic societies? Must we choose between a commitment to the life of Torah on grounds that undermine modernity, as Rosenzweig seems to do, or a commitment to an anarchistic spiritual life on grounds that undermine any form of Jewish community that takes seriously the imperatives of the Torah, as Buber seems to do? Is there not a third way between a traditionalist life of Torah and secularist humanism?

From the natural sciences

This is another way of stating the central question of this book. When I ask whether Judaism is believable, the obvious answer is – yes, at least on traditional terms, which means that if we believe in the total world and life view[17] of the pre-modern rabbis, then Judaism is imminently believable. However, I, and most other people, especially Jews, can no longer believe precisely what these rabbis believed. As we have seen, no voice of traditional Jewish belief is better than Maimonides', but even Maimonides' affirmation of the life of Torah cannot be affirmed independently of his entire philosophy, which is deeply rooted in a certain kind of worldview – a view whose origin is not the Hebrew Scriptures, but the science of the ancient Greeks, as that science was interpreted through a tradition of Christian and Muslim commentators. It is that worldview that no longer is believable, at least by most educated people in western civilization. Our choice is not just about what we must believe to affirm a life of Torah. It is rather a question of what we can believe, living today rather than when Maimonides lived, for what he could believe, especially about the sciences, we cannot.

Stated in more general terms, a belief in God is never an independent belief. The term "God" functions as a part of a system of beliefs that ultimately entails some belief about everything. The God of Judaism is at least the creator of the world who reveals himself through Torah to humanity. As such, God is a being who stands in some form of relationship to the world (as its creator) and to humanity (as its revealer). Hence, what we can believe about God is not independent of what we believe about the universe and human beings. The former is philosophically a subject of ontology, and that philosophy is dependent on what we learn about the world in all of the physical sciences (physics, astronomy, chemistry, etc.); the latter is philosophically a subject of ethics, a philosophy that is dependent on what we learn about being human in the life sciences (psychology, biology, anthropology, sociology, etc.). These sciences

---

[17] By "world and life view" I am thinking of the German "Weltanschauung" and "Lebenschauung." For simplicity of reference I will from this point on say "worldview," but my usage includes the meaning of both German terms.

inform a world view, and whatever we think about God is in relationship to that unified view. Our world view today is not the same as the philosophies that underlie any of the Jewish theologies so far considered, and it is to our view that I will turn next. What, in general, do we believe about the world and human life, and how does that set of beliefs inform what we think about a God who reveals a Torah to a Jewish people?[18]

From history

None of these questions are easy to answer. However, they do not represent as critical a problem for believability, especially of a theology modeled on a world view similar to Rosenzweig's, as do the problems inherent in modern academic history. And none of the problems of history are as critical for our Jewish theology as what modern historians claim about the Bible.

The problem of the academic study of history is simply this – history tries to model itself on modern science, and such a conception of history leaves no room for a viable conception of a God who reveals himself to the human within the world. Every science attempts to look systematically at empirical data in order to form theories that minimally make the data intelligible and ideally enable informed human beings to make practical predictions based on those theories. Furthermore, theories are ultimately about causes of events, and only certain kinds of causes are considered admissible, namely mechanical causes that can be expressed and tested in quantitative terms. In effect, modern historians assume that the study of history excludes from its domain any consideration of purpose in nature as well as any qualitative causal factors that are not reducible to quantitative judgments. Hence, so far as historians are concerned as historians, the universe is exclusively physical and inherently purposeless.

In making these assumptions as academicians, modern historians are no different than scholars in the human sciences, who also, in their hope to make their disciplines "scientific," model their conceptual categories as well as their investigative methodology on the physical sciences. The

---

[18] I have posed these questions about revelation in Jewish terms as questions about the intelligibility of God as the revealer of the Torah. Of course a similar line of questioning could be posed, in the case of Islam, about God as the revealer of the Koran. In the case of Christianity, however, just what it means to affirm revelation is significantly different. I will return in the final chapter of this book to that difference in comparison to what is said here about a believable conception of God as revealer in the case of Judaism.

hope of both the historians and the human scientists is that by imitating the methods of the physical scientists they can approximate (at least) their success.

Those scientists who are philosophically sophisticated and conceptually rigorous will claim that the exclusion of factors such as the spiritual (here meaning anything not physical, i.e., not extended in space and time) and the purposeful from their studies is purely methodological; it does not mean (and logically it should not mean) that the spiritual and the purposeful are not dimensions of reality. They only claim that these dimensions lie outside what they, as modern academics, can study. However, the implications of their chosen limitation are more radical than this, once we add an additional, philosophic (rather than scientific) premise – what does not fall within the domain of science cannot be known, and what cannot be known makes no difference in human existence in this empirical world.

All of the theologies I have considered, from the Hebrew Scriptures to Rosenzweig, make a radically different claim about the world, the human, and the interrelationship between them. They all posit a world that is purposeful, human beings who are more than extended objects in space and time, and – in addition to the world and the human – a God who created the world, who reveals himself to the human, and whose being is an essential factor in understanding both physical events in the world (viz., as created) and how human beings interact with each other (viz., as souls who love and are loved, by each other and ultimately by God). Clearly none of these claims can be rendered, in any meaningful sense, scientific. Clearly none of these claims can be said to be known in any sense that is acceptable within academic science. However, does that mean that such claims are not believable, even by people committed to modern academic science, that is, by reasonable people?

From biblical studies

If we assume, at least for the moment, that an affirmative answer can be given to this question, we still must face, in all honesty, the particular challenge to belief in a religious Judaism that arises from modern, critical biblical studies. For at least a century it has been almost universally accepted by scholars in this discipline that all of the books of the Hebrew Scriptures are a human product that exhibit not primarily the hand of God in history but the politics of (at least the leadership of) the Jewish nation in the ancient Near East. In other words, the study of the Bible is, in the modern sense of the term, scientifically modeled history, and not religiously motivated theology.

More specifically, the Hebrew Scriptures are an edited collection of works written much earlier than their editing, and the works included within the collection are themselves composed from earlier works, which are themselves composed from earlier works. While the many books of the Bible appear to be the work of single authors – divine or divinely inspired – they in fact contain within them many layers of earlier, independently written texts. Furthermore, at each level of compilation the editors (and they always seem to be plural) rewrote and reshaped the originals, transforming their content and form to express what the editors intended. The task of the biblical historian, so understood, is to isolate all of the different layers, locate each in the appropriate space and time, and tell us as much as it is possible to know about each group of author-editors in their historical location.

This most general understanding of biblical scholarship is called "source criticism." Its validity was debated with great vigor in the nineteenth and early twentieth centuries, but today it is taken for granted. As such, its role for biblical studies is comparable in status to the assumption of some form of theory of evolution by geneticists and even biologists in general.

Evolution

The theory of evolution, classically expressed by Darwin but adopted today by life scientists in a far more sophisticated form, is the core philosophical assumption that underlies modern biology, and it is an assumption that is especially troubling to many contemporary Christian theologians. They see evolution as the critical challenge to Christian faith in the sense that no one can seriously affirm Christianity who has not come to terms with what that faith means in the light of modern, that is, evolutionary, biology. Evolution and biology play no comparable role in Jewish thought. However, as I have argued here, modern (quantitative and causally mechanical) history, especially modern (source-critical) biblical history, is as crucial for considering what constitutes a believable Jewish faith as is evolutionary biology for Christianity.

In its most simplistic reading[19] evolutionary biology, especially as it is applied to the study of the human, that is, to anthropology, suggests that

---

[19] As in the kinds of interpretations presented by Richard Dawkins in *The Selfish Gene* (New York and London: Granada Publishing Co., 1978) and Daniel Dennett in *Darwin's Dangerous Idea: Evolution*

humans, like all other living things, are driven primarily by their desire to survive – in themselves in the present and through their offspring in the future. For many Christians – who believe that it is possible for human beings to transcend their mere physical natures and live their lives by a higher, trans-human, more divine, altruistic, spiritual standard – these biologically universal claims from philosophers of the life sciences are especially challenging.

However, there is no special challenge in these claims to biblically grounded Jewish theology. The claims of the modern biologists simply inform, even enrich, our understanding of what the Hebrew Scriptures mean when they say that the one commandment revealed to all living creatures is to procreate, a commandment no less fundamental to human beings who transcend the animal in significant ways but always remain animals. The issue is, what makes being human significantly more than being an animal? The prima facie answer of the Scriptures is that humans have seven commandments, six in addition to the one given to all life, and Jews as Jews are subject to the obligation of an additional six hundred and six commandments. However, these additional obligations are not a result of their biochemical make up. Their origin is in revelation, and revelation as such is independent of the claims of genetics. To a certain (admittedly minor) extent genetics confirms the Scriptures in the way that we have cited, namely, it makes sense of the first commandment (to be fruitful and multiply) as natural revelation by the creator deity, and is consistent with the textually recorded revelation of the revealer deity. In other words, there seems to be nothing in biology that is inconsistent with what has been discussed above about the God who reveals himself to the nation Israel in the Torah. However, source-critical studies of the Bible challenge this theology in a singular way that goes beyond any other challenge from any other modern academic discipline.

Source criticism

What the Jewish philosophers have to say about the God of revelation is not based on experience in the natural world. In this way we can come to form a reasonable belief about the God of creation, but not about the God of revelation. Rather, theological claims about the revealer are

and the Meanings of Life (London: Penguin Books, 1995) in their popular science publications. There is no necessity to interpret in the way that they do the implications of genetics and the other life sciences for humane (non-scientific) disciplines such as politics and ethics. However, their arguments are plausible inferences from the science which, as such, demand serious reflection by political theorists and ethicists, especially those who would like to put their philosophy on a more "scientific" footing than it has been on so far.

based on accepting the authority of the Hebrew Scriptures as a testimony to the claim that God does reveal himself to human beings in history.

As we have seen, the affirmation of the Hebrew Scriptures as a revealed text need not mean that every statement in it is true. Clearly, as I have cited above, many are not. Consequently, all who affirm the revelation of the Torah in some simplistic way – that God dictated the words of the Torah, that the Torah we possess is an accurate record of those words, and that any statement in the Torah, in its literal sense, is true – will have difficulty defending or justifying their belief. Fortunately, as we have seen, no serious Jewish thinker, at least since the time of the destruction of the second Temple, has read the Scriptures in this way. Their answer has been twofold. First, the written and spoken words of the Torah are a response to the encounter between God and Israel, and not a stenographic record. In this sense, revelation is to be understood in line with what classical liberal Judaism called "divine inspiration." Second, the Torah is a guide but only a guide to our understanding of God in his relationship to humanity and the world through revelation. As a guide we take what it says very seriously, where "seriously" means we try our best to understand what it means, giving it the best possible interpretation that we can, and then we raise the critical question – is what it says true? – tending always in our reading of the text to attribute to it a meaning that is true, or (at least) reasonable.

From a religious perspective, the statements in the Torah place a moral demand on us that they be taken seriously as authoritative for directing our lives and our thought about our lives. What source criticism challenges is not merely the truth of any particular reading of the Scriptures. That is easy to handle. Any reading that is not true cannot in principle be a proper reading. It is the task of Jewish theology to reread constantly the words of the Scriptures in order to find better – more true and more insightful – interpretations. Rather, the challenge is to taking the Hebrew Scriptures seriously, in any moral or intellectual sense, as an authority at all. I will explain.

There is no consensus among Bible scholars on where, when, and by whom critical events occurred in the evolution of our present texts of the Hebrew Scriptures, but all of them agree that the development occurred in something like the following way:[20] a group of Hebrew-speaking priests in the land of Israel collected together traditions about the history of their nation from different regions of the nation and put

---

[20] See chapter 8 "Are the Hebrew Scriptures revealed?"

them together in what at least appears to be a single, coherent story of their nation's history. The history itself serves as a background to give authority to what was their central concern, namely, to put down in writing the theocratic legal structure of the nation that they ruled. Many of the laws in this text had existed before these priests came to power, but other laws were innovations of their own. This distinction, between what is new and what is old, is intentionally hidden to make there appear to be a single expression of law, the authority for which rests on its ancient origin as the word of the deity of the nation to the people's ancestors. Its authority is that its precepts are ancient, those who accepted them were the founding fathers of the nation, and their author is the God who not only rules Israel through revelation but also rules the universe through creation. Eventually these priests are supplanted by other groups of priests who continue the process of papering over innovation by fusing the new elements that they introduce into the inherited elements synthesized by the priests they overthrew. Eventually the five books of Moses take on their present form, are wedded to other collections formed in the same way – the books of the prophets and the writings – and ultimately are edited into what is more or less our present Hebrew Scriptures, all of which become identified as the word of God revealed to Israel through its prophets.

How many such revisions took place and when they took place is a matter of debate. There is not even agreement on when the final codification of our present Hebrew Scriptures occurred. However, the common thread that runs through all of these accounts is that the act of editing was motivated by politics (viz., the desire to give authority in the guise of continuity with the past for what was in reality revolutionary), and that the intention of these creative editors was to deceive (viz., the political need to present a history as true that they knew not to be true).

This account is, admittedly, simplistic, and is so stated for the sake of emphasis. There are ways to soften this story, and some of these ways will be considered below. However, even when softened, the implication remains the same. The Hebrew Scriptures are not a response to an encounter between God and the human; they are in every respect merely a human product, and, more than that, a product by human beings whose intentions were politically selfish, without any positive valuation for telling the truth. As such, it is highly doubtful that what their words say deserve the attention of spiritually motivated people who read those words in order to determine what is right, what is good, and how human beings, under divine guidance, can help to bring about redemption.

SUMMARY

These, then, are all of the challenges to the account of the God of revelation that must be considered before it can be said that belief in him is reasonable. First, with specific reference to my judgment that the best reading of revelational theology in Jewish philosophy is Rosenzweig's, we must come to terms with his apparent racism and irrationalism, which at least threaten to entail some form of political and moral fascism. In this context I must consider whether Rosenzweig's verbal picture can be reformed to exclude these dangers without destroying the picture itself.

Second, beyond the specifics of Rosenzweig's theology, we must come to terms with the fact that the early twentieth-century science and philosophy which underlie Rosenzweig's religious thought is no less foreign to us today, at the beginning of the twenty-first century, than is the Platonic-Aristotelian philosophy and natural science that Maimonides used to state his theology. Questions will have to be asked about just how different modern philosophy and science are from those of Rosenzweig's day and how those differences affect our acceptance of Rosenzweig's picture of reality. Again in this context, I will have to consider whether this theology of revelation can be reformed to deal with those differences without destroying the theology itself. In this context I will look at what physical cosmology tells us about the world, what evolutionary psychology tells us about the human, and what analytic philosophy of religion tells us about God.

Third, and most critically, I will look to see if we can understand modern academic history and biblical studies in such a way that it remains intelligible for us to grant sufficient authority for our life and thought to the words of the Hebrew Scriptures to be able to say, reasonably and with honesty, that they are revealed. It is this third challenge that is the most critical to any contemporary affirmation of the central religious claim of all forms of Judaism – that God revealed the Torah to Israel through Moses.

PART II

Is the God of revelation believable?

CHAPTER 5

The challenges of political ethics – issues of racism and the irrational

TRUTH TESTS: CONSISTENCY, COHERENCE, AND HISTORICAL FALSIFICATION

How are we to judge the truth value of a worldview such as the ones considered in the first part of this book? A first test is whether the view is consistent and coherent. To the extent that it is not, it is problematic. "Problematic" does not mean that it is not true. There may be much in it that does deserve consent, but all of it cannot be affirmed, at least not without reservations. The assumption underlying this judgment is fundamental to reasoning. Two clear statements that contradict each other cannot both be true. They may both be false or one of them may be true, but not both. The views considered in part I were sufficiently sophisticated philosophically, including the worldview of the Hebrew Scriptures, to pass at least this first test. However, it is only a first test. A view that is consistent and coherent may be true (i.e., it is possibly true), but that does not mean that it is true. The biblical worldview, understood in the literal or plain sense of the text, was judged false not because it is inconsistent or incoherent in itself but because it was not consistent with observed facts.

The critical fact underlying its rejection in Jewish history was that the nation of Judea fought three wars against the pagan Romans in order to preserve and defend the legal system of the Torah; in all three cases the pagans defeated the Torah-true Jews, and this fact is inconsistent with central claims in the Hebrew Scriptures about the meaning of history – that those who obey the Torah will receive material rewards in this world and those who disobey the Torah will receive material punishments. The Romans clearly violated the Torah's provisions governing the nations of the world and Judah clearly followed the Torah's provisions governing Israel, but it was Judah, not Rome, who was punished with material failure (viz., its nation was destroyed), and it was Rome, not Judah, who was rewarded with material success (viz., its empire survived and even prospered).

Rabbinic Judaism is a reconstruction of the biblical view that over-comes this critical problem. It affirms the truth of the words of the Hebrew Scriptures, but it develops non-literal interpretations of those words. The classical worldview that philosopher rabbis such as Maimonides developed is coherent and consistent,[1] and it is not subject to the simple kind of empirical falsification to which a literal interpreta-tion of the Scriptures is subject. However, that does not mean that it is not falsifiable.

As we have seen, Maimonides' interpretation of the faith of Israel out of the words of the Hebrew Scriptures presupposes a general schema from the best science or natural philosophy (for present purposes these are two ways of saying the same thing) of his day, and it is this interpretive schema that is falsifiable. If Judaism is to be affirmed on Maimonides' terms, we must affirm his sciences – both the physical ones (notably his physics, astronomy, and biology) and the humane ones (notably his psychology, epistemology, logic, and ethics). However, few today would be willing to affirm the truth of his scientific worldview in the light of modern science. Clearly, modern and Aristotelian science make contra-dictory claims, so that while both may be wrong, both cannot be true. If modern science is believable, then in many critical claims Aristotelian science is not, and most of us, given this choice, will rely on modern over medieval science.

REASONABLE BELIEF RATHER THAN KNOWLEDGE

The modern theologies of Buber and Rosenzweig have the advantage over Maimonides' philosophy in that their claims do not rest on obsolete scientific views. Still, once again, that does not mean that they are true. My concern, however, is not to prove, in any rigorous sense, truth claims about the God of revelation. If that were possible, I would do so, but in principle it is not possible. I grant that claims such as those that concern us – that there is a God who both created the world and revealed the

---

[1] Or, more or less coherent and consistent. Chapter 3, on the modern move to theology beyond philosophy, isolated some problems of incoherence in the presupposed philosophy, notably in its theory of knowledge. Aristotelian epistemology defended a correspondence theory of truth, said that all that is knowable by the intellect are universals, and also claimed that what exists in reality is particular – and the conjunction of these three claims is incoherent. In the next chapter, on questions that modern science and philosophy raise about the truth of the present determined theology, I will consider other problems in the presupposed natural philosophy of Maimonides.

Torah through Moses to the nation Israel – cannot be proven, but neither can they be disproven.[2] That is because we moderns limit claims of knowledge to claims about logic and claims about science. The former are judged to be knowledge when they are certain, but the only kinds of statements that qualify as logical certainty are statements about language that in themselves have no application to anything beyond language. The latter (the claims of science) are judged to be knowledge when they have a significant degree of probability and they do yield relevant information about our world and our lives.

Just how significant a determined probability needs to be varies with the science. Certainly even the best (i.e., most probable) claims in biology have significantly less probability than the best claims in physics, but accepted (by the community of scientists) claims in biology have greater probability than their counterparts in fields like psychology and anthropology. However, none of these claims are relevant to this discussion of theology. As I discussed in the last chapter, modern science depends on a method of research that admits into its domain only questions about material entities (i.e., entities for which sense observation is relevant), where answers are dependent on quantifiable methods of research. What is inherently not quantifiable or not physical falls outside the domain of science. In fact this is one way to define the domain of modern philosophy – as a rational investigation of questions that fall outside the domain of any modern science. In this sense theology is philosophy, not science. Hence, given that "knowledge," as the term is used here, is not relevant to theology, my concern is not with knowing if what I have claimed about the God of revelation is true; rather, the question is, is it believable? To answer that question I cannot ignore modern philosophy and science, because some of their claims do seem to be incompatible with my religious claims.

THE CHALLENGE OF MODERN ETHICS TO JEWISH THEOLOGY

I will deal later with the questions that the modern sciences and natural philosophy raise, on which I must reflect before I can say that the revealer God of the Hebrew Scriptures is believable. In this chapter, my attention is limited to one modern branch of philosophy – ethics – because it does raise certain important objections to this determined theology.

[2] For an authority for this claim I rely primarily on a lifetime of such philosophic analysis in the writings of Richard Gale, especially his *On the Nature and Existence of God* (Cambridge: Cambridge University Press, 1991).

MORAL OBJECTIONS TO NORMATIVE
RELIGIOUS OBSERVANCE

For present purposes I judged the theology of Rosenzweig to be better than that of Buber. The former is better because it renders intelligible (i.e., reasonable), the commitment of all religious Jews – liberal and traditional – to be obligated in some sense to a code of Jewish practice that the rabbis developed out of their reading of the Hebrew Scriptures. On Rosenzweig's terms, this tradition of Jewish law is a proper response of the Jewish people collectively to the continuous self-revelation of the God of creation. On these terms *halakhah* (rabbinic law) makes some kind of proper moral demand on every Jew, "proper" in the sense that Jews ought to come to terms with those imperatives in their personal lives.

Prima facie those rules ought to be observed – "ought to be," that is, unless they cannot be (as, for example, in the case of priestly laws related to the destroyed Temple) or if they ought not to be for good reasons. All orthodox Jews will grant the first limitation on observance of rabbinic law in at least the example cited. What would count as other examples could be more controversial. For example, Conservative Judaism makes an exception of driving on Shabbat when the auto is used to attend communal-worship services in a synagogue. The movement claims that the conditions of modern life are such that it is not reasonable to demand that all Jews live within walking distance of a synagogue, and the value of participating in communal worship takes precedence over not driving on Shabbat. Orthodox Jews will argue against this analysis on grounds that all Jews could live near synagogues, if they gave Shabbat the priority in their lives that it deserves, and therefore there is no good reason to allow driving an auto on Shabbat, even to the synagogue. In this and all other similar cases, it is better not to participate in a communal service, which is not a legal obligation (since it is permissible to say the prayers in private rather than as part of a community), and instead observe what is a legal obligation (viz., not to do work by travel on Shabbat).

Note that claims on both sides of these, and similar, issues about observing the laws of the Torah are moral questions, and not just matters of personal preference or taste. If the Torah is divinely revealed, its provisions have the force of moral obligations. Either to violate or to observe them, therefore, is a moral question. When, then, would it be right or proper not to observe them? Two immediate kinds of answers suggest themselves.

WHEN YOU CANNOT DO WHAT YOU OUGHT TO DO

First, you are not morally obligated to do what you cannot do. In fact, to make an impossible moral demand on a person is itself immoral. Hence, it could be argued that given the reality of life in the modern world, it is functionally not possible for all Jews to live within walking distance of a synagogue, so that not to allow a provision for non-observance is itself immoral. It is immoral because the imperative itself makes a demand that is either psychologically harmful (it produces guilt where there is no viable way to remove the guilt) or it produces a further withdrawal from commitment to observance (since someone may feel, with justification, that if there is no way for me to be a good Jew, why bother even to try to be a Jew).

WHEN YOU OUGHT NOT TO DO WHAT YOU OUGHT TO DO

The second line of response to the question of when it is proper not to be observant is, for present purposes, more important. A law should not be observed if the observance itself is immoral. It is the more important claim for two reasons. First, in practical terms, it is this thesis that lies behind the single most divisive issue in contemporary Jewish communal religious life – the question of gender equality. Second, based on the concluding analysis in part I, it is the central problem with Rosenzweig's theology – it is suspect of racism and irrationalism. Both of these charges, if true, violate what most modern people would accept as positive moral values: to use reason as a primary tool for living life with other human beings is always a good, and discrimination against other people on grounds of race is always immoral. The primary interest in this chapter is with the second reason for claiming that observance of the Torah can be immoral, for it goes to the heart of the believability in general in the God of revelation. However, before I turn to the specific issues with Rosenzweig's theology, I will say a bit more about the issue of gender equality[3] as it relates to this theology of revelation.

---

[3] Logically one ought to distinguish between "sex," which is determined by biology, and "gender," which is determined by social behavior, and the two classes need not coincide. For example, a human being with a penis can be passive and compliant, and another human being with a vagina can be ambitious and aggressive. Similarly, a parent with a penis can stay at home to cook and to raise the children, while the first parent's partner, even though she has a vagina, may function in the family as the primary wage earner. In the light of this distinction, what will be said below in relation to Jewish practice has more to do with sex than gender. However, in most contemporary literature, academic and popular, no such distinction is made, and the term "gender" is used for both the biological and the functional distinctions.

THE LOGIC OF ETHICAL CHALLENGES
TO REVELATION

IN THE STRONG SENSE OF REVELATION

We may distinguish two forms of belief in revelation. One is a belief in revelation proper, namely, that the obligations determined by the tradition of rabbinic interpretation of the words of the Torah are themselves the word of God. On this view it should seem that whatever is determined to be the meaning of the Scriptures, its rules are binding on us, simply because they express the will of God. Even if we think they are immoral demands, they should be observed, for how can we say that anything God wills is not moral. In fact, if a determined expression of God's will seems to us to be immoral, we are obliged to reconsider what we think is and is not moral. In effect, this is a case of falsification of our ethics, not of the Torah. In logical terms, if a theory conflicts with observed facts, there is something wrong with the theory, and not with the facts; given that we know (at least in some instances) what is Torah, those instances (on the assumption of divine revelation in the strong sense, here called "revelation") constitute facts; hence, if our ethics contradicts moral facts, something is wrong with our ethics.

For example, few religious Jews will question the rightness of circumcising a son on the eighth day after his birth because sometimes some psychologists argue against its desirability from the perspective of mental health. It is not that these Jews reject the value of psychology in general. Rather, they affirm its expertise, but also recognize that the authority of its claims, while better than any other form of human authority, is based on a fairly low degree of probability, certainly too low to be accepted over the rabbinically determined will of God. Hence, they will continue to practice circumcision in full confidence that in time the psychologists will reconsider their judgments in this case and form better, more enlightened, judgments.

Note that those orthodox Jews who affirm the status of divine revelation as revelation, as the word of God, do not accept all rabbinically accepted interpretations of the meaning of the Torah. Restrictions placed on the application of the biblical laws of the Sabbatical year and the Jubilee are a case in point. While not denying the provisions, but recognizing the havoc that their enforcement would cause in the normal economic life of a community, those provisions have been sufficiently circumvented in law to make their observance inoperative.

The same procedure applies to cases where the Bible calls for a death penalty. Without denying the death penalty, the rabbis make the conditions under which someone could be convicted of a crime that requires capital punishment so severe that in practice no such cases can be tried. Presumably underlying these two and other examples of circumventing established laws, including laws of the Torah proper, the judgment of the rabbis was that, despite what the Torah says explicitly, enforcement would be morally wrong.

IN THE WEAK SENSE OF DIVINE INSPIRATION

I have not opted in part I for this strong interpretation of divine revelation. Rather, I opted for the other, weaker interpretation of revelation as divine inspiration, precisely because, in line with both Buber and Rosenzweig, I argued that even on a non-literal method of interpretation of the words of the Scriptures, at least some of its claims are not true. How many such claims there are is not relevant. It is inconsistent to claim that God in fact said anything that is either not true or not right morally. If any claims can be falsified in the Torah, no claim in the Torah can be said to be in itself a direct report of the will of God.[4]

The example of slavery

To take another example, while the Torah restricts slavery in a way that makes this institution less objectionable than it was in any other society at the time of the first two Jewish polities, both of which were based on the provisions of the Torah, it still condones the institution of slavery, and that condoning is in itself morally wrong. If the Torah is a response to God's will in a particular time and place in history, it is

---

[4] It can be argued that God may, for political reasons, express wishes that he does not will to come true. Consider, for example, the case of the leaders of the tribes of Israel inquiring of God at Beth El to attack Benjamin in Gibeah. This may be why, according to the biblical narrative, Moses is reluctant to accept God at his word when he says that he will prosper the people (Exod. 33:11–23, especially Exod. 33:15) since he had just before this promise spoken to Moses of destroying the people and starting over again with Moses' descendants. (Cf. Exod. 32:9–10 in connection with Exod. 33:3.) God as a ruler may tell his subjects what he wants them to do, but he may have his own reasons for wanting them not to succeed.

For the sake of simplicity, however, I will operate here on the assumption that what God communicates through revelation, if it has (as it does for Rosenzweig and most of rabbinic Judaism, but not for Buber) any content whatsoever, is what God believes and not merely what he thinks is useful for the recipient of his revelation to believe. In short, I will not complicate the discussion here with questions of divine esotericism.

perfectly reasonable that the Torah does not do away with slavery, but modifies it in a direction that can eventually lead, with human moral progress, to the complete elimination of the institution. This, in effect, is how Maimonides interprets the rabbinic expression that "the Torah speaks in human language."[5] He does not apply this rule to the case of slavery, which, being himself a product of his times, he did not consider morally objectionable. However, this is the way he interprets the Torah's provisions for sacrifice, an institution that he clearly considered inferior to worship through communal prayer.

The example of gender

The same kind of logic can be applied to what the Torah and rabbinic tradition say consistently about gender distinctions. Clearly in the Torah, and to an even greater extent in rabbinic law, the status of women is separated from the status of men, almost always to the socio-political disadvantage of the women. In effect, all of the liberal movements have argued that such discrimination may have been reasonable in earlier times, but we as a species have made sufficient moral progress that to continue the enforcement of such provisions now is immoral. The only question, at least today, is how far to extend gender equality under the law.

For example, the determination of who is a Jew by birth is based on gender differentiation. In the Bible Jewish identity depends on the male parent, and rabbinic Judaism (probably for reasons of legal clarity) changed that to the female parent. The Reform and the Reconstructionist movements have done away with even this kind of gender differentiation in a decision that is called "patrilineal descent," namely, that a child is Jewish by birth if either parent is Jewish.[6]

MORAL RULES AND GUIDES

Even more controversial is the question of same-sex marriage. It, too, is an extreme example of doing away with gender considerations under Jewish law. The question is whether cases of gender distinction are all like cases of racial distinction (viz. morally unjustifiable), or whether there are

---

[5] *Guide* 1:26 on Babylonian Talmud Yebamot 71a and Baba Metsia 31b.
[6] I have somewhat simplified this rule. In fact the judgment that the child of a mixed marriage is Jewish depends on the child being raised as a Jew. For present purposes, this condition unnecessarily complicates the example.

limits to the application of this rule. There are no clear answers, which is itself an interesting judgment about the nature of moral judgments, namely, that in many cases no clear rules can in principle be formulated in any mechanical way to guide determinations of what is morally right and wrong. In itself this is an argument for all moral rules – whether their origins are human, divine, or human responses to the divine – being treated only as guides and never as rigid formulations. General rules inform decision-making in concrete cases, but morality is always a value in concrete cases with specific people in relationship in specific times and places. Hence, it is coherent, possibly obligatory, to claim that at some times and in some places what is morally right violates general moral rules.

However, racism and irrationalism seem to be exceptions to this judgment about morality. It is never right to be irrational, and it is always wrong to be racist. Rosenzweig's theology seems to be subject to both charges, and it is to them that I will at last turn my attention.

THE QUESTION OF RACISM

At the very beginning of *The Star*, discussing the place of Nietzsche in his history of philosophy, Rosenzweig says "What he philosophized has by now become almost a matter of indifference. Dionysiac and Superman, Blond Beast and Eternal Return – where are they now?"[7] It is an amazing statement. In effect Rosenzweig says, writing in the 1920s, of everything that Nietzsche said, his racist exaltation of the evolution of a superior race of human beings will be the least remembered, least influential part of his philosophy. Rosenzweig makes this prediction about the impact of Nietzsche's philosophy on European culture less than a decade before Hitler established in Germany a state based precisely on the claimed identity of a new, purified German people as the fulfillment of Nietzsche's prophecy. At the least it says that despite all of Rosenzweig's learning, intelligence, and spirituality, he was no prophet. However, that is not the only troubling aspect of this statement. It is one clear indication that in

---

[7] William Hallo, English translation: *The Star of Redemption* (Notre Dame, IN: Notre Dame Press, 1985), p. 9. The original German reads "Beinahe gleich-gültig ist es schon heute, was er erphilosophierte. Das Dionysische und der Übermensch, die blonde Bestie, die ewige Wiederkunft – wo sind sie geblieben?" (*Der Stern der Erlösung*, in *Franz Rosenzweig: Der Mensch und sein Werk. Gesammelte Schriften* [Haag: Martinus Nijhoff, 1976], part II, pp. 9–10. All subsequent references will simply note *The Star* and give two page numbers – the first to the above-cited edition of the original German and the second to the above-cited edition of Hallo's translation. In the present case the citation is *The Star*, pp. 9–10/9.)

the struggle in European culture between liberalism and conservatism, associated with Ernst Cassirer's neo-Kantian rationalism and Martin Heidegger's existentialist romanticism, Rosenzweig's sympathies lay with Heidegger and not Cassirer,[8] and Heidegger became the philosophic voice of Nazism.

Of course this indictment of Rosenzweig is unfair. He was not the only European intellectual after World War I who believed that war to be a *reductio ad absurdum* of the rationalist liberal ideology that underlay the nation-states that produced the war. In fact, Rosenzweig's rejection of this establishment ideology is representative of the thinking of his time. In this sense what he says about Nietzsche is not exceptional. Therefore, it is not fair to condemn him for not being a prophet. He may speak about prophecy, but he does so only as a philosopher, who could not as yet see that the romanticism advocated as a corrective to the thought that brought us World War I would make a major contribution to the demonic political ideology in Germany that provoked World War II.

Still, we cannot ignore that the irrationalism and racism that Heidegger would voice, out of his philosophy in the 1930s, is not foreign to the intellectual sympathies of Rosenzweig in his philosophy. If philosophy has consequences for lived life, then the thought of Rosenzweig, no less than that of Heidegger, becomes suspect after World War II and especially after the Holocaust. Given, then, that both irrationalism and racism are serious infections in any system of thought, does Rosenzweig's theology show symptoms of this conceptual disease, and, if it does, can the philosophy be saved when the illness is removed from the thought? First I will consider the racism, and then the irrationalism.

THE JEWISH RACE

While Rosenzweig rejects the tradition of Platonic-to-Hegelian Idealism and extols the virtue of concrete thought over abstractions, in fact there is little space for actual individuals in his philosophy. His reality is constructed out of three elements – God, the world, and the human. None

---

[8] See Menachem Kellner (ed.), *The Pursuit of the Ideal: Jewish Writings of Steven Schwarzschild* (Albany: SUNY Press, 1990), "Modern Jewish Philosophy," pp. 229–233. Here Schwarzschild notes that in Rosenzweig's "last essay he awards the prize to Martin Heidegger over a 'scholastic' Cohen essentially because Heidegger himself had rebelled against (among other things) theoretical reason" (p. 232). In this quotation Schwarzschild is alluding to Rosenzweig's review of a famous debate between Heidegger and Cassirer where Cassirer was understood to be the voice for the rationalist philosophy of their teacher, Hermann Cohen.

of the three are concepts. He speaks of "the world" (die Welt) and "the human" (die Mensch) which, as his use of the definite article indicates, are individuals. However, they are abstract individuals. "The world" is not the class of all physical objects; it is an entity in itself. Similarly "the human" is not the class of all human beings; it is an entity in itself. Hence, individual things and people are not the elements of his ontology. In fact, they are barely situated in reality at all.

All physical things (presumably including human and animal bodies) are really processes of the world that arise as nothing out of the real nothing (space) and evolve in the direction of becoming a definite something as their end or goal, but that end is an asymptote – an ideal that in actuality is never realized. Similarly, all humans are really processes characterized by constantly changing states of consciousness whose self-consciousness is always a byproduct of becoming conscious of other states that are conscious of them. The human, no less than God, is defined negatively. I know myself to be something only when I know there is an other who radically is not me, whose existence as consciousness, as an other, makes moral demands on me. The demand is love. Love is the cause of the existence of every human, but the human so created is a not-anything. This is why the call to love provokes shame, for in that call we see ourselves as we are seen – as consciousness, which, in itself, is nothing. Hence, individual humans, like individual physical objects, do exist, but they are inherently insubstantial.

Given this ontology it is difficult to see how Rosenzweig could have a theory of human rights. Such a theory assumes that some things in virtue of existing are entitled to their existence without qualification. However, Rosenzweig's human beings are not things. In fact Rosenzweig does not discuss human rights. He neither denies them nor affirms them, but this omission cannot be treated as innocent. How could a philosopher who was writing when Rosenzweig wrote ignore human rights, given the conflict in political theory between democracy or republicanism and fascism or socialism in his day, as well as the conflict between religious Orthodoxy and liberalism in the Jewish thought of his day? It is not insignificant that liberal Judaism – whose major theme in its opposition to Orthodoxy was (and still is) the principle of autonomy[9] – is not even a topic for discussion in his word picture of absolutely everything.

In fact, there is a space for the individual human in Rosenzweig's thought, but that place is relatively minor. It is revelation that divides

---

[9] See Eugene Borowitz, *Renewing the Covenant: A Theology for the Postmodern Jew* (Philadelphia: Jewish Publication Society, 1991).

humanity into subspecies, and from this perspective there are only two subspecies – the Jewish people and pagans.

Note that the term "pagans" is plural, but the expression "Jewish people" is singular. There are for Rosenzweig only two kinds of pagans – Christians and non-Christians. What differentiates them is the revealed love-commandment. Christians are pagans who, by being loved by other Christians, are transformed into lovers who seek to love God and their yet-to-be-loved (which is to say, yet-to-be-redeemed) neighbors. Pagans belong to no collective entity other than the human. They come together into religious communities, but these communities have no ontological status. Rosenzweig's Christianity is not a community. It is, rather, a gathering of isolated individuals who through their mission to love one another strive to become a community. However, Christian community is an ideal, not an actuality, and, like all other worthy ideals, is an asymptote – an infinite project whose attainment will mark the messianic Kingdom of God as realized. Christians do not, at least in the present world, have a people. Rather, they are on a "way" – a path that leads eventually to a collective identity.

Only Jews are part of an actual people, because they and they alone belong to their collective by birth. In fact, they, unlike pagans, have within Rosenzweig's worldview no place of their own as individuals. Rosenzweig nowhere in *The Star* discusses Jews, only the "people." It is the people who are "eternal," not the individuals, and it is the people who have a "Jewish fate," not the individuals (*The Star*, pp. 331/298). Rosenzweig begins his discussion of the "eternal people" (das ewige Volk) in a paragraph that he entitles "Blood and Spirit" (Blut und Geist). Here he says:

> There is only one community in which such a linked sequence of everlasting life goes from grandfather to grandson, only one which cannot utter the "we" of its unity without hearing deep within a voice that adds: "are eternal." It must be a blood-community, because only blood gives present warrant to the hope for a future. (*The Star*, pp. 331/298–299)

What stands out to our post-Holocaust eyes is the identification of "the Jew" with "blood." It is no less a shocking reference than is the off-hand, unprescient way that Rosenzweig forgives Nietzsche's notion of a superman. Rosenzweig, no less than his intellectual teacher Nietzsche, seems to believe in a kind of superman, and that super-human seems to be the Jewish people. This, then, is Rosenzweig's interpretation of the call in the Hebrew Scriptures for the Jewish people to be God's chosen people.

What political liberals, especially the Jewish religious ones, and the Nazis share in common is their strong aversion to and condemnation of the traditional rabbinic doctrine that the Jewish people are an ʿ*am segulah*, a precious people whom God has chosen. However, the negative reaction to this concept by liberals and Nazis is for entirely different reasons. In the case of the Nazis, the objection is not to the concept of a chosen people *per se*. Rather, it is to the claimed identity of the precious one. For the Nazis it is the German people who are the chosen people, not the Jews. In contrast, liberalism is opposed to the very notion of a chosen people in itself. For liberalism, the claim is inherently offensive on moral grounds, because it falsifies a most fundamental assumption of modern ethics, both utilitarian and deontological – that all human beings are essentially equal before the moral law. There is one morality for all, and to claim otherwise is itself inherently immoral.

Both the Reform and the Reconstructionist branches of liberal religious Judaism have rejected the doctrine of the chosen people, and they have done so for the ethical reasons outlined above. To claim that any particular individuals or group of individuals have a special moral status is itself an inherently immoral idea, and where rabbinic Judaism advocates an idea or practice that is immoral, no matter how entrenched within the tradition that idea or practice is, it must be reformed or reconstructed.

It is not obvious, even within the canons of liberal ethics, that the doctrine of chosenness must be rejected, for classical rabbinic texts present interpretations of the doctrine that are not subject to the moral condemnation described above. Maimonides in particular argues that the only thing special about the Jewish people is that they stand in a tradition that goes back to the Torah, which is itself a humanly perfect legal code revealed by God through a humanly perfect prophet, Moses.[10] The suggestion implicit in Maimonides' analysis is that any people who accept the Torah are in principle no less chosen than Israel. In fact he may even believe that what defines a Jew as a Jew is not the mere accident of birth, but the intentional act of accepting on themselves the "yoke" of the Torah.[11] In this sense, Maimonides' chosen people are no less a community of faithful individuals than is Rosenzweig's Christian Church.

---

[10] See *Mishneh torah, hilchot yesodei hatorah* (Brooklyn, NY: Moznaim, 1989), ch. 7, paragraph 6, and all of ch. 8.

[11] See Menachem Marc Kellner, *Must a Jew Believe Anything?* (London and Portland: Vallentine Mitchell and Co., 1999), and David Novak, *The Election of Israel: The Idea of the Chosen People* (Cambridge: Cambridge University Press), 1995.

In fact, Maimonides' interpretation of chosenness seems (at least to me) to be more compatible with the words of the Hebrew Scriptures than is Halevi's "blood" interpretation that is the foundation of Rosenzweig's understanding of the concept. The Scriptures suggest no good reason for God choosing Israel. In fact, God himself seems to consider the choice of the nation of the patriarchs to be a poor choice, and he wants to start again with Moses, just as God repented and recreated humanity with the descendants of Noah after the flood. Staying with Israel as his chosen people seems to be more a favor granted to Moses than it is a decision of which God approves.[12] Furthermore, the Hebrew Scriptures have practically nothing positive to say about this people, who are seen to be in constant rebellion against God's will. At best the choice of Israel seems to be arbitrary. At worst Israel is not chosen because it is superior to other nations but precisely because it is inferior.[13]

However, this is not the line of interpretation that Rosenzweig adopts. Without reservation Rosenzweig's primary source for a theology of Israel, the Jewish people, is Judah Halevi, not Moses Maimonides, and Halevi clearly understands the Jewish people to be a race whose natural (birth given) disposition to be receptive to prophecy (to divine revelation) marks it racially as a distinct subspecies of the human species.

Rosenzweig does not claim that all Jews are holy and receive prophecy, any more than someone will claim that all humans are rational because he believes that "rationality" is the distinguishing mark that separates humans as a species from other animals. Some (maybe many) humans are in reality less gifted at reasoning than (at least) some animals. However, that is a judgment of how they are in actuality. Species are determined not by actual properties, but by dispositional properties. A particular dog (e.g., Lassie) may be smarter than a particular human master; however, the dog cannot get smarter than it is, precisely because it is a dog, whereas at least in theory the human can, which is precisely what makes the very dumb human human. Similarly, Rosenzweig seems to contend, following the theology of Judah Halevi, that Jews are born with a predisposition to hear the word of God, and this claim seems on moral grounds to be unjustifiable.

---

[12] Exod. 32:9–14.
[13] This is the thesis that the playwright, Paddy Chayevsky, advances in "Gideon." How better, his God character argues, could God show his greatness than by choosing as the agent of his salvation a savior who has no talent whatsoever for saving anything. Hence, Israel is a "holy" people, not because there is anything especially holy about it. On the contrary, few people, if any, have less natural disposition to be holy than Israel. All that makes it holy is that God chose it to be holy, so the credit for its holiness belongs to God, and not to the people.

RECONSTRUCTING ROSENZWEIG

Is it possible to reconstruct Rosenzweig's notion of the Jewish people in a way that preserves its central role in his worldview without the onus of immorality to which it seems justifiably subject? The key to a positive answer is that prima facie there is no reason why in his doctrine of chosenness Rosenzweig could not have followed Maimonides, just as he did in discussing the nature of God. He need not have rejected the doctrine of Israel as a chosen people. I see no reason why that claim should be seen to be morally offensive.

Empirically all people are not equal. Some people by birth have advantages over other people. Sometimes these advantages are genetic. For example, all other factors being equal, tall people are more likely to succeed at basketball than short people, and large people are more likely to succeed at football than small people. Of course there are exceptions, because "all factors" are never "equal." A very aggressive, highly motivated football player with a small body frame or a short basketball player will do better at their sport than a passive, relatively disinterested big competitor. All people, regardless of natural talents, are entitled to compete in these sports, and sometimes the less naturally endowed will succeed. It is opportunity that should be viewed as universal, not talent. Similarly, people differ in their talents culturally as well as genetically. Children born into families that value formal learning and have the financial means to support it have a definite advantage in gaining an education over children born into families that do not value this kind of learning or who do not have the financial means to support their children as students. There is no question that a student who can buy books and read them at home in good light in a quiet atmosphere will do better academically than students who cannot buy books and, even if they could, have no quiet space at home in which to read. These are inequalities of birth, but the inequalities do not determine fate. The disadvantaged student can be successful as a student despite the disadvantages, and it is morally reasonable for a society to make special efforts to "level the playing field," more (in my opinion) by giving special help to the disadvantaged than by placing special handicaps on the advantaged.[14]

These same considerations apply to judging and affirming the Jewish people as chosen. To be born into a home of parents who themselves are committed to and informed about Torah and who live in a Jewish

[14] See John Rawls, *A Theory of Justice* (Cambridge, MA: Harvard University Press, 1971).

community that can provide the necessary support for living a life of
Torah has, from the perspective of learning Torah, a definite advantage
over those less fortunate by birth. However, the superiority is cultural,
not genetic.

In the generations before the Nazis it was acceptable, for Jews as well
as non-Jews, to speak of a Jewish "race." However, those days are past. It
is a permanent (I hope) legacy from the Holocaust that the term "race"
can no longer be applied in any reasonable way to the Jewish people.

Jews are not members of a race. However, they are members of a reasonably large extended family in which members tend to marry other
members rather than non-members. Hence, there is something analogous to Jewish racial characteristics. There are, for example, certain
diseases towards which Jews are prone or not prone in disproportionate
numbers in comparison with their non-Jewish neighbors. In all such cases
genetics does have relevance as a basis of causal explanation. However,
none of these characteristics have anything to do with being a chosen
people. Intelligence is not racial, and neither is spirituality.

The critical institution that falsifies the charge of racism in rabbinic
Judaism is conversion. While Jews are born from Jewish parents, Jews
can also be Jews by choice, regardless of birth. Judaism has not been
for a long time a missionary religion, but the doors of entrance into a
life of Torah have always been open to all people through conversion.
Even Halevi grants conversion. For him the sole difference between a
Jew by birth and a Jew by choice is that the former and not the latter
has a potentiality for prophecy. However, since prophecy ended with
the destruction of the second Temple, it is a difference that makes no
difference. Furthermore, even this difference disappears with the children of converts to whom Halevi also grants a prophetic disposition.
That the children of converts are born with a disposition for prophecy
suggests that even this most extreme form of racism within the acceptable
boundaries of rabbinic Judaism is not a pure racism, and it is in no sense
comparable to the racism of the Nazi doctrine of German chosenness.[15]

---

[15] It is significant that Rosenzweig's discussion of the Jewish people says nothing about conversion,
either by non-Jews into Judaism or by born-Jews from Judaism. Can a Jew cease to be a Jew?
Judaism says no, and Rosenzweig accepts this judgment. However, in reality, it is possible for
Jews to cease to be Jews – at least sometimes. Certainly in modern America fully assimilated Jews
may remain in some respects, notably culturally, distinguishable as Jews, despite their efforts to
the contrary. However, these committed Jewish assimilationists can raise children who in turn
can raise children who are in no respect, even culturally, Jewish. Unfortunately such total escape
from Jewish identity is not merely theoretical. It is a fact that Jewish thought must accept in
making sense of what it means to be Jewish in the modern world.

In general, even in biology, the term "race," like the term "species," is problematic. These are fuzzy words taken from ordinary language that, because of their fuzziness, can hinder scientific progress. A case in point is debates in modern paleoanthropology over constructing the history of the human from archeological findings. There are a number of different characteristics that are used to designate some animal as a human ancestor. They include bipedalism, a large brain relative to the size of the head, the shape of the mouth and teeth relative to other features of a face, and other factors as well that go into judging some dead mammals to be more "human-like" than "ape-like." All of these features are said to be relevant to the development in some animals of the ability to work with complex tools, form complex speech, and form complex societies. Of course, just how "complex" does a tool, a society, or speech have to be for it to be called "human"? There are in principle no clear lines for making these distinctions. Furthermore, there seems from the fossil record to be no simple interrelated line of development for any of these skills. For example, animals can be bipedal with small brains, but they can also have larger brains and not be bipedal. In short, the interest of paleoanthropologists to present a clear picture of the evolution of human beings is barely, by any strict standards of what counts as science, scientific. The confusion led Ian Tattersall, the head of the Anthropology department at the American Museum of Natural History, to say

No energy need have been wasted on this empty argument (over whether certain fossils remain apes despite having certain humanoid features) if the various protagonists had taken a moment to consider how great a stumbling block the vagueness of the concept of "human" (and of "ape", come to that) is to the understanding of our evolutionary history.[16]

If it is not at all clear what a "species" is, certainly it is even less clear what a "race" is. These are terms best omitted from scientific vocabulary, and equally, for moral and political reasons no less than philosophical reasons, best omitted from popular thought, and, even more so, from theology.

This revision in no way compromises what is important in Rosenzweig's view of the Jewish people if we say that by birth Jews are born into a faith community and that that community supports in Jews the possibility of response to God's presence through the tradition of rabbinic thought and law. God is potentially present to all living persons.

[16] Ian Tattersall. *The Fossil Trail: How We Know What We Think We Know about Human Evolution* (New York and Oxford: Oxford University Press, 1995), pp. 74–75.

That presence calls for a response, and it is through our lives in communities that we learn how to respond. For those who have the good fortune to be born into a family of committed religious Jews who live in a community of committed religious Jews, it is the Torah that defines the moral response to God's presence.

This is not the only way to respond to God. Various forms of Christianity exemplify alternative ways. The same may be said, although Rosenzweig does not say it, for other religiously defined peoples as well, especially in the case of Islam. How we respond to the love through which we are related to God, our families, and our neighbors defines spiritual morality, and that response is guided by our written memory of how our people responded before us. In the case of individual human beings who by chance of birth or association end up as members of the Jewish people, that response is guided by Torah – "guided," but not dictated, for moral rules, while objective, are never, at least in principle, universal. What may be right (or wrong) in general may not be right (or wrong) at a particular time and place.

Rules are no substitute for openness to the presence of the other – both human and divine. Revelation is informed by rules, but not determined by them. We must be aware of the other, and, in that awareness, we must use our own judgment about what is right and what is wrong. For such judgment there seems to be no alternative, not even revelation, to rational thought, which brings me to my next major criticism of Rosenzweig's theology – his apparent irrationalism.

THE QUESTION OF IRRATIONALISM

REVIEW

I concluded part I with a qualified acceptance of Rosenzweig's formulation of a Jewish conception of the God of revelation. It was accepted, because, of the different views considered, his seemed the one that was most coherent with rabbinic Judaism and most likely to be true. That this conception of a revealer deity is compatible with rabbinic theology was settled in part I, but whether or not it is likely to be true remains an open question. A literalist interpretation of the Hebrew Scriptures was rejected, as in fact it was in Jewish intellectual history, because it fails to make sense out of human experience at all levels – in terms of our experience of physical nature, our sense of morality, and especially the history of the Jewish people. The other views considered are all at least possible views, and all of them have their advocates in the contemporary Jewish world. Most traditional religious Jews remain today by and large committed to Maimonides' religious philosophy,[17] and a considerable number of liberal religious Jews find the theology of Martin Buber adequate to make sense out of their lives, including the ways in which they find it meaningful to be spiritually Jewish. However, I concluded by preferring Rosenzweig's worldview to the philosophy of Maimonides and the theology of Buber.

Maimonides' view was rejected because it presupposed a general scientific view of the world, namely that of the Aristotelians, that no longer can be taken seriously by anyone who accepts the validity of the sciences as a way of knowing reality. His view makes sense out of being a religious Jew who has serious commitment to what rabbinic Judaism has defined as a life of Torah. However, the "sense" it makes – that is, the categories of physics, astronomy, biology, and psychology that it employs to explain the revelation through which God and Israel are interrelated – cannot be true. The reason why is evident. The science Maimonides uses, which was the best available to him in the thirteenth century, is far from the best science at the beginning of the twenty-first century, and the best science of our day is incompatible with Maimonides' science. In at least this respect the theologies of Buber and Rosenzweig are ruled to be preferable.

Buber's view was rejected for the opposite reason. While the science he presupposes is in contemporary terms compatible with his understanding of a spiritual life, it fails to make sense out of the life of any Jew who is committed to a path of Torah. On his view not only does revelation lack content but the association of content with this central experience of God's presence is the first step on an apparently inevitable path towards idolatry. To govern one's life by Torah – by a tradition that legislates behavior and belief through interpretation of the words of the Hebrew Scriptures in a communal context that has serious commitment in some form to past rabbinic reflections and judgments – seems in principle unjustifiable on Buber's terms. It is unjustifiable, first, because the notion of community in general is problematic in Buber's thought; second, and more importantly, because of the inevitable negative value that Buber's thought places on any association of content with revelation.

---

[17] See Menachem Kellner's *Must a Jew Believe Anything?* Kellner is an orthodox Jew who, despite the fact that he himself rejects Maimonides' authority on questions of dogma, grants this general claim.

As a consequence of the analysis in part I, I began part II by affirming Rosenzweig's theology. However, again, that affirmation was conditional, because the question remained open: is it true? I have so far considered objections that arise from moral sensitivity. I isolated two major problems with Rosenzweig's worldview, as it is presented in the words of *The Star of Redemption*: it seems to accept a form of racism, and it seems to embrace irrationalism. So far I have dealt with the charge of racism.

Rosenzweig separates the human as a distinct element of reality from both God and the world, and he then divides the human into two fundamental kinds of human beings – Jews and pagans. The difference between them is genetic. Pagans are born as individuals who have no innate capacity for revelation. To receive revelation – which here means to receive the love of another person, which is to say, of another conscious and willing agent who is conscious of themself[18] through consciousness of another person – the pagan must be loved by someone who has themself been loved. These lovers who are beloved are the Christians. They form a community, in what Buber calls "the Christian way," that reaches out to other pagans in order to transform them into new Christians in the way that the old Christians had been transformed. Jews, however, are different, and the difference seems to be genetic, for, on Rosenzweig's terms, Jews are born as members of a specific community of love, the Jewish people. What is morally offensive here is not Rosenzweig's human topology of pagans, Christians, and Jews; it is that the basis of the topology is biological rather than cultural – the result of what these humans are by birth rather than what they become through the influence of an environment – and this basis is racist.

TWO INTERPRETATIONS OF CHOSENNESS

The source of Rosenzweig's racism is an authentic Jewish tradition, whose major philosophic spokesman is Judah Halevi, that so interprets the root rabbinic belief in the Jews as God's chosen people. However, this is not the only line of interpretation available to Rosenzweig. There is also an equally authentic Jewish tradition, whose major philosophic spokesman is Moses Maimonides, that affirms and interprets this same root rabbinic belief in a way that is not racist. On this view it is the Torah and only the Torah that makes the Jewish people chosen. Those who are born of parents who are Jewish have the good fortune to be raised in a

---

[18] "Themself" is used rather than "himself" or "herself" or some other formally ungrammatical construct such as "him/herself" so that I may use the singular without being gender specific.

community whose life and thought is guided by the Torah. The parents themselves live by Torah for the same reason, in a chain of extended familial causation that goes back to what the story of Jewish religious history calls *torah mi-sinai* (Torah from Sinai), that is, God's revelation to the people Israel through the prophet Moses at a specific time and place in history.

I have asked whether Rosenzweig's word picture of reality can adopt this Maimonidean form of interpretation of the Jewish people, rather than the Halevi form of tradition, without changing his account of being human. Can he still maintain that the human, through relationship with God, evolves from a secluded element into a community of interrelated fellows who, through their own loving and being loved, love and are loved by God? Furthermore, can this evolution still be understood as involving two primary and mutually dependent ways of living in community – the Jewish and the Christian? My answer above was positive. Jewish community and the Christian way still constitute two different modes of responding to divine self-revelation, each needing the other to move towards an ideal of universal redemption that transforms the initial elements into something that fulfills all three. However – and this is why the view adopted here is a reconstruction of Rosenzweig's worldview rather than an authentic reproduction of it – in principle there can be more than just two ways of forming community. Furthermore, the birth of an individual does not entail permanent membership in a community.

Critical to Rosenzweig's understanding of revelation is that the experience of love is always concrete and not general. Hence, revelation does not occur in general; it happens only to specific people at specific times and in specific places. Therefore, since each such event is unique, in principle there is nothing to prevent the content-information response of the beloved to being loved from taking on a new pattern. There can be equally valid non-Christian and non-Jewish communities rooted in the experience of revelation. Similarly, there can be many, equally valid kinds of Jewish and Christian subcommunities. In short, there is nothing in Rosenzweig's theology that need preclude religious pluralism.

Furthermore, nothing precludes individuals who at birth are members of one religious community from becoming members of another religious community. In general, such movement is not likely, and it may even be appropriate for some communities, such as the Jewish ones, to obligate its individuals not to leave, but that does not mean that in every case such change is morally wrong. The test is whether or not the individual acts in a way that responds to the love received from the other, both human and divine. In general, it is not likely that there will be a positive response when the individual chooses to leave their community. However, this is not, and need not, always be the case.

What remains to be discussed in this chapter on ethics is the charge of irrationalism. First, is the charge true? Does Rosenzweig unjustifiably restrict the domain of what can be known through human reason, and is such a restriction a moral violation? Second, if the answer is yes to both questions, can Rosenzweig's worldview be reconstructed to eliminate this ethical lacuna without destroying the worldview itself?

THE LINE BETWEEN KNOWLEDGE AND BELIEF

The line between the first two parts of *The Star* is a line between what can be known and what can be believed. "Knowledge," Rosenzweig tells us, can be achieved through what he calls "silent language" (unhörbare Sprache), which corresponds fairly precisely to what analytic philosophers call a language of "propositions," whose truth values are determined through the employment of algebraic modes of expression. However, the content of such propositions is restricted to what in Rosenzweig's language are the elements of reality.

The logic for such an analysis uses as a model for a well-formed sentence – a sentence that expresses a "meaning" such that it can be judged to be true or false – only two terms ("A" and "B") and a single relationship between them ("="). The only possible well-formed sentences in Rosenzweig's silent language are "A=A," "A=B," "B=B," and "B=A." The "=" expresses a movement from a point of origin towards an end-limit. "A," taken from the two German terms used to express what is general and what has positive conceptual content (the "all" [All] and the general [Allgemeine]), expresses something general and/or universal and/or abstract. "B," taken from the German term for what is distinctive and specific (Besondere), expresses something concrete and individual.

The analysis behind Rosenzweig's linguistics in this case is a Cohenian interpretation of Aristotelian logic. Aristotle himself employs ordinary language to express his logic, but his use of it is in no way ordinary. His goal is to use language to say what is more or less precise, but ordinary language is always more or less imprecise. The difference is unavoidable. To determine the truth or falsity of a statement, the statement needs to be clear, and clarity requires statements to be as precise as possible. Hence, their meaning is generally (but not always) univocal, that is, something spoken in a single voice – the statement says what it says in all contexts and it never says anything else. Now, such precise statements have the virtue of being capable of rational truth-value judgment. That is why a scientific language should be univocal, because the sole legitimate purpose of linguistic use in science is to aid knowledge, to determine truth.

A model Aristotelian sentence has the form "S is P," where "S" is the subject term, "P" is the predicate term, and "is" expresses the relationship between the two. In Aristotle's semantics, an "S" is an individual substance that is itself a nexus of form and matter. The matter is nothing at all; it is that which takes what the subject is and locates it in time and space, that is, it materializes it. The form, which is what the subject is, is what a "P" expresses, namely a predicate expression of what is in itself a universal, whose function is to inform a subject. So far Aristotle is clear, but the "is" relationship between the individual substance and any of its definitions or characteristics is not clear. Consider the statement, "Socrates is a man." That says that there is an individual named Socrates who is a set of forms materialized by matter, or, which is the same thing, a material entity informed by forms. It also says that one of the forms constituting Socrates is a universal, "man."

Just what Aristotle meant when he said that forms inform substances is open to broad, not necessarily consistent, interpretation. Clearly, Aristotle meant that the referent of the P-term is at least part of what the referent of the S-term is. However, how is it the case that the P is what S is?

Rosenzweig's use of Cohen's method of reasoning is one, not unlikely, interpretation of how Aristotle understood the relationship between the subject and its predicate. "S" names something that in its concreteness has its material origin in nothing at all, and "P" names the (Platonic) ideal that functions as the end-limit of S. Hence, to say "S is P" means that S is an individual nothing that moves towards becoming the universal something, P.

Next, Rosenzweig says that this is all that logic can tell us. It tells us how, in a universe where relationship can only be bipolar, one term is defined by its movement towards becoming another term. In effect, logic can only deal with what a substance is and becomes. However, it can tell us nothing about how substances relate to other substances – not insofar as they are something (i.e., universal), but insofar as they are nothing (i.e., particular). The problem, he tells us, is that the language of scientific logic is a logic of pure reasoning, and reasoning takes place in the brain. However, a brain has no contact with anything, or, more importantly, has no communication with anyone beyond itself.

Rosenzweig's judgment of the limit of knowledge and reason draws from his knowledge of Kant, but combines that (accepted) knowledge with his own analysis of ethics, which is sharply critical of Kant. Implicit in Rosenzweig's arguments are the judgments that reality is to be grasped through ethical reasoning (from Kant), not from scientific reasoning (also from Kant), but that ethical thinking is inherently relational, so that no isolated person (i.e., conscious, willing being) can in isolation have a moral consciousness (in clear opposition to Kant).

For present purposes, the critical judgment is that ethical reasoning is inherently relational. Kant had argued that ethical thinking has to do with acts of will which can be judged good or bad depending on the universality of what the willing agent intends. Rosenzweig argues that such isolated acts of willing are not really moral. They arise from what persons desire for themselves. As such, they entail no real obligations, for, as the individual was free to create them, so the same individual remains free, without moral onus, to revoke them. Furthermore, what is right or wrong to will in any particular case depends on the specifics and not merely on the unconditionality of what is willed. Hence, a moral logic such as Kant's that reduces ethics to judgments of universality loses sight of just what precisely an ethical context is – one where a particular person stands in the presence of another particular person, and the presence of the other produces a sense of obligation that defines the standard for a moral judgment. Where there is no other person, there is no morality, only subjective desires.

As such, for Rosenzweig the grasping of reality, rather than mere elements about reality, requires thinkers to move beyond rational thinking ("silent language") into relationship with the radical other, ultimately with God. When the other is present to the person, that other manifests himself to the other, and that manifestation, which is what revelation is, is the only way that human grasping can be extended beyond the mere knowledge of elements of reality. However, receiving this revelation, this self-manifestation, from the other is not knowledge. We can be aware of what we receive from our interaction with the other, and we can believe what we received is right and/or true, but we cannot know that it is.

There is no knowledge here for at least three reasons. First, the content, even when it can be expressed in logical language, cannot be proven by logical rules, and therefore cannot be called "knowledge." Second, we cannot even be sure that what we think the other is saying, from our response to the other, is really (i.e., with certainty) what the other is saying, primarily because the other as other is not themself knowable. Third, the content may not be anything expressible as meaningful within the strict requirements for meaning imposed by an algebraic, scientific language. The expression is more likely to be myth (story) than a set of linear-in-relationship formal propositions. Stories are not simply sloppy ways of making scientific claims. They are used to grasp what science, rationalist logical thinking, cannot grasp – the course of life lived between persons. In this case belief is possible, for some stories are more believable than others, but they are not knowledge.

CRITIQUE AND RECONSTRUCTION

How, then, are some stories to be judged more believable than others? It is not by reducing them to logical claims subject to scientific analysis. This is the modernist answer, most intimately associated, in Rosenzweig's Jewish mind, with Spinoza. In his *Tractatus Theologico-Politicus*,[19] Spinoza argued that religions are elaborate imaginative myths intended to move philosophically and scientifically unsophisticated masses of people towards certain political ends. These myths are true or false if the ends intended are scientific, and true or false. Similarly, these myths are good or bad if the ends intended are political, and good or bad. However, only the scientist or natural philosopher has the skills to judge the veracity of conceptual claims and the value of ethical claims. This is precisely the view that Rosenzweig intends to reject, and in that rejection he seems (at least to me) justified.

The line of Spinozistic rationalism runs through Kant to Cohen's successor at Marburg, the secular humanist Jew, Ernst Cassirer. He dedicated his life to the critique of culture out of his determined neo-Kantian analysis of human knowledge. His last work was written after the Holocaust, in exile from his beloved Germany, in what was for him the intellectual wilderness of the United States (at Yale and then Columbia). Cassirer had believed that Germany was the most rational and intellectually sophisticated state in the world (which it may well have been), but that nation produced what may have been the most bankrupt and intellectually primitive state that the world had ever known: Hitler's third "Reich." From his exile at Yale, in 1946, Cassirer struggled to make sense of how this decline could have occurred. He decided that the

---

[19] English translation by A. G. Wernham (Oxford: Oxford University, Press, 1965).

fundamental error of all previous reasoning in the Spinozistic rationalist tradition of Europe was that it had ignored myth. However, Cassirer's own attempt to make sense of myth, his *Myth and the State*,[20] failed to enlighten the problem (or, at least so it seems to me).

Cassirer would have done well to read Rosenzweig's *The Star* with some care. For Cassirer, thinking mythically remains, as Plato called it, mere "bastard thinking," whereas Cassirer's Spinozistic goal was to advance reason sufficiently to be able to encompass myth. In this he failed. However, the failure was not because of any lack of reasoning skills. It was because there is, as Rosenzweig insisted, more to reality than what mere reason and knowledge can grasp, and grasping this more, which myth expresses, is vital to living. The life of pure reason, the ideal of Spinoza, ultimately is to be condemned because it is just too shallow. Reality is more than any science can contain, and this is especially true of the relationship between the human being and psychology.

Still, in some way myth must be able to be critiqued. Otherwise there is no defense against bad myth. This is precisely the failure of rational thinking in the case of Nazism. A false myth can be as powerful as a true myth, but whereas a true myth, in Rosenzweig's language, may put us on the path to redemption, the false myth, such as Hitler's, leads inevitably in the direction of human destruction and world damnation. Perhaps this is why Heidegger, whose thought is reasonably close to Rosenzweig's, could be attracted to Nazism. Reason as reason, the talent of the philosopher, provides no protection against radical evil when that evil is presented as part of a powerful myth.

In sum, Rosenzweig was correct to judge that there are radical limits on the ability of scientific reasoning and logic to grasp the lived world, as well as to see in a myth, such as the claimed Scriptures of the Jews and the Christians, a more powerful way for human beings to transcend the limits of their knowledge in order to grasp a proper belief in much more of reality. However, Rosenzweig failed to provide us with a way to distinguish between good and evil myths. That failure opens the door for very intelligent people to adopt a worldview, such as Nazism, that is inherently evil. The humanism of the Spinozistic secularist may condemn us to intellectual superficiality and conceptual triviality. However, the richer life of myth threatens us with emotional damnation and radical immorality. Better to remain trivial and superficial than to walk blindly into immorality and damnation.

[20] *Der Mythus des Staates* (Frankfurt a.M.: Fischer Wissenschaft, 1985). English translation, *The Myth of the State* (New Haven: Yale University Press, 1946).

I take this to be a strong argument against Rosenzweig's irrationalism or romanticism. It is an argument for a modified form of intellectual positivism. Science is all that we can know. However, there is more that can be believed than can be known. Yet, much that can be believed is evil, and, without some form of knowledge applicable to belief, there is no protection against the evil.

The critical clause here is "some form of knowledge." Rosenzweig, no less than contemporary logical positivists, makes too sharp a distinction between knowledge and belief. There are all kinds of knowledge, as there are all kinds of belief. Some kinds of knowledge are more certain than others, and some kinds of belief are more reasonable than others. The point is that knowledge and belief are not essentially different. They are imprecise terms that apply to the same continuum.[21] Some claims are clearer than others and some claims are more probable than others. No claims that are utterly unintelligible are either knowable or believable. That is because there is nothing clear enough in them to know or to believe. Conversely, no claims that are perfectly clear and absolutely certain are unknowable or unbelievable, no matter how trivial, and therefore uninformative, they may be. However, few candidates for knowledge or belief fall into these two extremes. Almost every claim that is interesting is somewhat but not perfectly clear, with some likelihood but no absolute certainty.

Another way to say "with some likelihood but no absolute certainty" is that the interesting truth claims have a probability greater than zero and less than one. The beauty of the probability metaphor in this case is that it illustrates that knowledge and belief are not radically different, but part of the same continuum. There is no sharp line between them. Some candidates for scientific knowledge may have less probability than some candidates for religious belief (as some liberal synagogues may be more traditional in their liturgical practices and religious beliefs than some traditional synagogues).[22] In this case there will be scientific purists who will say that the relatively low level of probability in some sciences (like physical cosmology or sociobiology) is so low that they ought not to be called sciences at all. Similarly, there will be some religionists who will argue that not all claims made in the name of a religion are faith

---

[21] See William Alston, *Perceiving God* (Ithaca: Cornell University Press, 1991). Alston argues that what we call "knowledge" is reasonably justified belief, and what counts for being reasonably justified varies, depending on what is the subject and content of the belief. Alston accuses analytic philosophers of applying these sliding standards inconsistently, demanding a higher standard of evidence for claims about religious experience than for claims about any other kind of experience.

[22] I will return to this judgment in the next chapter, on the challenges of modern science.

(i.e. belief) assertions. However, these are arbitrary judgments. Where the lines between science and religion, knowledge and belief, are drawn is of little importance. What matters is to recognize that both belong to the same continuum. What is considered most probable is called "knowledge," and the degree of probability of a claim is independent of its degree of importance, for there are many matters about which we must form judgments in lived life and the decisions must be made on relatively little evidence. Furthermore, all religious and moral beliefs can be subject to rational analysis of some kind. The last sentence expresses the theme of this book – an investigation of the degree of believability of a philosophically reasonable interpretation of the Jewish root belief in the God of revelation, whose form as belief is an affirmation, in thought as well as in practice, of a specific proposition – that God revealed himself to Israel through Moses in the Torah.

How believable this claim is, given the present reconstructed Rosenzweigian interpretation of this root-belief, is the subject matter of the second part of this book. So far I have considered the challenge to it from ethics, and that challenge took two forms: a charge of racism and a charge of irrationalism. The answer to the first was to modify Rosenzweig's notion of the Jewish people as chosen by opting for a Maimonidean interpretation that renders the people chosen in cultural terms as inheritors of the Torah. The answer to the second was to adopt a probabilistic model of reasoning that locates religious belief and scientific knowledge on a single scale of evaluation in terms of evidence.

I shall now leave ethics and consider challenges to this view of revelation from science itself. What do the modern sciences tell us, if anything, about the world, the human, and God that can and should modify what I have affirmed so far about how a self-revealing deity is related to a morally aware human, as both move towards effecting together a redeemed world?

CHAPTER 6

The challenges of modern science

REVIEW

This book began by positing that revelation is a critical foundational principle for a believable expression of all three Abrahamic faiths (Judaism, Christianity, and Islam). Furthermore, this belief must be compatible with the claim that the single deity who reveals himself also created the universe. Furthermore, in the case of any form of Jewish religion (traditional or liberal), it must be compatible with the claim that God revealed himself by means of Moses through the Torah. The first part of this book considered viable candidates for a conception of such a deity out of the sources of the Hebrew Scriptures themselves, and how Jewish philosophers and theologians have interpreted what those Scriptures say. In this case I focused on one major representative of classical rabbinic philosophy, the philosophy of Maimonides, and two major representatives of modern Jewish theology, the theologies of Martin Buber and Franz Rosenzweig.

ON THE EXCLUSION OF KABBALAH AND SPINOZA

It should be noted that I did not consider every possible conception of God that can be found in the tradition of Jewish thought. In particular I have not dealt with the tradition of Kabbalah in connection with classical Jewish religious thought, and I have not dealt with the more secular, humanistic tradition of Spinoza in connection with modern Jewish thought.

I will not discuss the philosophy of Spinoza in any detail in this book. I do acknowledge its importance. However, while I believe that Spinoza's theology may offer a reasonable conception of a God of creation, it does not present a viable conception of a God of revelation. In general, no secular theology can deal adequately with revelation, and Spinoza's

Jewish philosophy is ultimately just that – an expression (possibly the best yet written) of Jewish secularism. However, here, in this book on revelation, I limit my focus to non-secular Jewish theologies, notably, those of Buber and Rosenzweig, in the conviction that they and they alone can offer a reasonably believable conception of revelation.

As for the case of Kabbalah, it says everything and nothing about revelation. The central text of this tradition is the *Zohar*. In form as well as content, it is a commentary on the Hebrew Scriptures that presupposes that their words are revealed by God and that those words can be understood in a way that is distinctive to the *Zohar*. In this sense everything that this tradition says is about revelation. However, the doctrine of revelation and its correlated doctrine – that there is one God who is both the creator of the world and the revealer of the Torah – are neither questioned nor examined in the *Zohar*. Rather, these claims are treated as facts that are presupposed in everything that the *Zohar* asserts. Hence, this tradition contributes little if anything to the present project, because it is inherently philosophical in a way that Kabbalah is not. I will explain what I mean by this claim.

PHILOSOPHICAL THEOLOGY — THINKING CRITICALLY ABOUT THE UNCRITICAL

In most philosophy, we begin by assuming a critical posture towards claims that we are inclined to accept uncritically. A clear example of this is the way that Kant posed the problem that his *Critique of Pure Reason*[1] was intended to solve: how is it possible for there to be knowledge in the activity of physical, natural scientists? Kant does not ask if there is such knowledge. He assumes that there is. In this assumption his stance is uncritically affirmative. However, in asking how this assumption could be true, he assumes a critical stance towards what he believes, and it is that critical stance that makes Kant's *Critique* philosophy rather than apologetics.

A similar claim can be made about contemporary philosophers of science. While they do not pose the problem in the same way as Kant does, they do assume that science is a source of knowledge. The issue is not whether we know anything in this way. Rather, the question is, just what is it that we know and how is it possible for us to know it? Furthermore, a comparable claim can be made about what contemporary moral philosophers do. They also (at least in most instances) ask

---

[1] *Kritik der Reinen Vernunft*. English translation by N. Kemp Smith, *The Critique of Pure Reason* (London: Macmillan, 1929).

what it is that we know when we make moral judgments, and how it is possible for us, as reasonable people, to make these claims. However, they accept uncritically behind their critical stance that it is possible for reasonable people to make sound moral judgments.

I am engaged in this book in a similar philosophical enterprise, only in this case it is about religion, especially Judaism, rather than about science and ethics *per se*. However, as we have already seen, this enterprise in the philosophy of religion and Jewish philosophy cannot be conducted independently of philosophic considerations of both science and ethics. In discussing a literalist interpretation of the Hebrew Scriptures, I concluded – as did rabbinic and Christian tradition – that, so understood, the Scriptures are not believable. I concluded – again, as did the Abrahamic traditions – that in order to affirm the claim that the Bible is an expression of divine revelation, in either a weak or a strong sense of this expression, what the texts are intended to say is not what they literally say. I then considered how better to read the Scriptures on the claim of divine revelation. Both Buber and Rosenzweig were preferred to Maimonides on the grounds that the science presupposed by these theologians is more compatible with the claims of modern scientists than is the philosophy of Maimonides.

Rosenzweig was preferred to Buber, because Rosenzweig makes better sense than Buber out of the claim that revelation occurs as a relationship between God and a community that effects morally compelling content claims. In short, Buber's theology was faulted as the best option for an intelligible conception of revelation from the perspective of Judaism, because Buber's thought is too individualistic and too antinomian. However, Rosenzweig's theology raised moral problems of its own, specifically in relation to questions about racism and irrationalism that leave Rosenzweig open to charges of implicit fascism. These problems were addressed in the last chapter. The conclusion was a reformulation of certain critical aspects of Rosenzweig's philosophy, notably his notion of Israel as a chosen people and his radical conceptual separation of belief from knowledge. It is that reconstructed reading of Rosenzweig's philosophy that I will now consider in this present chapter.

THE CHALLENGE OF MODERN SCIENCE

Part I was an exercise in intellectual history, whose goal was to formulate a best possible understanding of the revealer God for a believable conception of the critical rabbinic foundational principle of revelation.

Part II is an exercise in philosophy, whose goal is to investigate critically how it is possible to believe what it is proposed to believe about the God of revelation and how he reveals himself to humanity, especially with reference to how the Hebrew Scriptures can be affirmed as a record of that revelation. In chapter 5 I considered questions of ethics related to Rosenzweig's conception that led to a modification of what he claims. In chapter 7 I will consider issues specifically related to believing in the Hebrew Scriptures as a record of revelation. In this chapter I now turn to questions or challenges that arise from modern science. The questions have the following basis.

I asserted that Maimonides' philosophy is sufficiently incompatible with modern science to require radical reformulation to be believable. Maimonides' understanding of the essential beliefs of Judaism presupposes a certain understanding of physics, psychology, and logic, all of which are drawn from the then reasonably believable Aristotelian sciences of the middle ages. The physics is the basis for Maimonides' understanding of what the world is, which is critical to his explanation of the doctrine of creation. The psychology is the basis for his understanding of what the human is, which is critical to his understanding of the doctrine of revelation. Furthermore, his understanding of logic and language is critical to his explanation of what it means to say that a single deity is both the creator of the world and the revealer to the human. However, these sciences are no longer reasonably believable; hence, Maimonides' interpretation of Judaism, based on that science, is no longer reasonably believable. These claims were made above in these most general terms, without any explanation. Now is the place to explain them, so that we can see if they can also be leveled against the theology of Rosenzweig, and, if they can, to what extent Rosenzweig's theology must be further reconstructed beyond the reformulation introduced in the discussion of ethics. First I will deal with physics and the world, and then with psychology and the human. Finally, in the next chapter, I will deal with logic, language, and how to interpret statements about God.

PHYSICAL COSMOLOGY – RETHINKING THE WORLD

The two primary challenges that modern science has raised for contemporary Christian religious thought have come from physical cosmology and evolutionary psychology. By "evolutionary psychology" I mean a philosophic inquiry that uses the life science of genetics (hence, the term "genetic") as well as the social science of paleoanthropology to con-struct a picture of the origin and development of humanity, in order to make judgments about all aspects of human nature (hence, the term "psychology"). By "physical cosmology" I mean a philosophical inquiry that uses physics (hence, the term "physical"), with a special emphasis on astrophysics, in order to construct a conception of the origin and gen-eral nature of the universe (hence, the term "cosmology"). I will discuss physical cosmology first before turning to evolutionary psychology.

CREATION AND CHRISTIAN THEOLOGY

The challenge that physical cosmology raises for at least some Christian theology has to do with the origin of the universe. Until the latter third of the twentieth century the dominant scientific view in cosmology was what is called a "steady state" theory. According to this view, the universe has no significant history, which is to say that the way the universe is now is the way the universe has always been. However, since the mid sixties[2] the dominant view has been any one of a number of variations on what was initially called "the big bang theory." On this view the universe began with an infinitely small quantity of positive energy, which was infinitely dense at infinite temperature and which imploded and began to expand.[3] Since then the stuff of the universe has become increasingly less dense and cooler as everything that is expands further apart. As everything expands, there begin to form very small particles (such as quarks and antiquarks, electrons and positrons, etc.) that are subject to gravitational forces. Subsequently, elemental particles become subject to weak and electromagnetic interactions, which (with subsequent expansion) lead to the development of nuclear particles, matter, atoms, compounds, and our present universe.

In contrast, a literalist reading of the Book of Genesis, which some Christians still accept as the true and therefore authoritative reading of the Bible, posits that the universe in its present complex form was created less than six thousand years ago. Some Christian thinkers may derive solace from the fact that few cosmologists believe anymore that the universe we occupy is uncreated. However, it is vastly older than

---

[2] The critical event I have in mind is the 1965 mathematical prediction of the presence of cosmic background radiation by James Peebles at Princeton University, and the empirical confirmation of the prediction later that year by Penzias and Wilson at the Palmer Physical Laboratory of the Bell Telephone Company in Princeton.

[3] See Steven Weinberg, *The First Three Minutes* (New York: Bantam, 1977).

any literal reading of the Bible proposes. Hence, modern cosmology raises serious challenges to how these religious Christians, as religious Christians, see the world.

CREATION AND JEWISH THEOLOGY

As I explained in my *Judaism and the Doctrine of Creation*,[4] this question of dating the universe has never been a problem for Jewish philosophy, ultimately because that philosophy, like rabbinic Judaism in general, has never taken the literal meaning of the Bible to be its revealed, true meaning. From the influence of Aristotle, in fact, the tendency of all Jewish thought about creation has been to view it as an atemporal event. Hence, classical Jewish philosophy is most compatible with a steady-state view of the universe. The reason for this is not just scientific. It is also the most reasonable consequence of rabbinic Judaism's conception of God.

God being perfect in every respect means that God is absolutely simple, and this absolute unity means that what God is and what God does are one and the same thing. Hence, God is not a creator who creates the world in the sense that there is a distinction between God as the agent of creation and God's act of creation. The verbs that describe what God does are no less God than the nouns classical Jewish thinkers used to locate God in the universe.

It is a consequence of this radical notion of divine oneness that God can have only a single act that is not subject to change of any form. Hence, the one thing that God does, which is what or who God is, is eternal. That single act can be described as creating or revealing or redeeming, but these are differences only from our human perspective. In reality they are one thing. Hence, the term creation expresses a relationship between God and the world that is an eternal relationship. Creation did not occur thousands of years ago (as some Christians maintain). However, neither did it occur millions of years ago (as many cosmologists maintain). Rather it is always. Hence, in some sense, since the world is the term towards which God is directed in the relationship of creation, the universe – no less than God – is eternal.

There are many ways to interpret what it means to say that God eternally creates the world. The standard philosophic reading is that the verb "to create" is not subject to time (past, present, or future) modifications. However, it may also be interpreted in the way that some midrashim

---

[4] Cambridge: Cambridge University Press, 1994.

suggest,[5] namely, that our present world, which begins with the story of the garden of Eden and ends with the redemptive establishment of God's kingdom on earth, is not the only world. There are at present many worlds other than our own, as there were many worlds before ours, and there will be many worlds after ours. Not every midrash suggests a many-universe cosmology, a reality in which our visible universe is just one among many. It is not the case that a committed Jew has to accept this view in order to affirm the doctrine of creation. However, the same can be said of physical cosmology. Some cosmologists claim that ours is one of many, infinitely expanding universes. In fact this kind of view, simply called an "expanding universe theory," is most widely accepted today by physical cosmologists. However, this view may also be rejected without major consequences for their commitment to their most general conception of the nature of the universe. On any of these interpretations, scientific or Jewish, the kind of problem that Christians have with the current (or the past) scientific accounts of cosmogony (the theory of the origin of the universe) does not exist for Judaism.[6]

THE WORLD ACCORDING TO BUBER AND ROSENZWEIG

So far, just as there is no conflict between the claims of modern cosmology and classical Jewish philosophy about creation as the origin of the universe, so there are no conflicts with either of the modern theologies (Buber's and Rosenzweig's) that were considered in part I. First, Buber is a phenomenologist, and, as such, he does not discuss how the physical world is, but how conscious persons perceive the world. Whatever the claims of physics, past or present, what it describes falls under his topology of the I–It relationship, and his interest religiously is in the I–Thou relationship, which, being non-objective, makes no claims about knowledge whatsoever, including claims about creation. Hence, Buber, in radical separation from the Jewish tradition before him, practices theology without any claim about creation. His God is a revealer and

---

[5] See Samuelson, *Judaism and the Doctrine of Creation*, ch. 4, "Classical rabbinic commentaries," esp. pp. 113–115.

[6] There are some contemporary traditional rabbis who read Scripture on creation in the literal way that these Christians do. However, I do not think that this reading is authentic to rabbinic Judaism. It is rather a consequence of Christian influence, viz. politically and culturally conservative rabbis taking upon themselves, probably unconsciously, the agenda of Christian clergy with whom they share a common political and cultural agenda. My argument for this claim is based on my reading of the classic midrashim, medieval commentaries, and works of medieval Jewish philosophy discussed in *Judaism and the Doctrine of Creation*.

a redeemer – whom he discusses as the God of the patriarchs. However, his deity is not a creator – whom he identifies with the God of the philosophers.

For Rosenzweig, creation is a central term of his word picture. Yet, insofar as vision is focused somewhat exclusively on God the creator, there is no significant difference between Rosenzweig and the classical Jewish philosophers. He, like them, affirms creation not as an event in time, but as an eternal relationship between God and the world, one concerning which science is capable of yielding at least some knowledge beyond belief, and belief is able to expand into a fuller, richer picture than can be achieved by unaided science, that is, by science not informed by revelation.

The kinds of challenges that physical cosmology raises for Christian faith are not the kinds of challenges that science raises for Jewish philosophers, who are steeped in classical as well as modern Jewish philosophy but are as yet (at least) untainted by the political-cultural influence of some conservative Christian educators. That is not to say that there are no challenges from modern science for Jewish belief in creation. Those challenges have to do with modern science's radical separation of the ethical from the physically real. I will explain.

AMORALITY AS THE CHALLENGE OF PHYSICS

The Jewish Aristotelians – necessity versus purpose

Maimonides believed[7] that there was a radical difference between what he called the philosophers' view of an eternal universe and what he called the Torah's commitment to creation. There is no consensus among scholars about what Maimonides actually believed, and there is some unclarity in what he actually says in the details of his view.[8] However, at a more general level, what he explicitly says he means is clear. Reason, and therefore science, is in no position to give us knowledge about the origin of the universe, because all human reasoning is dependent for its premises on sense experience; sense experience is reliable for physical

---

[7] *Guide* I:13.
[8] Personally I think he believed in some form of Platonic view of eternal creation, which for him is reducible neither to the "Torah" view of creation nor to the "philosophers" view of eternity. I present my reasons for this judgment in "Maimonides' Doctrine of Creation," *Harvard Theological Review* 84,3 (1991), 249–271. However, not everyone is convinced that I am right. Ken Seeskin offered his reasons for rejecting my view in *Searching for a Distant God: The Legacy of Maimonides* (New York and Oxford: Oxford University Press, 2000).

dynamics within the universe, but it is not reliable for any dynamics of the
universe as a whole, since it is logically invalid to infer from what is true
of parts what is true of the whole. Since reason cannot settle the issue,
we should follow the literal meaning of the Scriptures, which supports
the Torah view of creation out of nothing. However, there are some texts
whose literal meaning supports a non-temporal view of creation, which
entails that the Scriptures alone cannot settle what we should believe
in this case. How, then, should we choose between a view that says the
universe is created and one that says it is eternal? The issue seems to be
independent of questions about time, since, on both views, there is no
temporal beginning to the universe. His judgment is that the Torah view,
which he equates with creation, leaves room for the possibility of miracles,
whereas the Aristotelian philosophers' view, which Maimonides equates
with eternity, does not.

As Gersonides subsequently clarifies Maimonides' position, the issue
is not about miracles as such, but about contingency. Miracles on this
Jewish understanding are not events that contradict the laws of nature.
Since the laws of nature express divine will, for God to act in such a way
that he contradicts his own will would be tantamount to God not being
God. Rather, miracles are possible events that God is able to will, if he
so chooses, that are not part of his general legislation of the universe. In
other words, what Maimonides means when he says that creation leaves
open the possibility of miracles while Aristotelianism does not is that the
view of the philosophers is totally deterministic whereas the Torah view
admits contingency.

As Abraham ibn Daud argued explicitly,[9] what is ultimately important
about contingency for rabbinic philosophers is that without it the notion
that God commands laws is unintelligible. Divine governance of the
universe is such that obedience to his will and laws brings reward, and
disobedience results in punishment. The value of reward and punishment
is pedagogic. Rewards reinforce desirable behavior, and punishments
discourage it. However, if everything is determinate in a strong sense, so
that nothing is contingent, there is no room for real education. People
do what they must do, and since they must do it, being commanded,
which means having choice, is irrational. Furthermore, it is unjust, for
no one deserves a reward for doing what they could not help but do,
and, conversely, no one deserves punishment for what they could not

---

9 In al-ʿaqida al-rafiʿa (The Exalted Faith), Book 2, Basic Principle 6, ch. 2. See Abraham ibn Daud,
  The Exalted Faith. English translation by N. Samuelson (Rutherford, Madison, et al.: Fairleigh
  Dickinson University Press, and London and Toronto: Associated University Presses, 1986).

help but do. The philosophers' view is totally deterministic, and hence raises challenges to the coherence of a Torah conception of the universe, which we would have to face if the philosophers' view were knowledge. However, it is not knowledge. It is only speculation, and therefore, as such, offers no compelling reason to reject what the Torah says.

Gersonides[10] makes his version of the Maimonidean claim even stronger. It is not, he argues, that reason is neutralized between the options in cosmogony. While no definitive argument can be given, it is clear that insofar as we can tell, armed with the best astronomy of our day, much that is true of the heavens is contingent, for there is no good logical reason why it should be one way rather than another.[11] Hence, the belief in contingency is more reasonable than the belief in necessity, and contingency verifies the thesis of creation – that the world runs not just by mechanical principles that necessitate whatever is – and falsifies the eternity thesis – that there are mechanical principles by which everything that happens, independent of purpose, is caused, that is, is necessitated. In sum, the universe of the medieval Jewish philosophers is a universe where things in nature happen for a purpose, for not everything occurs by necessity, and it is this purpose that expresses the will of God. It is in this sense that creation is also revelation, for nature itself manifests the mind of God.

Modern physics and natural philosophy – necessity and contingency

In contrast, modern physics, at least since the seventeenth century, admits only mechanical causes, and affirms the possibility of perfect knowledge of the causes of everything, an ideal that means that everything happens by necessity, which further means that nothing has purpose. Spinoza in *The Ethics* gives the strongest statement of this natural philosophy. Everything that is exists as a modification of God. Everything happens by a necessity whose first and completely determinate cause is the will of God, but his will is purposeless, since God being God must do what he does and must will what he wills. Newton, for religious reasons, objected strongly to this view of the universe, which he called "mechanical philosophy" and associated with Descartes and Leibniz rather than Spinoza.[12] However, the worldview that Newton published in his final version of

---

[10] Levi ben Gershom, 1288–1344, Languedoc.

[11] See *The Wars of the Lord* (*milhamot adonai*) Treatise 6, chapter 1. Cf. Maimonides, *Guide* II:19, and my discussion of both texts in *Judaism and the Doctrine of Creation*, pp. 95–97.

[12] Richard S. Westfall, *Never at Rest* (Cambridge: Cambridge University Press, 1980), esp. pp. 301, 390, 454–458.

the *Principia Mathematica*[13] seems no less "mechanical," or at least that is how the *Principia* has been transmitted down to us as what is now called "classical" physics.

The modern science that at least holds out the promise of being able to inform us about everything in the universe is physics. That science employs mathematical models to interpret all events. Insofar as the subject matter purports to be concerned with reality, reality consists of motions that are to be understood in terms of interpreted calculus equations, equations that describe continuous change in terms of integration and differentiation. The most fundamental model for an explanation, comparable in its form to Rosenzweig's "x = y" as a general form or pattern for all meaningful scientific-knowledge statements, is the equation for average velocity as an integration equation concerning movement of an extremely small particle in an extremely small unit of time.[14] From this model Newton expresses three laws of motion, all of which in form are integration functions, and one law of gravitation. Beyond Newton's own work these principles of understanding the physical world are applied to everything else – thermal dynamics, waves, electrostatics, electrodynamics, optics, and so on. What emerges from all of these branches of classical physics is a view of the universe in which everything is a composite of increasingly smaller particles that are governed in their motion through force fields by strictly deterministic mathematical laws. In such a universe, despite Newton's protests to the contrary, there is no room for purpose, and, without purpose, there is no room for ethics in the sense that ethics has nothing to do in any way with what occurs. Hence, this universe may have a God, but it is an entirely a-moral God, for his will, expressible as the mathematical principles of the universe, has nothing to do with ethics.

Quantum mechanics – chance without purpose

It is true that the above picture is transformed somewhat when classical physics is modified by considerations of quantum mechanics. At its most fundamental level what occurs in the universe is not determined, because the laws that rule here are probability equations. Probabilities give us information about sets of particulars, but not about the particulars themselves. Hence, the modified view of the Newtonian universe that

---

[13] *Philosophiæ Naturalis Principia Mathematica.* English translation by I. Bernard Cohen and Ane Whitman (Berkeley: University of California Press, 1999).
[14] This is my verbal interpretation of two equations – $v = dx/dt$ where v is average velocity, and $a = d^2x/dt^2$ where a is acceleration or instantaneous velocity.

emerges through quantum mechanics is a world far more amenable to an Aristotelian view than the classical Newtonian picture. In an Aristotelian universe, contrary to what Maimonides seems to have claimed, there is irreducible chance and indeterminacy, because particularity is a function of matter and matter as matter is in principle unintelligible. So too in the quantum universe the ultimately small particle building blocks of the universe are unintelligible.

Still, while the universe of contemporary physics admits chance, it does not admit purpose. The laws remain mechanical, which in this case means mathematical. Certainly this is no universe familiar to Maimonides and the Maimonideans. However, it is not foreign to the world of Rosenzweig.

The world of Rosenzweig

Rosenzweig's element "world" is constituted by infinite vectors, arising out of the nothing of spatial-temporal location, moving beyond their initial nothingness in the direction of becoming something. This "something" is not what they are; it is what they are directed to become. It is their end-limit. As each concrete particular emerges, it fills the infinite space-time plenum towards the end-limit of the world itself, as a whole, also becoming something, an ideal ever approximated but never achieved actually in space and time. Rosenzweig's world is a world of motions, not things, as it is in modern physics, and the motions in the world as such, again as in physics, are purposeless. However, unlike modern physics, Rosenzweig's universe exhibits purpose. The purpose is to fill the plenum, and, in doing so, become, so to speak, the actualized body of God, for in the idealized end the three distinct elements – God, the world, and the human – become one. However, this end that directs physical motion is not something knowable by the "silent speech" of science. Hence, there is no incompatibility in claiming, as Rosenzweig does, that there is in nature itself directed movement, and claiming, as modern physics does, that there is no purpose that can be found in nature by means of science. The end becomes visible through belief, not knowledge, and the source of the belief is God's revelation of himself to the human, which, in principle, while not incompatible with science (Rosenzweig's or quantum mechanics), is not to be found anywhere in science. The source of this belief in a moral-valued, purposeful universe resides in the human and in the divine, not in the physical *per se*.

Rosenzweig makes a radical separation, at least in terms of origins, between the human and the physical world. In so doing, Rosenzweig, in psychology at least, separates himself clearly and sharply from the worldview of the Maimonideans. I turn now to what can be learned from evolutionary psychology about the believability of either Jewish theory of psychology.

EVOLUTIONARY PSYCHOLOGY – RETHINKING THE HUMAN[15]

THE SCIENCES OF THE HUMAN

Of all the views considered, Rosenzweig's conception of the God of revelation is most applicable as a base for constructing a contemporary conception of the Jewish dogma of revelation. First, unlike Buber's theology, Rosenzweig's is consistent with an understanding that both the Torah itself and the tradition of rabbinic commentary on it are manifestations of some initial experience of a relationship between God and the Jewish people, that this relationship is not just a single event in the past but is alive and continuous into our own day, and that the nature of this ongoing encounter provides an intelligible and believable understanding of the auxiliary rabbinic dogma of *torah mi-sinai*, namely, that God revealed himself to the Jewish people through the prophet Moses at an event associated with a more or less specific time and place called "Sinai." Second, Rosenzweig's religious thought is consistent with the claim that this deity of revelation is also the deity of creation, and his conception of the Jewish dogma of creation is intelligible and believable in a way that the philosophy of Maimonides is not. The fault with Maimonides' philosophy in this case is that his conception of creation is tied to a natural philosophy that was eminently believable in his own day, but is no longer acceptable by anyone familiar with modern physics and cosmology as a true account of the nature and origin of the created universe.

Rosenzweig's philosophy is subject to no such criticism. His view of creation is a picture of a universe of dynamic motions out of the nothing of an origin governed by no principles other than mathematical conceptions of chaos and chance. What Rosenzweig interprets the Hebrew Scriptures

[15] The presentation in this section grew out of discussions with colleagues in Jewish philosophy and in the life and physical sciences at two workshops, in 1999 and 2000 in Tempe, AZ, sponsored by the Harold and Jean Grossman Chair of Jewish Studies at Arizona State University with support from the Academy for Jewish Philosophy and from the Department of Religious Studies at ASU.

to mean by the primordial nothing of the space out of which God creates is compatible with the claim of modern physics that what begins as pure energy becomes transformed in its motion into positively and negatively charged forces governed by the fields in which they are located. Furthermore, not only is the physics compatible with Rosenzweig's account of creation; it constitutes an insightful elaboration of just what intelligent, informed committed Jews can mean when they, as religious Jews, affirm that the God of the Torah created the world out of nothing.

What physics cannot provide is a purposeful direction to these motions that constitute the universe. That purpose, Rosenzweig tells us, transcends the scientific and the knowable. It is not a subject for knowledge; rather, it is a dictate of belief. It cannot be learned from observing nature; rather, its content depends on the interpretation of a revealed text. That text is the record of a relationship between God and human beings.

How believable this claim about revelation is depends on a number of factors, two of which we have already looked at – what the implications of this theology are for our sense of ethics, and how this picture agrees with what we believe on the basis of modern science to be the best account of the nature of the world. What remains to be seen is how believable is the claim that the Torah itself is a manifestation of revelation and how Rosenzweig's theology conforms to what we learn from other branches of science. The question of the believability of the Torah as a true expression of divine revelation will be the most difficult issue to be considered, for even if we believe in revelation, that does not necessarily mean that our Torah is revealed, and it is because of its difficulty that I have put off this subject to the last. However, for now, I will look at what the other sciences have to say that is relevant to this consideration of revelation and the revealer deity. The last section dealt with the physical sciences that purport to inform us about the world, whose relevance is primarily to questions about creation. Here I look at the humane sciences, especially psychology and biology, which purport to inform us about the human.

What I will look at here is a set of different sciences that deal with different aspects of the conception of the human. Of notable importance are biology, genetics, anthropology, sociology, paleoanthropology, anatomy, cognitive sciences, and informational sciences. All of them contribute to forming a picture of what a human is. Whatever else human beings may or may not be, they are animals. As such they are subject to all the laws that govern the rest of the animal kingdom, and notable in this respect are the laws of genetics. Hence, an adequate conception of what it means to be human requires some knowledge of biology, anatomy, and genetics.

Furthermore, humans live in communities of other humans through which they interact with each other and their world. No understanding of a human as an isolated individual can adequately capture what it means to be human. Hence, an adequate conception of what it means to be human also requires some knowledge of sociology.

Furthermore, what a human is now is not what a human always was. Humans, no less than all other forms of life on our planet, have evolved, and knowing how they have evolved so far is critical to considering how they will evolve into the future. To be human is not something static. Humans, no less than all other compounded forms of positive energy, continuously change. Hence, an adequate conception of what it means to be human requires some knowledge of paleoanthropology. As for their future, the conception of what it means to be human has always, as we shall see, been tied to conceptions of human cognition, and that conception is changing in the light of contemporary studies in cognition, especially in the informational sciences.

I have collapsed all of these very different disciplines together for present purposes into a single, collective view of what modern science teaches about the human under the label "evolutionary psychology." I have singled out evolution for emphasis in this picture, in much the same way that I singled out cosmology from the list of physical sciences in the last section, because evolutionary biology and anthropology more than any other branches of the life sciences raise most directly questions about the viability of the classical Aristotelian conception of the human that past rabbinic theology has adapted to its interpretation of revelation through the Torah. I begin with a summary of how the classical Jewish philosophers understood what it means to be human. Then I will consider what modern evolutionary psychology says, and finally, what the differences between the modern and the classical entail for a contemporary Jewish theology of the human.

CLASSICAL VIEWS OF THE HUMAN

The Hebrew Scriptures

One way of reading at least the opening chapters of the Book of Genesis[16] is as a drama about the creation of the world as a dialogue between God (its creator) and the human beings whom he makes responsible for

[16] Chapters 1–3.

governing the earth. It is this responsibility that provides the primary definition of what it means to be human. All of the universe is created through divine speech. God takes the pre-existing space, divides it into separate domains (notably the sky and the earth), generates lights to dwell in the sky, and orders the earth to generate living entities composed from the earth. The sun and the moon are singled out among the celestial lights to govern the sky in accordance with God's will, and the human (*ha-adam*) is singled out to govern all the life forms on the earth.

The sky is the background for the text's focus on the earth. On earth the kinds of creatures are differentiated by their laws and their function. The single command given to everything that the earth generates is that it should reproduce its kind. The plants reproduce to provide food for the animals, and at least a certain segment of the animal population reproduces to provide food for the humans and sacrifices for God. That humans prepare the sacrifices for God, in whom the food chain ends, is another way that humans are distinct.

There are a number of details to add to the above, most general, picture of the human in the Bible that bear specifically on how these Scriptures conceive of human beings and how subsequent rabbinic commentators interpreted them. First, the focus of the Scriptures increasingly becomes more microscopic as the biblical story of reality unfolds. I have already noted that once the sky and the earth have been separated, the narrative focuses on the earth. Once the earth generates its life forms and the human is created, the focus becomes only the human. Then the humans are differentiated into nations, and once the nation of Israel is created, the focus becomes exclusively Israel. The universe is considered in the whole of the Scriptures only as background for discussing the earth, which is a background for discussing the human, which, in turn, is a background for discussing the nation of Israel.

Second, since the universe exists by divine will expressed as speech, the primary way that things are defined is by the commandments that they receive, through nature, from God. Non-living entities – stars, planets, mountains, valleys, rivers, and so on – are commanded to remain within specified domains. In the case of spatial objects, it is their spatial location that defines them. Living things upon the earth, as we have seen, are defined by their commandment to reproduce their own kind, and, in so doing, fulfill their function as part of a cosmic food chain. Similarly, humans, who, like other animals, are composed from the matter of the earth, also are commanded to reproduce their own kind. However, they, unlike any other earth creature, are not created to be food for anyone or anything. Rather, they are ordered to govern the earth and to prepare for God his food from the creatures (vegetable and animal) whom the human governs in service to their creator.

Third, it is not unreasonable to assume that the hierarchy of commandments given to living things reflects their status in God's universe. This universe can be conceived of as a state whose government is a monarchy (i.e. ruled by a single person). That ruler is God. At the bottom of the hierarchy is space and inorganic matter. Next in order are the living things, who have a single commandment. Next are the human beings, who, in addition to the one commandment that they share with the animals, have other commandments.[17] These laws, known subsequently as the Noachite code, can be read in a number of different ways. Rabbinic tradition interpreted their number to be seven. One is the commandment to reproduce, and the remaining six are understood to be general moral rules to govern human society at all levels. Next in order are all the descendants of Abraham, who, in addition to the seven laws of Noah, are commanded to circumcise their male children. Finally, there are the people who descend from Abraham's grandson, Israel, who, once formed into a nation by the revelation of the Torah through Moses at Sinai, are defined by the legal system outlined in the major body of the Pentateuch. Rabbinic tradition counts these laws to be 613, of which seven are the laws governing all human beings.

Fourth, the Hebrew Scriptures do mention something that can be called "species," namely "kinds" (*minim*). One primary use of the term is to say that all things are to reproduce only with their own "kind."[18] It is in this respect that the term "kind" can be understood to be a species, for what primarily defines a species in terms of biology is the ability of (at least sexual) things to reproduce through intercourse with each other. If, then, the Bible can be said to have species, they are defined by the function of reproduction. Hence, the human is a species, and, as such, their definition is no different than that of any other earthly conceived animal. Gender, then, is central in the Bible to what makes human beings human. However, once the original human is separated into two kinds of human beings, one male and one female,[19] the focus comes to fall exclusively on the male, with the female human – like the sky, earth, plants, and animals – forming part of the background of the narrative.

Fifth, while the human is an earth thing created from the earth, there is something special about them. To say that humans are defined by

17 Gen. 1:28.   18 Gen. 1:24.   19 See Gen. 1:27 and 2:22–23.

the number and content of their commandments places humans on the same level with all animals. The difference between them is primarily quantitative rather than qualitative – other animals have only one commandment from God while humans have no less than seven. However, there are two ways that the biblical story suggests that humans are qualitatively different as well. One way is that humans get to name all of the other animals.[20] A second (and more important) way has to do with how the human is created. In the case of the animals, the earth in response to God's word generates them; but God himself participates in the creation of the human.[21] While it is true that at least in part (how large a part we are not told) the human is a creature of the earth no different than any other creature of the earth, it is also true that the human is at least in part divine.

Sixth, that God's participation in their creation means that there is something more than earthly about the human is reflected in God saying that they are created in his "image." What this means, beyond the method of origin, is not spelled out in the text, for we are not told what "parts" of the human are created directly by God rather than indirectly by his servant, the earth. It would not be unreasonable to infer that the human distinctive ability to name the animals is an expression of this divine part.[22] However, this act of naming may indicate something more general, namely, that human beings have, like God, the power of speech, so that they, again like God, can relate to others by uttering commandments. God commands but cannot be commanded; humans can both command and be commanded, while all other creatures may be commanded but cannot command. This way of distinguishing the human may be the most important way in the biblical text, which is, after all, primarily a narrative about law, where the drama between God and the human, and especially between God and Israel, is presented as a flawed love story, characterized by success and failure of the human in heeding the revealed word of the divine other.

The Jewish philosophers

I think that the summary I have presented above of the biblical view of the human accurately reflects most of the biblical text – most, but not all. A notable exception, and there may be others as well, is the Book

[20] Gen. 2:20.   [21] Gen. 1:26–27.
[22] See Howard Eilberg-Schwartz, *The Human Will in Judaism: The Mishnah's Philosophy of Intention* (Brown Judaic Studies 103; Atlanta: Scholars Press, 1986).

of Proverbs. In Proverbs the conception of the Torah as a dynamic legal expression of relationship between God and his creatures is transformed into a Platonic ideal. I will illustrate my claim with just one, familiar text from Proverbs.

Proverbs 8:22 reads "The Lord made me the beginning of (*reshit*) his way, the first of (*qedem*) his works from of old." The rabbis rightly noted the parallel between this verse and Genesis 1:1, which reads "at the beginning (Be-*reshit*) God created the sky and the earth." The problem in the Genesis text is that *reshit* is generally a construct form of the noun *rishonah*, and, as a construct, there should be another noun for it to modify. Hence, more literally, Genesis 1:1 reads, "at the beginning of God created." The question is, at the beginning of what? Whatever the candidate is for the what, it must be something other than God that, in some sense, also is identical with God. The rabbis who wrote this midrash[23] reasoned as follows. Since the text that we have was written (in some sense at least) by God, it contains no errors. Hence, whatever the term *reshit* modifies could not be missing because of an error in transmission. The only reason for its absence would be that to state it would be superfluous, because, whatever it is is God. The midrashic commentators found the solution to the problem in the above text from Proverbs. The missing term is "his way" and (from the parallel second half of the verse) "his works."

I think this midrashic reading reflects the actual intent of the author of the Proverbs texts, that is, that the quoted verse was written with the Genesis text in mind. In this case, the way/work intended is "wisdom" (*chokhmah*), here reified into something like a Platonic form. Furthermore, this Hebrew term for wisdom (*chokhmah*) is in extension synonymous with the Hebrew term *torah*. Hence, Torah, the word of God, is not a book; it is an entity. That entity is the model that God employed to create the world, and that model is in some significant sense identical with God.

Personally I believe that the author(s) of Proverbs, as well as the authors of other books not in the canon from the period during which Proverbs was composed (viz., from what is called the "wisdom literature"), had already made the judgment, probably under the influence of some kind of Platonic philosophy, that wisdom is a form, that to know it is the highest human end, that in attaining wisdom one attains knowledge of God, and that it is through wisdom that the world is created and governed. However, even if this is not a correct interpretation of

---

[23] See both *Bereshit Rabbah* and Rashi on Gen. 1:1, especially the interpretation of Rav Oshaya. Cf. N. Samuelson, *Judaism and the Doctrine of Creation*, p. 114.

Proverbs, it is an interpretation that becomes authoritative no later than the age of classical Jewish philosophy.[24] This moral-religious judgment about a reified wisdom as the ideal end of human behavior informs – or better, transforms – the Jewish understanding of what it means to be human.

Drawing upon their knowledge of the philosophical traditions of both Plato and Aristotle, the classical Jewish philosophers[25] presented the following conception of what it meant to be a human being in God's created world: every individual is defined by a complex form that is expressed in language as a species; a species is a compound of two simpler (but not necessarily simple) forms, one that is expressed as a genus – what the members of this class share in common with members of some other larger class, and another that is expressed as a specific difference – what the members of this class share in common that they do not share with other members of their genus. In the case of the human, the genus is what is an animal, and the specific difference is whatever it means to be rational.

Equating the philosophical term for rationality with the biblical term for "speech" (*dibbur*), these rabbis identified what it meant to be specifically human with speech, so that to speak is to be rational. Hence, they read the biblical texts discussed above to say that the way that the human being is created in the image of God is that only the human, like God, is rational, which they took to mean, a thinker, which they took to mean, someone who can speak. The question now becomes just what is involved in being rational, for both God and humanity, and how this rationality relates these two very different kinds of persons (conscious entities).

Everything is a form, matter, or a compound of form and matter. Only God the creator, in his radical simplicity, is purely form. Conversely, only space, independent of anything occupying it, is purely matter. Furthermore, since form alone expresses what something is, only form is intelligible, so that something is itself intelligible only to the extent that it is informed, that is, that it has a form. All the forms in the universe exist unified as a single form that is identical with God. From this form God performs his two primary activities in reality – creating the world and revealing himself to the human. As something created, everything

---

[24] For the development of this history of wisdom ethics in Jewish philosophy see Hava Tirosh Samuelson's *Think Happy* (forthcoming).

[25] From at least Saadia onwards, but possibly even earlier, as in the work of philosophical theologians such as Philo. See Hava Tirosh-Samuelson, *Think Happy* (forthcoming).

that is, insofar as it is, is what it is because of its form, and that form is ultimately identical with the form of God.

Consider, for example, a particular tree. What makes it particular is that it is materialized, but what makes it a tree is that it has the form tree. This form exists absolutely in God in unity with all of God's forms. However, when matter modifies that form, it becomes one form among many in one created thing among many. In other words, the tree (a form) becomes a tree (a particular substance). This, then, is how God creates trees. He informs them, and, insofar as these creatures exist, they are God – only they are what God is materialized, whereas God is all of them in unity and radical simplicity as an absolutized form.

When a particular human comes to know a tree, what occurs is that the images of the tree, formed from sense reports about the tree, are purged in the human intellect of everything material, that is, everything that makes it an image. What remains is the form of the tree without its matter. As such, that form is what we know about the tree – a concept of the tree. As a concept it is a form that is the same form as the form that exists absolutely in God and materially in the physical world, but, as it resides in a human intellect as a concept, the form exists mentally. Hence, our concept of a tree, the physical tree, and the form of the tree in the mind of God are all a single thing – the form tree. They differ only in their mode of existence – mentally in the intellect, physically in the material world, and absolutely in God.

Furthermore, in knowing any form, such as that of a tree, God is the immediate agent that causes the human to know the form. When the human mind is prepared for conceptual knowledge through the acquisition of sufficient relevant memories of sense images, God activates in that human's intellect the form of the objects in question. Then, and only then, do humans know what otherwise they can only imagine through remembered images. This activity of God actualizing concepts in intellects that otherwise only have the potential to so conceive is the model employed by the classical Jewish philosophers to explain revelation.

In God's single activity of being God, he creates creatures and reveals knowledge. For human beings, given the imperfection of their being situated as material animals in time and space, the effects of this single act appear (to both the imagination and the intellect) to be separate activities. However, in (absolute) reality, the two are the same. Creating and revealing are a single act, differing only in the object to which the divine action is directed – creation in physical matter, and revelation in the intelligent mind.

The critical point for present interest in this account of knowing is that it is this capacity of the intellect to actualize concepts from God, that is, in its capacity to receive revelation, that defines the human as a human and not as just another animal. Furthermore, in knowing (i.e. in grasping concepts), the real object of the knowledge is God. All knowledge is knowledge of God, because all forms known are identical with the form of God. In fact, the more you know the closer you come not just to knowing God but to being God, for the form that you know is the form that is God – but it is it in an inferior way, namely, as a one among many.[26]

For all these reasons, knowing becomes for the classical Jewish philosophers the highest form of moral activity. Knowledge as the good follows from both their philosophical ethics and their philosophical religion. In terms of ethics, something is called "good" or "evil" relative to the end that appropriately defines the thing in question. In this Aristotelian universe substances are defined in terms of essential movements, and its end defines motion. What brings the substance closer to its end is good. Conversely, what removes it further from its end is bad. In the case of the human, what brings them closer to ultimate knowledge is good, and what removes them further from this end is bad.

This ultimate end, called "happiness" (*eudaimonia*) by the philosophers, is identified with the end of the religious life. In terms of religion, the end of human activity is the imitation of God, which means, becoming more like God, which, as we have seen, means for the Jewish philosophers coming in actuality to know God. Hence, since the knowledge of anything is knowledge of God, and since to know God is to become God, there is in principle (at least in the minds of the classical Jewish philosophers) no conflict between the ethics of philosophy and the values of the religious life. Both have the same end: knowledge of Torah.

This last point brings me back to the starting point in this section on classical Jewish ethics. Revelation defines humanity. The human being is the only creature in the material world to whom God reveals himself. He does so by causing the prepared human to know God's created

---

[26] This account may fit Maimonides' theological epistemology, but that is debatable, since what Maimonides says in this case is not straightforward. Insofar as he describes God's knowledge, it would fit this model. However, he also emphasizes that God's knowledge is so radically different than human knowledge, that human beings can in no way conceive of what it is. In this case I am following Gersonides rather than Maimonides. Gersonides is clear and it is not impossible that what Maimonides believed is what Gersonides said. In any case, even if he did not, Gersonides' account of divine knowledge makes more sense out of the classical tradition of Jewish philosophy than do Maimonides' words. See N. Samuelson, *Gersonides on God's Knowledge of Particulars* (Toronto: Pontifical Institute of Mediaeval Studies, 1977).

world. Knowledge is revelation and revelation is God. Hence, Torah, intellectual knowledge of the world and of God, and divine revelation are a single activity. This single reality also defines the human, and defines the human in such a way that to be human is to be becoming divine.

From the perspective of psychology, the keys to all of these identities, so crucial for classical Jewish ethics, are the judgments that humans as a species are distinct, what defines the human is rational knowledge, and knowledge is a prime example of revelation. All of these key assumptions about being human are subject to doubt in the light of the modern sciences of psychology. Furthermore, this understanding of what it means to be human is critical in this religious philosophy's understanding of revelation. Hence, doubts that arise from modern psychology about the classical view of the human also constitute a serious challenge to how classical Jewish philosophy interprets revelation. I will now turn to what these issues are before I consider the view of the human in Franz Rosenzweig's theology.

MODERN VIEWS OF THE HUMAN

The sciences

What I will now present is a summary of what I have learned from a variety of contemporary life sciences about what it means to be human, with specific attention to what the Hebrew Scriptures and classical Jewish philosophy affirm about the human as the recipient of divine revelation. These claims are that human beings constitute a distinct natural species, that rationality is the most distinctive human characteristic, and that the proper understanding of ethics rests on the foundation of this conception of the human.[27]

---

[27] For my presentation of the life sciences I rely heavily on Steven Pinker, *How the Mind Works* (New York: W. W. Norton & Co., 1997). However, there are other works that have special importance as well. For paleoanthropology I rely on Richard Leakey, *The Origin of Humankind* (New York: Basic Books, 1994) and Ian Tattersall, *The Fossil Trail: How We Know What We Think We Know about Human Evolutions* (New York and Oxford: Oxford University Press, 1995). I use these two books, together with Pinker's, to present a picture of the genesis of humanity. They do not agree in the details, but I think that for present purposes those details do not matter. Where I think that they do, I will so indicate.

For evolution, I rely on a number of different works of popular science, including many of the publications of Edward O. Wilson, Richard Dawkins, and Daniel C. Dennett. Of special relevance are Dawkins, *The Selfish Gene* (New York and London: Granada Publishing Co., 1978; Dennett, *Darwin's Dangerous Idea: Evolution and the Meanings of Life* (London: Penguin Books, 1995), and Wilson, *On Human Nature* (Cambridge, MA: Harvard University Press, 1978). As in the case of paleoanthropology, the emphasis in my summary will be more on what these biologists share in

Epistemic qualifications

The story of the origins of humanity is constructed primarily from the study of scattered ancient animal bones, thousands to millions of years old, that have managed to survive and to be discovered. Both factors, survival and discovery, are historical accidents. For such old bones the conditions for survival are rare. If, for example, they are exposed to the atmosphere, they will decay, and if the materials that conceal them are too dense, they will be crushed. The discovery of these relatively few remaining bones is also a matter of chance. Something must happen to expose them to the atmosphere, and this exposure must occur at a time when they will be discovered by some human being who will correctly assess their value and preserve them for scientific study.

These facts mean that all reasonable judgments of early animal history are skewed. If the remains that we discover are a good sample of what in fact occurred, we can make reasonable judgments. However, the conditions for survival and discovery are so unlikely that the judgment of ancestry based on these data has limited probability. Furthermore, it is rare that entire skeletons are discovered. In general, paleoanthropological data are more like pieces in a very advanced jigsaw puzzle. Randomly dispersed bits and pieces must be put together, and it is not difficult for perfectly good expert researchers to put together pieces from one animal with pieces from another animal. Furthermore, all the pieces may not be originally from the same places, because, for example, many of the discovered sites are by rivers that brought the bones to where they are from upstream. For the same reason, all the pieces may not be originally from the same time.

None of this means, of course, that it is illegitimate to draw conclusions about the origins of human beings and the historical development of species of animals. Reasonable judgments are always to be based on

common and less on how they differ. My selection is with a mind to the theological implications of their work for many academic disciplines, including philosophy and all of the life and social sciences. Stephen Jay Gould's many publications present a significantly different interpretation of both evolution and its relevance to other disciplines, and Gould's influence can also be detected in what I will say about evolution.

For the theological implications of evolutionary psychology, my summary is informed by a number of studies on Christianity and science. Notable among them are Philip Hefner, *The Human Factor* (Minneapolis: Fortress Press, 1993), Ted Peters, *Genetics: Issues of Social Justice* (Cleveland: Pilgrim, 1998), Holmes Rolston, *Genes, Genesis, and God: Beyond Selfishness to Shared Values* (New York: Columbia University Press, 1997), and Ursula Goodenough, *The Sacred Depths of Nature* (New York and Oxford: Oxford University Press, 1998). How I assess the scientific data is significantly different from what they say, but the difference is primarily about how my Jewish sources differ from their traditional Christian sources. However, the differences are not so great that their insights could not, and did not, help me in making my own assessment.

the best available evidence. However, how probable a most reasonable judgment is varies with the epistemic quality of the data on which the judgment is based, and in the case of paleoanthropology the level of probability of any judgment is necessarily extremely low (at least by the standards of judgments in physics), so low that it is not at all surprising that in any age different researchers disagree about the significance of their findings, and consensus about findings can undergo radical change from one generation to the next.

The above summary of the epistemic state of the field of paleoanthropology must be kept in mind in the story I am now going to present. It is based on the best research in the field at the time of the writing of this book. However, the epistemic value of the story – beyond the fact that I am summarizing (and therefore simplifying) accounts that are themselves summaries of original research, research that I personally have not examined – is low, and that too will be a factor in comparing the claims of modern science with those of Jewish philosophy about the origins of humanity.

The origins of the human
With these qualifications in mind, I will now tell our story. It begins with two accidents. The earth core is a rugged sphere surrounded by a ring of water. Because the surface of the core is rugged, some of it reaches out sufficiently high to extend through the surrounding ring of water into the atmosphere. These extensions of the core into the air constitute the surface, what the Hebrew Scriptures call "dry land" (*adamah*), upon which we and all other animals live. That surface is slowly (in our human time frames) changing, because shifts occur in the crust of the earth. Our story begins with a change that took place about twelve million years ago. That change took the region of land surface that we today call Africa and divided it into two separate regions – east and west. Until then, with reference to evolution, there was interaction between all members of any species, including what we commonly call apes. However, after this change, interaction, and therefore mating, between the apes of these two regions ceased to be a realistic possibility. Hence, these two groups of apes developed significantly different genetic histories, which means that changes that occurred on one side of the mountains dividing Africa into two had no effect on the inhabitants of the other side. For present purposes, the group that matters is the apes of East Africa.

The next major accident occurred some three million years ago. During the nine million years in between, both groups of apes lived in thick, rich forests. There our ancestors lived primarily on fruit, which they picked from trees that protected them at the ground level from predatory animals as well as from the flying predators in the sky above the trees. This necessity motivated them to develop a keen sense of depth vision as well as the ability to discern colors. Both skills enabled them to organize what their eyes saw into distinct objects, so that swinging through the trees they could use their depth perception to avoid crashing into them, and seeking fruit they could use their color perception to distinguish fruit from other forest objects.

It is this development of a strong sense of depth and color that underlies the first major human intellectual talent – the ability to see the world in terms of things called "objects" that are located in something called "space." Hence, if this account is right, the brains of our ape ancestors had formulated their first abstract ideas – space and spatially located objects.

The development of vision is a skill that should not be undervalued. In the words of the artificial-intelligence researcher, David Marr, vision is "a process that produces from images of the external world a description that is useful to the viewer and not cluttered with irrelevant information."[28] It begins with how the brain determines depth (stereovision) from the data provided by two eyes through what is best described as trigonometry. A similar mathematical approach is taken to explain how the mind determines perspective through judgments of shade and shape. Therefore, vision itself is an activity whose performance requires what amounts to, in human terms, a highly sophisticated ability to use mathematics. Hence, the development of the powers of vision, motivated by the search for food in forests, is the first major step by our ancestors to becoming intelligent animals.

Three million years ago the second geological change in our story separates the development of the East African apes from their cousins in West Africa. At that time changes in the earth's crust led to major regions of East Africa losing their forest coverings and becoming large grasslands, or savannas. This change forced our ape ancestors out of the woods into vastly more dangerous territory. Now they no longer had the protection of the tall trees and thick forests. However, with the danger came new opportunities for food and development. Their advantages in the new environment were their superior depth and color perception. And there were other advantages as well. They could stand erect, and they had highly developed front paws (what we call "hands").

---

[28] Quoted by Pinker, *How the Mind Works*, p. 213.

Just when our ancestors developed useful hands and an upright posture is a matter of debate among scientists. Pinker, following Darwin, says that it happened when our ancestors were forced to live in the savannas. Pinker claims that we stood erect in order to see above the grass of the large plains, which gave our ancestors an advantage in identifying the approach of enemies as well as an advantage in identifying animals sufficiently weak for them to eat, because the major change that took place when apes began to live on the plains was that meat was added to their fruit diet.

A value of Pinker's account is that the development of hand dexterity and an upright posture coordinates with the development of other skills developed in the savannas that become distinctive marks of being human, notably the use of tools. However, Richard Leakey reports that bipedalism, standing erect on the hind two paws (which we call "feet"), is found as early as seven million years ago, long before our ancient apes adjusted to life on the plains. If Leakey is correct, a reasonable evolutionary account of the development of these first two humanoid-like traits has to do with swinging through the trees. The hands developed to grasp the tree branches, and the erect posture was a consequence of the hand swinging.

In either case all of our scientists agree that the move from forests into plains promotes major changes in the genetic development of East African apes that propels their distant offspring on a path that leads to becoming human. On the plains fruit is rare and meat is plentiful, but meat takes more talent to catch than does fruit. To be successful at it our apes would either have to become stronger or faster than they were or find some other way to hunt. In fact they did not become sufficiently strong or fast to be anything more than good food for other, more fitted-to-survive, animals. It may be the case, in fact, for reasons of weakness, that the meat they did begin to eat was taken from the discarded remains of other more talented hunters. In other words, our fruit eaters became scavengers. However, in time our ancestors did develop one new skill that enabled them to actually hunt. They learned to hunt together. In other words, they learned how to live in a society.

Society is a major development. For it to occur, our ancestors had to be able to agree on divisions of labor, so that females would remain at some relatively permanent place that we could call "home," and there give birth to and raise children, while the males could go off to hunt and return to share what they hunted with the females and the children. To work together in this way they had to be able to exchange information, and to be able to do that, they had to develop larger brains to carry out the increased demands for thinking.

To be sure, the thinking was primarily practical. They knew what space and objects were, but they thought about them not as space and objects but as enemies, friends, and food, judged at distances that determined courses of action. Enemies far removed were no threat, and living food too far away could not be attained. Conversely, you had to flee enemies near by and you could hunt food close at hand. Still, practical thinking (what Pinker calls "ecological intelligence") is no less thinking than is pure thought (what Pinker calls "modern academic intelligence"). Both are sophisticated and require brains far more developed than the forest apes had.

The desire for meat required larger brains that in turn, because of the amount of energy they burn, required better (i.e. more efficient) sources of energy through food than fruit can provide. Hence, the more they ate meat, the more they needed larger brains, which in turn required more meat. Furthermore, larger and better brains required larger skulls to contain them. Larger skulls however had their own problem. The larger the skull the more difficult it became for females in the species to give birth. Female pelvises increased in size to accommodate the larger offspring, but there were limits on how large the pelvises could become. In any case, as ape brains increased, so did gender differentiation. Nature's solution to apes producing very large fetuses was for children to be born prematurely, well before their brains could become fully developed. However, premature births meant that the females who bore children had to become more sedentary: while the children were carried within their mother's womb, the females had a certain freedom to move about, as did the males; the larger the fetuses became, the less freedom the females had to move, but even so, more movement was possible while they were carrying their children within the womb than was the case when the children were born prematurely, for the newly born offspring had to be nurtured outside the womb to the level of maturity they had once reached within it. These changes meant that the females had to remain more or less in the same place for up to two years, and during this period of time they and their children became totally dependent upon the males to protect and feed them. The result was that the males became larger and more aggressive, that is, better hunters (or killers) than the females, while the females became more social than the males.

Society is a byproduct of gender differentiation. While the women resided at "home" raising their children, they had the opportunity to develop their skills of communication. That skill is coordinated with the development of speech, because speech is the primary tool that our ancestors used to transmit information. As the skills of communication increased, so did the complexity of their society, which in turn stimulated the development of the brain, which in turn stimulated the use and development of tools – tools used for preparing the food that the males brought back from their hunts and tools that the males themselves used to improve their ability to fight predators and to be themselves predators. Hence, brain size, gender differentiation, social development, speech, and the use of tools were coordinated into a bond of mutual dependence and ever increasing complexity that propelled our ancestral apes in the direction of becoming more intelligent, and therefore, more human. Intelligence is correlated with humanity, because these scientists, no less than the classical philosophers, see in intelligence the critical feature that defines a human as a human.

Critical reflections

Sight versus hearing

This emphasis on intelligence is not the only respect in which evolutionary psychology's picture of what it means to be human matches what the Jewish philosophers said. Another notable example of parallel is the emphasis that the above modern scientific story places on vision. Maimonides, for example, hierarchically ordered the senses from touch to vision, making excellence of vision the highest natural precondition for rational thinking.[29] However, it should be pointed out that Maimonides' emphasis in this case, as in many others, differs from at least the biblical understanding of the human, where the emphasis is clearly given to hearing over seeing.

With very few exceptions (the most notable of which being the so-called "account of the chariot" in the first chapter of the Book of Ezekiel), the Hebrew Scriptures read as if they were written by someone who was blind. In general we are told what players say, which is oral, but we are told practically nothing about what they looked like. For example, we know a great deal about what Moses said and what kind of a person he was. All of this is learned both from what he does and, more importantly, from what he says. On the other hand we have no way to tell from the

---

[29] See Maimonides, *Guide* II:41, 45 (esp. the eleventh degree of prophecy). Of the different senses associated with prophecy, vision is noted as the highest. "Vision" is generally the sense associated metaphorically with intellection (*Guide* I:4).

text itself how tall he was, or how fat he was, what color his hair was, or even what color was his skin.

The same can be said for all the central figures in the biblical narrative, most of all for God. More precisely, what we do know about God is that in his case there is nothing to see. We may see his accompanying cloud and even his "glory," but not him. In fact, any deity who can be envisioned is not God, and to worship any visually perceivable entity is idolatry. God "appears" to prophets, but that appearance almost always (again the Ezekiel exception) is described exclusively by what God says.

Some scholars[30] argue that what is true of the Hebrew Scriptures is true of the rabbinic literature as well. Certainly the fact that the term used to identify "thinking," which most classical Jewish philosophers at least believe is the primary human excellence for achieving happiness, literally means speaking (*dibbur*), and speech can only be heard, not seen. However, other scholars argue that this is too broad a generalization,[31] and again Maimonides (as I have noted) certainly is an exception.[32]

However, this contrast is somewhat simplistic. In spite of his emphasis on the value of sight, Maimonides associates speech with reasoning and vision with imagination, and reasoning is in his judgment vastly superior in every way to imagination. Similarly, he also says that at the highest level of conception, namely that of the prophets, those who only hear God's words are at a higher level than those who see visions,[33] and at the highest level of prophecy and human perfection (viz. that of Moses) only reason and no imagination at all is involved.

The same complexity of the relationship between hearing and seeing is present in the scientific story of the human given above. While the emphasis in the story of evolution is placed on the development of abstract thinking in terms of visual judgments of space and color, thinking about space and things in space is, at its highest level, pure geometry. While geometry may employ visual images to illustrate what it claims, its objects are purely abstract, and, as such cannot really be seen. Furthermore, the development of speech is tied to the development of society and information sharing. As such, it is a higher form of development,

---

[30] See Lionel Kochen, *Jews, Idols and Messiahs: The Challenge from History* (Oxford and Cambridge, MA: Basil Blackwell, 1990).
[31] See Kalman Bland, *The Artless Jew: Medieval and Modern Affirmations of the Visual* (Princeton: Princeton University Press, 2000).
[32] Kabbalah also is a counter-example. In fact it is a better case of the primacy of the visual over the oral than is Maimonides' philosophy, since it consistently presents its speculations about the nature of God, the human, and the world as visual images.
[33] *Guide* II:45.

"higher" in the sense that it is a more advanced step on the road of humanity developing its most distinctive characteristic – at least for both the classical Jewish philosophers and for evolutionary psychologists – the power of the brain to reason.

Ethics and the emotions

This emphasis on the developmental superiority of reasoning in the human species points to another similarity between modern evolutionary psychology and classical Jewish philosophy. What the above story says explicitly about human development entails a judgment about ethics, even though most psychologists will insist that ethics is a subject of philosophy that lies beyond the domain of what they can say with authority as scientists. The story suggests that to the extent that a human improves their ability to reason they are a better person. This is notable in psychological discussions of the nature of the emotions by psychologists such as Pinker. In marked contrast to the Romantic tradition of the late nineteenth and early twentieth centuries in which Rosenzweig participates (and possibly with this tradition in mind), Pinker takes a strong stand against viewing emotions as something contrary, in both function and value, to reason. He argues that emotions play a vital role in thinking in that they provide both the goals and the motives of rational thought, and in at least this respect they are intimately connected with, rather than opposed to, rationality.

What these psychologists say about the emotions in this connection closely parallels the philosophy of one Jewish philosopher whom I have intentionally removed from the discussion of Jewish views of the human – Baruch Spinoza. I did not exclude him because he does not have a place of importance in an intellectual history of Jewish thought, but because his philosophy can offer no useful model for understanding revelation. That modern scientific thought about the human is close to what Spinoza believed in itself suggests a challenge that evolutionary psychology raises against forming a viable (i.e. reasonably believable) conception of revelation. I will discuss that below. For now, however, I will first say more by way of a description of evolutionary psychology's Spinozistic conception of the emotions.

We feel pleasure in what we judge contributes to our desire to exist and prosper, and we feel pain in what we judge to endanger these desires. These are the base feelings. All other emotions are complexes reducible to pleasure and pain. In this way the evolutionary psychologists attempt to explain feelings that are subject to moral judgment, such as altruism, revenge, honor, love, grief, and self-deception. Altruism is an illusion of wishful thinking. Our brain is wired to be selfish, not generous. However, genes are not people. Altruism is a highly complex way for people, living in societies, to ensure their own survival and physical prosperity. The same method of analysis is used to explain feelings of affinity with family and friends, as well as to engage in such seemingly non-survival-related activities as producing art, humor, religion, and philosophy.

In sum, society and culture, including ethics itself, are survival mechanisms of the species. They develop because they are useful, and their value lies chiefly in their use. Should they fail to meet the environmental needs of the species, then the species will discard them in favor of better survival techniques, or the species will join many other different species before them and simply pass out of existence.

This account makes no explicit moral claims. It could be argued, for example, as some philosophers do, that use entails truth, or, even more strongly, that what it means to judge something to be true or false is that it is or is not useful. However, if it is true that all the values of society and the conceptions of culture – including religion, philosophy, and (why not also) science – are illusions devised by our very creative brains to improve collective survival, then they are not really believable. They are not believable, because we are not (at least yet) so sophisticatedly cynical that we can believe something, no matter how useful, that we know not to be true.

This judgment certainly plays a critical role in at least some expressions of what we today call "postmodern" thought, and it is anything but rationalist. It does not say, as Rosenzweig does, that reasoning is too limited to grasp all of reality; it says that there is no reality to be grasped. Nor does it say, again as Rosenzweig does, that while there are truths to be known through reason, there are even more important (i.e., vital to life) truths to be reasonably believed through revelation. Rather, what it says is that there are no truths at all other than successful and unsuccessful techniques of survival. This implicit skepticism is a critical challenge to all Jewish thought, especially thought about revelation.

This challenge will be taken up in discussion below of what the Jewish theologians have to say about being human. First, however, I will continue my description of what modern evolutionary psychology has to say about being human. I still have not looked at what in my judgment are the most critical, at least for present purposes, claims of the academic field of evolutionary psychology. They are, first, how do we know how to classify humans as distinct from non-humans?; and, second, what makes "evolution" evolution?

Classification
Charles Darwin claimed, first, that the most distinctive traits in becoming human are bipedalism, technology (viz., using and creating tools), and having an enlarged brain, and, second, that these three characteristics are mutually dependent and therefore historically they developed simultaneously. Pinker agrees with Darwin. However, if there is no mutual dependence between these traits, as Leakey claims, which of them defines what it is to be human?

Ian Tattersall suggests that there is something fundamentally wrong with this entire way of thinking. For example, in the 1940s and 50s there was a major debate among anthropologists about whether the fossil bones discovered in Sterkfontein, South Africa were the bones of early humans or of apes. Like apes, the new discoveries had small brains, but, more like humans, they could stand erect and they had human-like teeth. Tattersall comments that no "energy need have been wasted on this empty argument if the various protagonists had taken a moment to consider how great a stumbling block the vagueness of the concept of 'human' is to the understanding of evolutionary history."[34] Furthermore, on whether the mark of being human is bipedalism, a large brain, or reduction of face and teeth associated with advancements in tool-making, Tattersall comments, "Of course . . . the term 'human' had been deprived of any hope of precise definition as soon as it was realized that people have an evolutionary history."[35] In other words, the term "human" is itself not an especially scientific term, and science would do better to exclude it entirely. Certainly what (at least some of) those whom we today call "humans" do is reason, but so do other biological kinds. Why make reasoning our distinctive characteristic? The answers are historical and philosophical, but there is no scientific reason for doing so, and, if Tattersall is right, to introduce the term "human" as a technical term into evolutionary psychology does a disservice to science as science.

If the above analysis is correct and psychology properly conceived cannot tell us anything about what it means to be human, the question to be raised is why there is a discussion of evolutionary psychology at all in a book on revelation. The answer is as follows. I am discussing what would be a reasonably believable conception of revelation, and have so

---

[34] Tattersall, *The Fossil Trail*, pp. 74–75.   [35] Ibid., p. 114.

far concluded that revelation is to be understood as an intimate personal relationship between God and people. To understand revelation is to understand this relationship, and to understand the relationship requires some understanding of its two terms – God and the human. The focus in this chapter is on the human element of the concept. In the end I may conclude that modern psychology is of no help. I suspected that it would be helpful from the example of the analysis of the concept of creation as a relationship between God and the world. In that case physics was helpful in forming a reasonably believable conception of creation, because it informed what it would mean to think of the world as created. The question now is, does psychology inform what it would mean to think of the human as a recipient of revelation?

The tentative conclusion that "human" is too crude a term to be useful for evolutionary psychology, even if it turns out to be true (and that is a matter for psychologists to decide, not philosophers and theologians), does not mean that modern psychology cannot inform our view of the human. Evolutionary psychologists study life forms which evolved in earth history into mammals with relatively large brains that they use to make tools and share information. These functions have proven to be useful to their survival, for, if they were not useful, whether or not the species would have survived, the functions would have ceased to be operative. What we non-scientists call humans belong to the class of these life forms. As such, what psychology can tell us about such beings tells us something about ourselves that may or may not (that remains to be decided) contribute to a reasonable belief in humans as recipients of divine revelation. However, the classification itself is fuzzy.

For example, do humans have to be mammals? Not if what defines them is reasoning. Suppose, for example, that we can develop non-organic forms that do at least what we call reasoning. Computers seem to have that capacity, and in some cases the capacity has become actual. Given this form of progress, some philosophers[36] have argued that information (what computers transmit) is an entity in its own right, ontologically distinct from mind and body or even from substance and process. Furthermore, these philosophers argue that what it means to be rational is to be able to receive and transmit information, and this computers already can do; in fact in many respects they do it better than the organic forms that we call humans. Why, it may be argued,

[36] See Brian Cantwell Smith, *On the Origin of Objects* (Cambridge, MA: The MIT Press, 1996).

does the definition of what it means to be human have to include, as a precondition, being organic?

Similar questions can be raised about each of the other so-called identification marks of what it means to be human. What we can learn from evolutionary psychology is at least that, contrary to classical Jewish philosophy, there is no sharp line between members of the human species and members of other species. Humans may reason, but so do machines, and so do other animals. What makes human ability to reason distinct is the kind of body and physical environment that human beings have. We speak in a certain way. That speech is determined not just by the size of our brains, but by the kinds of sounds our bodies enable us to make and by the kind of information we have to share because of the kind of world in which we live. Change either our anatomy or our environment and our speech will become radically different.

Would the speech then not be rational? How could such a question be answered without prejudice? What this discussion suggests is that this whole way of thinking about what is human and what is not human may be misguided. I will return to this judgment later when I discuss what modern Jewish theologians have to say about being human. For now, I turn instead to a last critical reflection about modern evolutionary psychology, namely, what it means to call it "evolutionary."

Chance, evolution, and purpose

It is important to note that the first two events that begin the story of the genesis of the human do not involve human ancestors and are accidents – two shifts in the earth's core, one twelve million years ago and the other three million years ago. The events are "accidents" in two respects. First, the laws that govern geological changes are purely mechanical. They have nothing to do with purpose in any respect. Second, these particular changes have nothing directly to do with any life forms on the surface of the planet, including those apes who are our ancestors. With respect to this geological beginning, no scientist would call the change "evolution." It is simply change.

The term "evolution" is introduced into the story once we begin to talk about living things. This very description already organizes our thought about this history of life into a story of something less (such as an ape) becoming something more (such as a human). In other words, it is not just a story of change; it is change with a direction, a purpose. If this description of evolutionary psychology is correct, as science it is problematic, for science as science is committed methodologically to the judgment that the only causes appropriate within its domain are mechanical ones. Either the term "evolution" has to be understood in a radically different way than the ordinary use of the term suggests, or what these scientists describe ought not to be called "evolution," or their science ought not to be called "science," or we must reconsider what it means to call an academic discipline a "science."

What makes "evolution" evolution, and not just a record of chance change, is that the change is characterized as natural selection. Calling it such suggests that there was purpose. However, whatever the purpose is, it should be clear that it does not occur because one group is in any sense superior to another. Only the apes of East Africa developed into humans, because East African forests became savannas and West African forests did not. There is nothing about East African apes themselves that makes them more disposed than West African apes to development into humans. In a sense the one group is chosen over the other to evolve, but there is nothing about the one that makes it more worthy of selection than the other. It is an important point to remember when thinking about what it means for any group to be chosen. No one deserves it; it is only an accident of history.

However, is there evolution, purposeful change in the direction of an end-limit, at all? It is a reasonable question that Pinker discusses. His answer is yes, and that answer depends on his analysis of ordinary human reasoning.

The problem is not new. In Darwin's own time Alfred Russel Wallace, himself a believer in some form of evolutionary biology, objected to Darwin's account of human evolution on purely logical grounds. It simply did not make sense that, if natural selection is right, human beings needed such large brains just to enable them to forage. He saw Darwin's account as what we today would call a "Rube Goldberg" solution, that is, an excessively inefficient and unnecessary way to solve a problem that could have been addressed more directly and more simply. Certainly, Wallace reasoned, nature could have found an easier way to accommodate hunting.

Pinker's answer to Wallace is that foraging is no less difficult an intellectual activity than is academic reasoning. Both equally require considerable intelligence. In other words, while nature could have solved this problem in different ways, because nothing need be the way that it is, the solution that nature did find, namely, growth in brain size and all that that growth entails (gender differentiation, the formation of a society to share information, tool making, etc., to sophisticated culture in general with its complex ethics and religions) is reasonable. It only seems unreasonable because we do not fully appreciate how difficult practical thinking is.

This is an important insight. There is a debate that begins with Plato and runs through the history of western philosophy, including Jewish philosophy, about the relative value of practical and theoretical thinking. How major figures in classical Jewish philosophy stand on this question is not always clear, and contemporary scholars differ about what rabbis such as Maimonides intended to say. Some say he thought speculation about the universe and its meaning was more important than trying to improve society, while other scholars make the opposite judgment.[37] Still others say that at its highest levels, notably in the case of Mosaic prophecy, the distinction collapses and there is not real difference between the two.[38] This seems to be the conclusion that Pinker reaches about ordinary thought – it is complex and valuable, be it about finding fruit in trees or solving problems in trigonometry.

In this respect again the evolutionary psychologists are closer to the classical philosophers than they are to the authors of the Bible. However, the comparison in this case is mixed. The Hebrew Scriptures posit a view of the human in the world where to be human is not to be naturally distinct (all living things are generated from and by the earth), but politically distinct in that only humans are ruled by multiple commandments from God and are charged to govern the earth surface of the planet. Here reasoning as reasoning plays no distinctive role. Evolutionary psychology also affirms that what we are physically is no different from any other animal, that what we are as animals is essential to being human, and that as human animals our first duty to what it calls "nature" and the Bible calls "God" is to preserve our species (whatever it is) through procreation. However, evolutionary psychology identifies human uniqueness and value neither in ethics nor in politics as such but in our general ability to think rationally, be it in practical or purely theoretical terms. In contrast, the Jewish philosophers posit a view of the human in the world where to be human is something naturally distinct, and what makes us distinct is our ability to reason.

Evolutionary psychology affirms the value here placed on reasoning, but it rejects the claim that what is most valuable about human beings is

---

[37] Notably, Howard Kreisel in *Maimonides' Political Thought: Studies in Ethics, Law, and the Human Ideal* (Albany: State University of New York Press, 1999).
[38] Notably, Kenneth Seeskin in *Searching for a Distant God: The Legacy of Maimonides* (New York and Oxford: Oxford University Press, 2000).

anything uniquely human. Here humans are not creatures purposefully created to govern the earth. Psychologists posit no counterpart to the philosophers' divine right of humans to rule over the earth. At bottom all creatures are the same kinds of chemicals who come together to be genetic codes that determine each new entity to be the kind of thing that it is. If the Jewish philosophers posit a cosmic monarchy where revelation functions as the way for God the king to govern his hierarchically ordered subjects, evolutionary psychology posits a democracy in which all things are created on an equal footing, differentiated solely through accidents of change in a chemically based genetic code.

What remains to be seen is how all of this discussion of what it means to be human applies to Rosenzweig's conception of the element, the human, for it is his theology that I have judged to be the best available in past Jewish thought for thinking about revelation. In the light of psychology, can Rosenzweig's thought about the human stand basically unchanged, as it can in the light of what physics tells us about the world, or must it be reconstructed as was necessary in dealing with the challenges of modern ethics.

THE THEOLOGIANS

Review

Buber and Rosenzweig

There are close parallels between what Buber and Rosenzweig say about the human. The parallels come from the shared intellectual and spiritual origins of their ideas, namely the use of a Cohenian interpretation of the philosophy of Kant in the light of the Romantic critique of philosophy to interpret the Hebrew Scriptures. However, there are differences as well, due primarily to differences in ontology and in their judgments about community in general, Jewish community in particular, as well as the value of the rabbinic development of interpretation of the Hebrew Scriptures. I have already discussed these differences at the end of chapter 5 as well as above in this chapter, when I discussed the challenges of modern science in relation to physical cosmology. Those considerations led to a preference for Rosenzweig's theology as a framework to explore a believable conception of revelation over those of both classical Jewish philosophy and the theology of Buber. The question now is, given what we can learn from evolutionary psychology, does Rosenzweig's theology require further reconstruction? It needed no revision for physical cosmology, but did require important revision in the light of contemporary ethics.

Now is the time to make these kinds of judgments about Rosenzweig's conception of what it means to be human. We have seen that evolutionary psychology raises significant challenges to the classical philosophic interpretation of the human. I will summarize those challenges before moving directly to answering the question about Rosenzweig's psychology.

Human uniqueness
Evolutionary psychology emphasizes the uniqueness of the human ability to reason, as does classical Jewish philosophy. However, it also emphasizes distinct functions of the human body and tends to see reasoning as one of those physical functions. What is critical about being human is having an upright posture, dexterous hands, a distinctly shaped jaw, and a large brain. These characteristics are the basis for explaining human advanced thinking as well as the unique abilities of human beings to form social organizations and share information through the development of speech. Ethical thinking also plays a role in describing what makes the human human, even though ethics (strictly speaking) falls outside the proper domain of these sciences. However, the ethics that emerges is significantly different from both the biblical ethics of duties through interpersonal relations and the Aristotelian virtue ethics where the standard for judging the good becomes happiness defined as wisdom. In the case of the evolutionary psychologists a more naturalist, utilitarian ethics is adopted, very similar to (if not identical with) the modern Jewish ethics of Spinoza.

A number of discordances between classical Jewish philosophy and evolutionary psychology were discussed above. The critical challenge comes down to this: for the classical Jewish philosophers the definitions of both ethics and what it means to be human are mutually dependent, and the critical disposition that defines both is rationality. Because humans are rational they are a distinct species from other animals; because they are a distinct species, actualizing this ability to reason constitutes what it means for a human to be good. For the evolutionary psychologists humans do reason, but so do other creatures. They seem to be less developed in it than humans are, but the difference has to do almost entirely with differences in their relative anatomies and environmental needs. The difference is not qualitative, and, as such, does not constitute a species distinction in the strong sense of species that the classical philosophers intended.

The same is true of the other differences as well. Humans are different from animals, but the differences are not qualitative. From a cosmic perspective, we are animals, living forms composed from the same chemical elements from which all other life forms are composed, nothing more, and, as such, subject to the same laws. In this respect, there is nothing morally or spiritually unique about being human. There is certainly nothing about humans to suggest that they are more than this. In other words, contrary to the claims of both the Hebrew Scriptures and Jewish philosophy, human beings are not in any part divine.

The classical Jewish philosophers considered reasoning to be the highest disposition of the human soul, both in terms of development and in terms of moral and religious value. "Soul" is a term that I have not yet considered and it is central to Rosenzweig's conception of the human, for it is with respect to the concept of soul that human beings can be called "created in the image of God," which here means being in part divine as they are in part physical. I turn now to Rosenzweig's psychology and begin with his account of the relationship between the human body and soul.

Rosenzweig's psychology

Rosenzweig's discussion of the element, the human, begins with the classical Jewish distinction between the body and the soul. It is the soul, he tells us, that receives revelation, and it is the soul that is immortal. Still, what is judged and valued about any human being is neither the soul nor the body, but the "self," which is the conjunction or unity of the soul with the body.[39]

Body and soul

Rosenzweig makes these judgments in the first part of *The Star*, not the second, so he is speaking as a philosopher, not yet as a theologian. The philosophy he has in mind is medieval, both Jewish and Christian. In their shared Platonized Aristotelian ontology the universe is divided into two

---

[39] See Franz Rosenzweig, *Der Stern der Erlösung*, vol. II of *Franz Rosenzweig: Der Mensch und sein Werk, Gesammelte Schriften* (Haag: Martinus Nijhoff, 1976), Part I, Book 3, "DER TRAGISCHE HEROS: Psyche," pp. 86–87, and the commentary on this section in N. Samuelson, *A User's Guide to Franz Rosenzweig's Star of Redemption* (Richmond: Curzon Press, 1999), p. 76.

distinct realms, the physical and the spiritual. The human body is part of the physical, and, as physical, it generally shares the fate of everything material, that is, it is generated and it corrupts – "generally," but not entirely. Both Jews and Christians shared a belief in a resurrection of the dead that will take place when a promised Messiah comes (in the Jewish view) or returns (in the Christian view).

This belief in resurrection is solely theological, drawn exclusively from Jewish and Christian readings of their revealed texts, and not philosophical. With respect to science and philosophy, energy may be incorruptible and therefore recyclable in a way that could support some religious notion of reincarnation, but the recycled energy cannot in any meaningful sense be called the same "person" as the composite energy form that died. In physical terms all human beings, like all other life forms, are a composite. Birth is the forming of more basic elements into an organic whole; death is the breakdown of that unity. The "self" is associated with the composite and not the elements, and this physical self does not return. However, beyond (but not necessarily incompatible with) any claim of natural philosophy, there can be a self that returns that is a new self, formed from a new body united with an immortal spirit that persists through the existence of both the body of this old world and the body of the new coming world.

It is in this spiritual soul that the medieval philosophers located intellect, and many of them, depending on how rigorous they were as Aristotelian philosophers, were even willing to concede that the development of intellect alone, divorced largely from questions of personal religious observance and piety, determines the extent to which any individual in this world can persist through death to the next world. It is this consequence of Aristotelianism – that one is immortal to the extent that one becomes intellectual – that Rosenzweig rejects. Hence, what Rosenzweig means by "soul" is not what these philosophers meant.

Personality
The world is constituted by an infinite series of movements from nothing towards something, where the "something" is always a physical body, something positive that occupies and moves through space and time. The way that humans are in this world is through their bodies. Insofar as the human is part of the world, what they are is a body, and nothing else. More precisely, what a human body is is what we are in the world.

It is also with respect to the body and the world that, as Rosenzweig uses the term, a human is said to be a "person." "Personality" is the quality of an individual human body that makes it unique. As such it is a relational term, for what we are as persons is determined by how we are related to other bodies in the world.

The will

A personal body is not all there is to being human. Following his philosophical Kantian tradition, Rosenzweig asserts that a human is most distinctively what they will, and the will is not physical. It is the will that defines the human beyond their relations to the world as what they are in themself, and the self is a unity of will with body. The history of the self in the world is a story of the personality of a particular body in the world, but the history of the self in itself is a story of a dynamic movement of will from an origin towards an end. This movement, in Rosenzweig's symbolic language, is "B = B."

"B" here is taken from the German term "Besondere," meaning something totally distinctive or individual, which, as such, is inherently meaningless, accidental, and even unintelligible. It is a radical individual but real nothingness. The human is a vector whose origin and end are both in nothingness. In the case of the body the origin is physical birth, and the end is physical death. In the case of the spiritual (i.e., non-physical) component of the human self, the origin is in pure will and the end is in a will that becomes a soul. Hence, the non-physical component of the human is a soul, but, as in the case of Aristotelian definitions, the term "soul" defines the human not in terms of what it is in actuality but in terms of the end-limit towards which the course of the will's movement is directed.

To say that the will begins "pure" means that it is entirely free. To be "free" means to be able to have choices, and to be purely free means that the options are unlimited. At the moment of birth each of us is free to be anything. However, at that very same moment the first choice is made – to be human – and that choice constitutes the first limit on choice. Hence, with respect to origins, the human is both like and unlike God. Like God, in their origin, humans not only have but are unrestricted choice. However, unlike God, human choice limits the chooser. God remains through the course of his life unlimited, because nothing that is (nothing that he creates) is him (because what defines him is not being whatever comes to be); humans through the course of their life become increasingly defined, because what comes to be through their will positively defines them.

The first self-determination of the originally pure human will is to be defiant. In this case the source of Rosenzweig's insight is Nietzsche, and it is perhaps the most important influence that Nietzsche had on shaping Rosenzweig's worldview. Once born, what every human will share in common is defiance. The object of the protest is God. Both God and the human differ from the objects of the material world in that both can and are defined by will. However, what God wills is. God speaks (wills), and what he says comes to be. Humans speak (will), but rarely does what they say come to be. Humans are not God, and for that reason they cannot forgive God. That God's willing determines physical reality is why God is the creator, and his effective creation is what relates him to the world. However, human will determines little or nothing in physical reality. Hence, when the human in defiance of God wills to will despite its ineffectiveness, the human defines themself as human, but the self so defined is alone, is unrelated to anything but itself. We can, and do, will to be God, but the world we will into existence has no existence outside our will. Hence, the original human who was secluded becomes defiant, but, in their defiance, they remain secluded, from both God and from the world.

The soul

The act of defiance changes the seclusion in a way that enables the will to overcome it and achieve relationship beyond itself. At least in defiance, precisely because it is defiance, the will knows and acknowledges that there is more to reality than itself. All that it lacks to be able to relate beyond itself is humility. With humility the will abandons its desire to be God and accepts that it is human, less than God. In that admission the will opens itself to be loved by another, and that openness is a necessary precondition for receiving the love of another. In being loved the will becomes capable of love, and in loving another as another loves it, the will becomes a "soul."

The German term for soul is "Seele." It is also a verb, "beseelen." "Zu beseelen" is "to soul." The will becomes a soul when it learns to soul. This act of "souling" is the end that defines the human, and it is with respect to this end that Rosenzweig spoke at the start of this discussion of the human. It is the soul that receives revelation, that is, love from God, and it is the soul that is immortal, for it is nothing in, and therefore nothing subject to, the endless flow of physical origin in nothing and end in nothing.

Hence, the soul is separate from the body, but the separation is in no way as radicalized as it is in classical Jewish philosophy. First, in Rosenzweig's ontology, there are no substances of any sort. Hence a soul, while non-physical, is not any kind of "ghost in a box," as some philosophers have said, for a soul is not a thing. Similarly, a body is not a thing. Rather, the self is a movement defined by two aspects, one that characterizes it within the world of physical objects, and one that describes the direction of the movement, namely, from self-absorbed will towards loving and being loved by others, both human and divine. If the body is a motion in space and time, the soul is the vector of the motion that describes its direction, from origin to end.

Evaluation

I think the above suffices for a description of Rosenzweig's view of the human as recipient of revelation. I now turn to evaluation. How does this conception function as part of a conception of revelation? How does Rosenzweig's view of the human contribute to an understanding of a human of revelation who stands in a relationship of revelation to a God of revelation? Is this view viable Jewishly and epistemically – "Jewishly" in the sense that it is consistent with a view of revelation that makes sense out of the critical claim that God revealed himself to Israel in the Torah, and "epistemically" in the sense that it is a believable concept. "Believable" in this case has to do directly with the subject matter of this chapter. If this view is consistent with Judaism, it can be affirmed as true, that is, it is believable, if there are no challenges to it from science, which in this case means evolutionary psychology, to which it cannot respond in a coherent and believable way. As we shall see, I may give an affirmative answer to all of these questions.

Jewishness

Rosenzweig's understanding of the human is Jewish, at least in the sense that it is consistent with the Hebrew Scriptures and a rabbinic understanding of *torah mi-sinai* (Torah from Sinai). It is also believable in its own right, at least in the sense that there is nothing in evolutionary psychology that would in itself raise doubts about this view of what it means to be human.

What Rosenzweig's psychology does is establish an essential link between being human and being ethical, where ethics is understood to be evaluative judgments of good and bad in terms dictated by concrete relations between willing entities (whom I would call "persons"). The critical point is that it is ethics, not rationality, that defines humanity.

In conceiving of both psychology and ethics in these terms Rosenzweig reflects what has become a dominant philosophic trend in contemporary Jewish thinking, in which the major spokespeople are, along with Rosenzweig, Martin Buber and Emmanuel Levinas.[40] As we have seen, this tradition is a major break with classical Jewish philosophy, which presents a radically self-focused interpretation of ethics by identifying happiness with wisdom, and understanding wisdom to be primarily an intellectual accomplishment.

The new theology that Rosenzweig represents is also closer to what we have seen to be the view of the human and ethics in the Hebrew Scriptures. In this sense Rosenzweig's psychology, like that of Buber and Levinas, represents a return to biblical ethics. "Return," however, needs qualification.

If we take what the words of the Hebrew Scriptures say literally, they cannot be affirmed to be true, that is, they are not believable. There is a consensus, at least in Jewish religious thought, that what these texts say is authoritative in some sense for belief, but there is no consensus about how they are to be understood. At least on the basis of what I have argued here in this book, an adequate (i.e., believable) interpretation cannot be what the classical Jewish philosophers claimed it to be, and that is as true in ethics and psychology as it is in physics and cosmology. What Rosenzweig presents is a new way of interpreting the Scriptures that is both believable and closer to what the Jewish sacred texts actually say than were the traditional interpretations of the classical Jewish philosophers. It is in this sense – that it is "closer" to what the Hebrew Scriptures literally say – that his psychology represents a return to biblical ethics.

This virtue of being biblical, however, could be taken to mean that it is not Jewish, if "Jewish" is defined exclusively by rabbinic tradition, which includes the classical Jewish philosophers. For clearly, and intentionally, for all his indebtedness to Maimonides, Rosenzweig breaks with him on ethics. However, it can be argued, and I would want to do so, that Rosenzweig's ethical psychology is Jewish even with respect to the rabbinic tradition, for what Rosenzweig does as a theologian is what the rabbis did, and in precisely the same spirit that they did it, that is,

---

[40] In the case of Emmanuel Levinas I have in mind basically four books – *Nine Talmudic Readings* (English translation by Annette Aronowicz [Bloomington: Indiana University Press, 1990]); *Totality and Infinity: An Essay on Exteriority* (English translation by Alphonso Lingis [Pittsburgh: Duquesne University Press, 1961]); *Time and the Other* (English translation by Richard A. Cohen [Pittsburgh: Duquesne University Press, 1987]); and (most importantly) *Ethics and Infinity* (English translation by Richard A. Cohen [Pittsburgh: Duquesne University Press, 1985]).

they took the Scriptures seriously as divine revelation and considered the tradition of rabbinic commentaries on those texts to be part of the revelation. "Traditional" need not mean believing the conclusions of what the tradition believed. To be traditional we need no more do that than the rabbis were obliged to accept the conclusions of the textual interpretations of those rabbis who came before them. Certainly Maimonides was not traditional in this way, and we may be traditional in the same way as he was – we may read our tradition in order to determine how to understand it in a way that is believable.

Believability

Rosenzweig's ethics, no less than Buber's and Levinas's, is also a major break with the tradition of philosophical ethics in the western world. In fact, this way of conceiving of ethics constitutes a conceptual revolution. I will briefly explain what I mean.

For at least the past century, ethics has come down to debates about the viability of competing sets of rules. For example, utilitarianism, which is the dominant philosophical position adopted in ethics by the evolutionary psychologists who were considered above, judges good and bad on the basis of a calculus whose source is feelings of pleasure and pain. In general these kinds of ethicists do not mean to say that "good" simply is pleasure and "evil" simply is pain. Rather, these emotions provide the foundation for using quantitative techniques to determine general rules, where what is good is judged to be in accord with the rules, what is bad is judged to be what violates the rules, and what is not moral is what the rules do not cover. In this respect the various forms of deontology, the major competitor of utilitarianism in modern ethics, are the same. What both kinds of ethics share in common is that they present a calculus whereby actions can be judged good and evil by universal standards. Deontologies reject pleasure and pain as the foundation for the formulation of these rules, but they accept the claim that only what can be judged by objective, universal rules can be called good or bad. Some form of modern, neo-Aristotelian virtue ethics offers a different approach to the action-centered judgments of both utilitarianism and deontology, for here what is judged is the actor rather than the action. However, again the standard of judgment remains universal and objective.

In contrast to all these forms of modern ethics, what Rosenzweig captures from the words of the Hebrew Scriptures about ethics are three major points. First, moral judgments are not universals. Rather, they are rooted in concrete situations. Nothing is generally good; ethical determinations are always relative to a particular time and place with particular people in particular circumstances. Second, while different moral judgments differ in their degree of clarity and certainty, they are nonetheless objective. No matter how morality is to be judged, it is never merely opinion. Third, what enables one to affirm a contextual understanding of ethics without subjectivity is that ethics is relational and not autonomous. Good and bad are judgments based on an individual person's ability to respond to the obligations that arise in relationship to other individual persons in specific times and places. They are expressions of the will, as they are for Kant, but the will here, in marked opposition to Kant, is not autonomous.

Individuals may will what they may will, but as such there is nothing moral about what is willed. Moral duties only arise from the (implicit or explicit) will of another, and we are to be judged morally by how we, as persons, respond to these duties. The good and the bad are values related to concrete obligations that arise in specific relations between two or more persons, where to be a "person" means to be able both to initiate and to receive the moral commands.[41] More precisely, a person is the kind of entity who can participate in a moral relation, where the real source of the obligation is the relationship rather than either entity or term of the relationship.[42]

It is being a person in this sense of the word that defines a human as being human, a "Mensch." In general, to be human means what the evolutionary psychologists say it means. It means having an upright posture, dexterous hands, and a relatively large brain. However, agreeing with Rosenzweig, these are marks only of what it means to be a human character in the world. This way of defining the human defines them as a body among bodies, and this way of thinking is not in itself objectionable. In fact it can be useful to think of the human in these terms. Yet, the evolutionary psychologists do not exhaust everything that there is to say about the human; what they leave out is what is

[41] The reader will note, hopefully without confusion, that the way I am using the term "person" here differs significantly from how Rosenzweig used the term. "Person" for him, as we saw above, is associated with the body and the way a human is in the world. His word for what I call "person" is a "soul." I prefer not to stay with his terminology at this point. His German has different associations than my English. That he uses the terms "person" and "soul" in the way he does made sense in the context of his writing. I think, however, the use of the two terms has sufficiently changed that it would be better not to use them the way he used them.

[42] Robert Gibbs struggles to develop such an ethic in his *Correlations in Rosenzweig and Levinas* (Princeton: Princeton University Press, 1992) and *Why Ethics? Signs of Responsibility* (Princeton: Princeton University Press, 2000). So does Edith Wyschogrod in her *Saints and Postmodernism: Revising Moral Philosophy* (Chicago and London: University of Chicago Press, 1990).

most distinctive about the human, namely, that they are (in Rosenzweig's language) souls, beings who can love and be loved by God and by each other.

A prime example of a moral context is what the doctrine that I have identified as *torah mi-sinai* (Torah from Sinai) expresses. In this case the commanding person is God and the person who receives the commandments is the nation Israel. This command-defined relationship is not a particular moment in history. Revelation is no less a continuous event throughout time than creation is eternal. Rather, revelation describes an ongoing process in which a particular people opens itself to each other's love through the gift of divine love, and that reception of love opens the people to a concretized sense of duty to God and to each other.

As such, Rosenzweig's psychological ethics also presents us with no less of a new way to understand what Jewish thought has traditionally called *ta'amei mitzvot*, giving reasons for the commandments. Rosenzweig's theology is no less radical as Jewish theology than it is as philosophical ethics. It is, in effect, an account of the system of Jewish law (*halakhah*) as a system of ethics, for here ritual commandments have no less moral force than do the commandments that regulate the way we humans are to relate to each other. However, the understanding of *ta'amei mitzvot* presented here supports a liberal religious understanding of them in line with the weaker interpretation of revelation as divine inspiration.[43]

God, for Rosenzweig no less than for Buber, does not command content. Rather, what he does is make himself present to us. That presence is God's love, and the commandments are our concrete, specific response to that loving presence. As such, the content is human, not divine. However, that does not mean that the content is not revelation. It is revelation, for it is our response to God. As such the content places on us as Jews an obligation, and that duty is moral. However, because the obligations are also human, what their value is, though objective, is time and place dependent, so that what may be moral in one context may not be moral in another.

The interpretation presented here of divine revelation is the deep insight of liberal Judaism. It is not a denial of Torah, and it is not a denial of *halakhah*. It is rather an affirmation that the process of reading

---

[43] In my *An Introduction to Modern Jewish Philosophy* (Albany: State University of New York Press, 1989), ch. 5, "Jewish Religion," pp. 68–71, I explain the difference between orthodox Judaism's commitment to "revelation" in the sense of something that God creates and humans receive and Reform's commitment to "divine inspiration" in the sense of something that emerges from the active interrelationship between both parties of the relationship, God and the human.

and rereading our record as a Jewish people of relationship with God is an ongoing process that will never stop, at least not until the end of days. It is not just that new situations will require new laws; it is also that new situations will require rethinking old laws. As in law, so in belief. To think critically as well as constructively about what the tradition has determined to be true belief is inherently to be traditional. It is authentic in a way that any version of Judaism is not when it demands blind acceptance of what past rabbis claimed to be the good and the truth of the Torah. Thus, I see the reconstruction of the Jewish doctrine of revelation in this book to be an inherently traditional as well as authentic way of practicing Jewish thought.

CHAPTER 7

The challenges of modern philosophy – rethinking God

REVIEW

This book is a study in the philosophy of religions and its central concern is to develop an interpretation of revelation out of the sources of Jewish philosophy that is believable as a foundational principle for Judaism. To serve as a basis for Jewish belief the principle must make sense out of the claim that God gave the Torah to Moses at Sinai, and that a tradition of rabbinic interpretation of the Torah is in some sense authoritative for religious Jews in their decisions about what they ought to believe and do. All versions of Judaism agree that whatever is the sense in which this tradition has authority, it does not involve any literal reading of the Hebrew Scriptures in the simplistic way that some Christians read them. However, there is no consensus, in either rabbinic history or the present, on what these Scriptures do mean by which they can be considered authoritative. The critical divisions are between secular Jews, orthodox religious Jews, and liberal religious Jews.

SECULAR JUDAISM

For secular Jews, both the Torah and rabbinic tradition may have some authority as a personal ancestral record. These Jews have a strong sense of familial identity with the Jewish people, and, as such, they value all records of their family's past. These religious documents hold a special place of importance. However, it is not reasonable to say that they are in any viable sense authoritative for belief or practice.

You may be very interested in what your ancestors did and believed because they are your ancestors, but the mere fact of familial lineage is no reason for you personally to believe anything they said. In fact there is no reason why these Jews should not take literally what the Hebrew Scriptures say, since their value has nothing to do with their truth. Hence, secular Jews may, and often do, read the Scriptures in much the same way as Christian fundamentalists do, although with different intentions and different consequences for belief and behavior.

The most sophisticated readings of the Hebrew Scriptures in this tradition are those of the academic biblical critics, for whom the Bible is read solely as literature or solely as documents for constructing Israel's ancient history. It is this group that raises the most serious issues for the theological enterprise of this book. I will consider these scholars in the next chapter, when I will deal directly with the question of whether the Hebrew Scriptures are revealed.

ORTHODOX AND LIBERAL RELIGIOUS JUDAISM

For now the question remains, what is the most believable way to interpret the claim that the Hebrew Scriptures are revealed? It is this question that divides liberal from orthodox religious Jews. The central difference between them, insofar, that is, as the difference is conceptual and not merely political, has to do with whether we take the notion of revelation in a strong sense, as the orthodox do, or in a weaker sense, as the liberals do. The strong sense of revelation says that the content of the Torah, as the rabbis through the centuries have interpreted it, is in fact the word of God. "Word of God" means that in revelation it is God who is the active agent and Israel is its passive recipient. Hence, the content is authoritative in a strong sense of authority: what it says, when properly interpreted, must be true and must be good; therefore, its belief claims ought to be believed and its behavioral imperatives ought to be observed.

In contrast, the weak sense of revelation, which I have identified as "divine inspiration," says that the content of the Torah, as the rabbis through the centuries have interpreted it, is a product of an ongoing relationship between God and Israel. Its words are neither the dictate of God, as the orthodox claim, nor the creation of Israel, as the secularists claim. Rather, it is a product of the interaction of these two persons, where "persons" are understood to be conscious, willing entities who are capable of awareness of the presence of another person and sensitive to the demands that that presence places on them – that is, willing, sensitive beings who think and feel, and who in consequence care about the values of both truth and the good. Truth is to be found in openness to what an-other reveals, and what is revealed calls for a moral response. Relationship entails responsibility as its immediate consequence; that responsibility involves a duty to think what is true and do what is right; and the concrete nature of this general responsibility is a further consequence of the relationship.

This liberal understanding of revelation is far subtler, and therefore more difficult to accept, than the position of either the orthodox or the secular Jews. Perhaps its difficulty explains why today liberal Jewish religion seems less attractive to large numbers of Jews than do the extremes of secularism and Orthodoxy. However, I have opted in the course of this book to focus on it, primarily because I find it to be the most intelligible, and therefore the most believable, option for believing in revelation, and, grounded in that belief, for affirming a commitment to Judaism.

The critical question upon which the difference between the orthodox and the liberals rests is the nature of God as a revealer. Part I was a summary of what Jewish tradition says about God in this respect – in the Hebrew Scriptures, classical Jewish philosophy, and modern Jewish theology. I examined their views of God as the single critical component in understanding their views of revelation. On all interpretations revelation is a relationship between God and the human in which some kind of information arises. What that information is depends on the nature of the relationship, and what we can think about that communication depends on what we think about the natures of both God and the human. How believable any conception of revelation is depends on how believable it is to claim that God and the human can stand in such a relationship.

In chapter 6 I focused on what kind of conception of the human we must have to believe that human beings can receive revelation from God. That discussion led to a consideration of challenges from political ethics and the life sciences. Now, in this chapter, the focus shifts to the other pole of the relationship – God. Can we believe that there is a deity who reveals himself to human beings, and, if we can, what form must that belief take? It is the answer to this question that lies at the core of the differences between liberal and orthodox Judaism. Both claim that God is the revealer, Israel is a recipient of that revelation, and the Torah is an expression of what was and continues to be revealed. However, for the orthodox, that content is not subject to change, while for the liberals it is. It is not for the orthodox, because they affirm it to be the word of God. It is for the liberals, because they affirm it to be a human response to God's presence.

DOES GOD SPEAK?

How the issue is to be decided between the liberals and the orthodox, in so far is it can be settled by reasoning, rests on what each believes about the nature of God. The argument that will be considered here in this chapter claims that any interpretation of divine speech in revelation that makes the consequent claims of revelation incorrigible – that is, not subject to change in the light of new human insights – is not believable, because it presupposes an understanding of who God is that is not believable. Furthermore, with respect to this claim, there is no difference between the classical Jewish philosophers and the modern Jewish theologians. Hence, an affirmation of revelation as divine inspiration is more "traditional" than the position of the contemporary orthodox, because it is the liberal position that best reflects how pre-modern rabbinic tradition has interpreted what it means to say that God is the revealer of the Torah.

JEWISH PHILOSOPHY

In chapter 2 I looked at how Maimonides interpreted what it means to believe in God. His explanation presupposes the worldview of the best natural philosophers (i.e., scientists) of his day, and that worldview is inherently Aristotelian. If this physics describes what the universe is like, God is to be understood as in some way analogous to a first mover. As a first mover, God is an incorporeal substance whose unity is so radical that who he is is what he does and what he does is a single activity that never changes, is without beginning or end. This single activity is expressible, due to the limits of human understanding, as diverse acts, some of which can be called "creating" (viz., what God does vis-à-vis the world of physical objects) and some of which can be called "revealing" (viz., what God does vis-à-vis human intellects), but these acts, which seem to us to be diverse and plural, are in reality a single act: God being God.

In fact the above view is not precisely that of Maimonides. Rather, it is Gersonides' reconstruction of it. Maimonides' position is more radical. He denied that there can be any analogy drawn whatsoever between God, who is the creator, and anything else, which is a creature. He argued that the distinction between creator and creature is so fundamental that no comparison is possible. Rather, what we literally know about God is that anything of which we can conceive could not be God, since the basis for conception is the imagination, and there are only images of creatures. Certainly, on my Maimonidean view it cannot be said that in any positive sense whatsoever, God speaks. If, in fact, it is claimed that God speaks through prophets, just what that means cannot be understood. However, given Aristotelian astronomy, we can explain what it means for a prophet to receive information from one of the separate intelligences that are the messengers (*malachim*) through whom God communicates his creating and revealing. Maimonides accepts this analysis for all prophets at a lesser level than Moses, and Gersonides accepts this analysis for all prophets, including Moses. On Gersonides' reconstruction of Maimonides' view, the intellect that governs our universe is the Active Intellect, which is that celestial being with whom the rabbis are said to have associated God's presence (*ha-shechinah*). She governs by thinking the forms of everything in our universe. Those forms are what inform matter to be material entities, and those forms are what inform the human intellect to be thought. These thoughts are "beamed," so to speak, eternally from God's presence, and when a human intellect is sufficiently mature to grasp (i.e. to receive) these communications, it does so. On this analysis there is no real difference between receiving revelation from God and grasping concepts. Hence, revelation and conceptual knowledge are the same thing.

Certainly there were rabbis who objected to the philosophers' equation of what they do best, namely reason, with divine revelation, not to mention objections to making reasoning the highest standard for judging human value. However, that is beside the point here. One of the reasons for preferring the theology of Rosenzweig to the philosophy of Maimonides is that it devalues the exalted status that the philosophers gave to human reasoning. This preference was primarily for scientific reasons: from what we learn about the human from evolutionary psychology, there is no justification for making human reason qualitatively superior to animal thinking. We need not wed ourselves to justify belief in revelation to the epistemology of the Jewish Aristotelians.

The concern here with the classical Jewish philosophers is only relative to the claim that the weak interpretation of divine revelation as inspiration is an authentic rabbinic interpretation of this core doctrine. We exhibit its authenticity by highlighting the fact that they endorsed an understanding of revelation which, while affirming its divine origin, equated its content with human knowledge. In effect, in response to the question whether the content of revelation is human or divine, it affirmed both – human because it is no different than any conceptual human knowledge, and divine because the source as well as the object of all conceptual knowledge is God. Certainly this view of revelation is more coherent with the liberal Jewish conception of divine inspiration than it is with an orthodox strong interpretation of revelation.

JEWISH THEOLOGY

What is true in this case for classical Jewish philosophy is equally true for modern Jewish theology, as exemplified in the reflections of both Buber and Rosenzweig. In fact, their conception of revelation comes, with little conceptual revision, from a weak interpretation of Maimonides' view, weak in the sense that it follows the epistemologically more moderate position of Gersonides. For Maimonides, we know nothing about God; for Gersonides, what we know is that God is the standard of perfection for our imperfect world, such that (given the difference between us and God) what for us defines God is that whatever it is of which we can conceive, that is not God. In Buber's language, that means that God is always an I–Thou and never an I–It, so that being eternally I–Thou is what defines God. In Rosenzweig's language, God is the radical other who is in origin totally free, a freedom that becomes restricted as he continues not to be each particular something that comes to be in the world. As such, God is the absolute real nothing, and, as nothing, God is inaccessible to knowledge, although he is accessible to belief.

What makes belief possible is revelation. However, what is revealed has no content. The totally other deity of Rosenzweig can no more literally speak words (i.e., cause sound waves to arise so that the human recipient hears words) than can the revealing deity of Maimonides. What God reveals are not words or imperatives or propositions. What God reveals is himself. In becoming aware that there is more to reality than what we can perceive and know, we become aware that we stand in the presence of a presence (a *shechinah*). What we know of her is that she is radically different from us; that knowledge, the awareness of the divine presence, is received by us as a challenge, a challenge to which we first respond with guilt and which we then translate into a personalized, individuated content. Hence, the content, no less than it is for the classical Jewish philosophers, is an expression of the relation between the divine presence and the human. It is not the product of the activity of either alone. Rather, it is our response to God's love. In the religious language of the Jewish liberals, it is divine inspiration.

THE PHILOSOPHY OF RELIGION – PROOFS
THAT GOD EXISTS

INTRODUCTION

Let this suffice for the claim that an interpretation of revelation as divine inspiration, that is, in the weak sense of the term, is in rabbinic terms the most authentic interpretation, the one that most corresponds to what the most sophisticated of religiously committed Jewish thinkers have had to say about God as the revealer. In this case no distinction need be made between the positions of Maimonides and Rosenzweig. They are the same. The question remains, however, irrespective of its authenticity, is it believable? Maimonides' analysis is rooted in an Aristotelian theory of the universe and human knowledge, both of which are obsolete. Is Rosenzweig successful in freeing this notion of God the revealer from its dependence on an obsolete natural philosophy? On the answer to this question rests the claim of believability for the doctrine of revelation as I have reasoned it out of its Jewish/rabbinic philosophical and theological sources.

Where now do we look for a source external to Jewish texts for a standard of comparative analysis? In the case of our view of the world we turned to astrophysics, and in the case of our view of the human we looked at modern evolutionary psychology. Is there a comparable science to look at for our view of the divine? The answer is an unqualified no.

By methodological definition, questions about God lie outside the domain of what we today call "science." However, they do not lie outside the domain of modern philosophy based on modern science – the Anglo-American tradition of linguistic and logical analysis. If any tradition of academic thinking will present objections to this view of the God of revelation from our Jewish sources, it is this philosophic tradition, and, for that reason, it is the tradition I will now examine.

In this case there is a vast literature of essays and books that explore in great detail classic arguments for the existence of God. In some cases new arguments are also constructed, both for and against this existence claim, and often the presentation of old arguments has been so refined, given the more powerful tools of twentieth-century logic and linguistics, that they constitute new arguments.[1]

[1] What I will present here is an overview of how contemporary analytic philosophers who are interested in religious thought argue for and against God's existence. A more detailed statement of both the arguments and the logic underlying them is given in Richard Gale's *On the Nature and Existence of God* (Cambridge: Cambridge University Press, 1991).

The arguments to be considered are of two forms. There are atheological arguments, intended to demonstrate that God does not exist, as well as theological arguments. I will consider the theological ones first. Of these there are four types. The first are analyses of the different forms of cosmological arguments that the Aristotelians (Jewish, Muslim, and Christian) employed. Then there are versions of the ontological argument that the medieval Christians constructed. Next are two modern forms of arguments for God's existence – one based on religious experience and another based on pragmatic calculation.

I will conclude this chapter by considering the atheological arguments, because they, for present purposes, are more important. My claim is that belief in God as a revealer is an obligation of Jewish religious belief. If this claim is correct, it is important that such a belief be reasonable. However, it need not be demonstrable. My concern, then, with the theological arguments has more to do with determining their relevance to the question of belief in the God of revelation. As we shall see, these arguments speak of God in a very generalized way. Their intent is to broaden analysis beyond the theology of individual religious thinkers, invariably Christian, to theology in general. It may be the case, since the orientation is to Christian thinkers, that these arguments have little or no relevance to a philosophic discussion that focuses on the God of Judaism. If that is so, it is important to look at the atheological arguments, since, then but only then, if these arguments are valid, a belief in a God of revelation will not be believable.

The Hebrew Scriptures and historical argument

The earliest formal proofs of the existence of God are found in Treatise I of Saadia's[2] *Book of Beliefs and Opinions* (*sefer emunot ve-de'ot*) in the tenth century. However, informal arguments occur earlier in both the Hebrew Scriptures and the Midrash. A notable example occurs in the Book of Isaiah.[3] What he offers is a kind of argument on the basis of history. He presents, in effect, a sacred history in which all events, from the creation of the world through the rise and fall of the first Jewish state, are presented as a story of unrequited love between God and the nation Israel.

---

[2] Saadia Ben Joseph, 882–942, Egypt. The English translation, *The Book of Beliefs and Opinions*, is by Samuel Rosenblatt (New Haven: Yale University Press, 1948).

[3] That Isaiah's recounting of human history throughout this book is an "argument" is indicated by expressions like "Come now and let us reason together" (Isa. 1:18), as well as "Don't you know (and) don't you pay attention? Has it not been told to you from of old?" (Isa. 40:21), and "Listen you who are deaf, and look to see you who are blind!" (Isa. 42:18).

The story is a challenge to an audience that assumes the existence of multiple deities of which Israel's God, *yhvh*, is one among many. The challenge is that this history and only this history makes sense out of the events of the world. In this sense it is a sort of nascent argument from design: if you look at the history of the world, the most intelligible understanding of what has happened is this story in which the main players are a deity, who created the world, and the nation he loves, Israel, who has not yet proved capable of accepting the responsibility that God's love entails. However, it is not formally an argument from design, not only because it is presented as a reading of history and not as a philosophical argument but also because it takes for granted the existence of multiple deities, including the God of Abraham, Isaac, and Jacob. As such it is not an argument for God's existence – that there exists at least one deity – but an argument for God's unity – that there is only one real deity and that is *yhvh*. In this sense the entire Hebrew Scriptures can be read as an attempt to demonstrate God's unity, for everything in them is either a narrative that states the history, so constructed, or an explanation of the narrative, as is the case of the cited passage from Isaiah.

As such, the biblical account of theological history fails. It could even be read as an atheological proof, a proof that the deity literally described in the Hebrew Scriptures does not exist. If this deity exists, the world was created so that a Temple could be built with a nation to administer it from which God would derive his sustenance. Hence, if such a deity existed, then either the Temple would not have been destroyed or, if it were destroyed, the world that God created would have ceased to exist. However, the Temple was destroyed (twice) and the world continued to exist in very much the same way that it had existed while the Temple stood. Hence, this deity of Israel's history does not exist.

However, even on these terms, the biblical narrative with its interpretation is not really a proof. First, what the text says is not what the text is taken literally to mean. Second, even taken literally, the form of argument is rhetorical and not demonstrative – it is not a form of argument intended to prove anything; rather, it is intended, and solely intended, to persuade.

Midrash and arguments from design

The same logic applies to the less historically oriented kind of argument for God's existence found in the Midrash. A typical example is the following:

A scoffer asks the rabbi to show him that God exists. He tells the scoffer to return on the next day, when the rabbi compliments his guest about his garment and asks if anyone made it. The scoffer replies with amazement, "What do you mean, did anyone make it? Can't you see that it is a garment? How can there be a garment without a maker?"; to which the rabbi responds, "And can't you see that the world is created? How can there be a creation without a creator?"[4]

Here we do see an argument, but the argument is argument by analogy, and such arguments – found most commonly in the way lawyers advocate their positions in courts or politicians their issues in parliaments – are clearly rhetorical, not demonstrative. In form it says that the world exhibits an order or intelligibility similar to the order or intelligibility of some artifact, and, as the order of the artifact requires an artist who crafted it, so the intelligibility of the universe requires a creator.

The logical problem is that the world may be like an artifact, but it is not an artifact. In general, two things are alike and not dissimilar if they share some characteristics in common, and, conversely, two things are only alike and not identical if there are some other characteristics that they do not share in common. To construct a demonstrative argument it would be necessary to distinguish between these characteristics and argue strictly on the basis of the characteristics shared in common, rather than on the basis of an analogy between the bearers of the characteristic. That being a certain kind of thing, A, means that something else, f, is true of it, need not mean that f is true of some other similar thing, B. It does only if both A and B share in common some characteristic, g, and g means f. Then, however, the argument is a strictly formal deduction and not a mere analogy. Then and only then the argument would be a demonstration and not a mere analogy.

All forms of arguments from design – that the world exhibits a kind of order and having order entails the existence of some intelligent being who imposes the order – are in structure purely rhetorical. There can be all kinds of reasons for something exhibiting order. One possibility is that an artist created it, but that is only one possibility. There are many ways that a thing can have order.

For example, the order of an egg, because it is an egg, entails the existence of some kind of creature like a chicken who laid it. Our world also exhibits an order like that of an egg – both are organic, alive, and oval. However, it does not follow from this analogy that the creator of

---

[4] I have taken this story from the Ch. N. Bialik and Y. Ch. Rabinitzki edition of *sefer ha-aggadah* (Tel Aviv: Dvir, 1956), *ma'ase-bereshit ve-dorot harishonim*: Beriyat-Ha-'Olam 1:6, who cite their source as "*midrash temurah.*"

this world is something like a chicken, and the way that he created it is by laying it.

I am not aware of any people who have so imagined the relationship between the creator and his creation. Yet, there have been many peoples who have taken the similarities between organic life and the world as a whole to assume that the world was born from a sexual act between deities, just as animals are born from sexual acts between animals. In principle, there is no more and no less reason to assume that the world is like a chicken egg than it is like an animal.

Furthermore, things that come to be solely by chance also can exhibit order. In fact, certain kinds of order can be seen solely because the events so made intelligible have no cause. For example, if ping-pong balls are shot at random into a narrow, rectangular opening separated into columns of equal dimensions, the distribution of the balls will eventually exhibit the shape of a bell curve, where the greatest height is in the middle and the height decreases in proportion to the distance the column is from the center. The bell curve is a clear example of order, but it is an order that entails no causal determination by any intelligent agent, that is, it was clearly not created by a God. It is rather the order and structure of pure chance.

The modern world of chance

As far as I know, no nation or culture ever seriously considered the possibility that what occurs in the universe occurs solely by chance. To be sure, there were some natural philosophers in the pre-Socratic Greek world and there were some popular philosophers (the Epicureans) in the Roman world whose only causal principles were mechanical, so they believed that everything that happens does so ultimately for reasons that have nothing to do with the creative actions of gods. However, these were even then only the views of relatively few people in nations and cultures that accepted, mostly uncritically, that what occurs in the universe in general occurs for a purpose imposed on events by the will of an intelligent being.

To this generalization there is one notable exception, and that is the western civilization of the modern world. Even here most people, at least until the twentieth century, including most scientists and philosophers, affirmed the existence of a creator deity as a dictate of reason. However, at least since the nineteenth century (if not earlier) the dominant view in science has been that only mechanical explanations can count as scientific accounts and only what counts as scientific can be called "knowledge." Hence, while belief in at least a creator deity was widespread throughout western civilization, including among scientists and intellectuals, such an affirmation has been widely accepted as belief and not as knowledge.

It is a distinctive mark of the modern western world that doubt about the existence of a creator deity is considered reasonable. That reasonableness is based on the wide acceptance of two philosophical assumptions of the positivists: first, that the domain of science is limited to judgments about chance occurrences, because the only admissible objects for judgment are physical (i.e., objects that occupy space and time of which there is in principle sense experience); and, second, that the principles of explanation are quantitative.

All of the forms of demonstrations of the existence of God that the classical Jewish philosophers developed presupposed a world and a science radically different from the one of modern western philosophy. In the universe conceived of by the Aristotelians, events have final causes, purposeful ends towards which they are directed. Ultimately there is an identity between the sought-after entity as a final cause and the prime mover of the events themselves, and this originative and consequent cause is something willful and intelligent. Hence, given the presupposed universe of the proofs, proof was superfluous.

Ultimately, it could clearly be said that there is a God, because there could only be such a universe if there existed such a God. All that the proofs do is make explicit the premises of the very rules of argument, for those logical rules are dependent on the presupposed ontology of those philosophers who formulated the arguments.

However, it is not insignificant that no matter what kind of civilization we consider, all of them entail the existence of one or more deities, with the sole exception of our own. It is important to ask if our philosophical view of the nature of the universe is no less theologically biased than was theirs. Is it or is it not the case that just as their proofs of the existence of God beg the question because their underlying conception of the universe – both ontologically and epistemologically – presupposed necessarily some kind of deity, so any modern consideration by contemporary philosophers of proofs for or against the existence of God beg the question for the same reason? If the only kind of knowledge is scientific knowledge and if science is defined as a discipline that can deal only with the material and with mechanical principles, does it not seem obvious that there can be no creator God who is an immaterial being of intelligence and will who, in virtue of these traits, generates the world ? In other words, given the terms of the discussion in modern western philosophy of religion, discussions of God's existence are pure question-begging, futile enterprises.

There are a significant number of Anglo-American philosophers who would disagree with this conclusion. Some of them claim that it is possible to reformulate the classical proofs for the existence of God in such a way that the reasonableness of such belief can be affirmed without rejecting the ontology and epistemology underlying modern scientific thinking. Still others claim on the same terms that it can be demonstrated that no such deity exists and to do so does not beg the question.

I will now consider both sets of arguments, first the theological ones and then the atheological ones. The theological arguments constitute, in effect, a reformulation of the arguments of the medieval Muslim, Jewish, and Christian philosophers for God's existence. As such, they also suggest how we could reformulate what the classical Jewish philosophers affirmed about God. This reformulation would be relevant at least to what they said about God as a creator, and may possibly be relevant to what they said about God as a revealer. However, it is too soon to raise this question. First we must look at just what they prove, if anything.

COSMOLOGICAL ARGUMENTS

The first theological argument to be considered is the cosmological argument.[5] It is the one form of argument shared in common by all three Abrahamic faiths. In all of them it is assumed that there must be a sufficient reason of some sort for something to exist, and that this reason, whatever it is, depends on something that exists other than what it explains, which, on the same grounds, requires its own sufficient reason. The result is an apparently endless chain of existing things, each requiring something else to exist in order to provide a reason for its existence.[6] As such, this chain of reasoned things constitutes a unity which itself, it is assumed, also requires a sufficient reason of some sort, with the same consequence, ad infinitum – a chain of reasoned things infinitely dependent for its reason on higher infinite chains of reasoned things.

---

5 The versions of the argument here considered are presented by Alvin Plantinga in *God and Other Minds* (Ithaca: Cornell University Press, 1967), Richard Swinburne in *The Existence of God* (Oxford: Clarendon Press, 1979), and William Rowe in *The Cosmological Argument* (New York: Fortress Press, 1975).

6 I.e., for any t_n there must be another thing, t_{n+1}, that provides a sufficient reason for the existence of t_n.

Consequently, it is inferred, there must be something that provides a reason for everything else that is its own reason, and, therefore, as such, brings the list of reasons to a conclusion, so that at least in principle there is a reason for everything.

That a number of steps in this generalized form were listed as assumptions indicates that it is at least possible to negate what these steps claim. The assumptions are as follows. First, there must be a reason for anything that happens to happen. This assumption, called "the principle of sufficient reason," applies equally to aggregates of events and things and to individual events and things. Second, nothing actual is infinite. Hence, if the chain of reasons is infinite, the reasons are not based on anything that is actual. Third, to know something is to know every reason for it.

Infinity

The second assumption is the least important for present purposes. It rests on an understanding of infinity that is not the only way to conceive of infinity. In fact, as any one will know who has studied infinite series in mathematics, things can be infinite in many ways. For example, some infinite series have infinite ends, but others have finite limits, and, as we have seen in the case of the discussion of Rosenzweig's use of Cohen's infinitesimal calculus, end-limits of infinite series can be real. In fact, the application of calculus to solving problems in physics presupposes just that, namely, that the determination of a limit in problems like velocity and acceleration or area and volume determines something actual and not just ideal. Hence, contrary to all versions of the cosmological argument, there is no reason why in principle a series of reasons or causes cannot be infinite and still be the real reasons or causes of some actual and finite determination within the series.

The principle of sufficient reason

For present purposes the first assumption, the so-called principle of sufficient reason, is more important. In an Aristotelian universe this premise is unquestionable. For anything to be, it must have a form, and the form itself is something intelligible that constitutes a reason for the thing being. The premise would also hold if we were to assume, as Spinoza did, that everything that exists is either a substance or a modification of a substance, and that there can be only one substance. However, neither world is the world of modern science, where there are posited to exist multiple discrete entities (be they objects or motions), all of which arise for no particular reason.

It is important to highlight why that is the case. In modern science to say that a is the cause of b means that there is an observed conjunction of occurrence between a and b such that a relatively high degree of probability can be assigned to the conjunction of their subsequent appearances. Hence, what the word "cause" means in modern science is radically different from what this word means in either Aristotelian science or Spinoza's transitional worldview into modern natural philosophy.

For Aristotelianism the assertion of a causal relationship between two things assumes some real connection between them such that the existence of one is dependent on the existence of the other. Given such a notion of causation, it does necessarily follow that nothing can exist without a reason, for its existing is either self-determined or dependent on something other than itself. However, there is no reason for making any such assumption in a universe that presupposes that what falls within the domain of modern science is all that there is, and what counts as an explanation in modern science is the only kind of explanation that there is.

Hence, the cosmological argument is a valid argument in an Aristotelian universe or in any other similar kind of universe (i.e., those considered by pre-modern, non-positivist natural philosophers) but it is not valid in all possible universes, for it is possible to conceive of at least one where the argument is not valid. It is a universe in which there is no principle of sufficient reason, and it is not impossible that such a universe is real.

Knowledge as necessity

The last two sentences point to what is problematic about the third assumption about knowledge itself. It implies that for a proof of the existence of God to be valid it must be universally valid, valid for all possible (i.e. in principle conceivable) universes. Then and only then is what is claimed necessarily true, and only what can be legitimately claimed to be necessarily true can be judged to be demonstrated. The medieval Abrahamic-tradition philosophers believed that if something is necessarily true of an Aristotelian universe, then it is necessarily true, because they believed, based on the science of their day, that the Aristotelian universe is the real universe. It is this assumption, even more than the others, that marks the difference intellectually between us and them.

We no longer share their confidence that science can tell us with any real degree of certainty what is the case. The claim is not that there is some better way to know than that provided by science; rather, the claim is that nothing is better than science for knowing anything, but not everything can be known, and even what can be known cannot be known with the degree of certainty that our intellectual ancestors thought was possible.

Belief and probability

For the classical Jewish philosophers anything that cannot be judged to be certain cannot be considered knowledge. For them anything less than necessarily true is merely opinion. However, they also recognized that not all opinions are the same. Some are better (i.e., more reasonable) than others. In modern terms, there are no necessary truths that are informative, that are about anything other than games we play with humanly invented language. When it comes to information, claims vary in degree of probability, and no claim has a probability of 1. Hence, there is no real qualitative separation, contrary to the pre-modern philosophers, between belief and knowledge.

All beliefs vary in degree of probability, and those that we call "knowledge" come closer to (but are always short of) ultimate probability (i.e., 1) than others. However, "closer to" is a relative judgment. A certain kind of belief, which is closer to 1 than others on the same topic, may be called "knowledge," because of its fairly high probability relative to currently conceived alternatives. The line between opinion and knowledge depends on what is being considered. Where a high degree of probability is possible, a lower degree (say, n) is not considered knowledge. However, where a far lower degree of probability is all that is possible, a belief of significantly lower probability (say, n-m) could be considered knowledge. That is certainly the case when we compare the kinds of claims that pass as scientific knowledge in the different sciences.

Consider a single example. Because of the considerably different qualities of data for judgment in physics and paleoanthropology, a claim that can reasonably be called "knowledge" in the latter would be considered only an opinion in physics. I discussed the reasons for this difference above in chapter 6, on the human. This is not anything against paleoanthropology. Physics deals with claims about events that are constantly repeatable, that can be tested under carefully controlled conditions, where every variable can be controlled except the two factors being correlated.

Such control and such repeatability are in principle ruled out in pale-oanthropology because of its subject matter.

What is interesting for present purposes in this discussion of relative probability is the high standard of likelihood required for statements to support the existence of God. In effect, to count as a proof, the conclusion must not merely be probable relative to contrary claims but must be necessarily true, that is, have a probability of 1, that is, be true in all possible worlds. Otherwise, it cannot count as a valid proof. The source of this "higher standard" of demonstration is the classical proofs themselves. However, the application of that standard to modern reconstructions of the classical proofs is unjustified.

The classical proofs assumed, incorrectly, that we know what the universe is really like. Hence, to prove that something necessarily is true conditionally on an Aristotelian universe – to prove that something necessarily is true if an Aristotelian universe is the real world – is to prove, without precondition, that it is necessarily true. We, however, know better (at least in this respect). Hence, as we reconstruct our versions of the classical proofs to evaluate them epistemically, we must also reconstruct what we count as proof, and in general this is not done. Proofs of God's existence function more like "Jim Crow laws," rules so defined at such a high standard that qualification is functionally impossible. As such, these proofs constitute more of an exhibition of the prejudices of contemporary Anglo-American philosophers against religious claims than they are objective discussions of the reasonableness of religious beliefs.[7]

What, then, would be a more reasonable test for judging the validity of this argument? The answer turns on what we mean by "sufficient reason." Need there be an explanation for everything, or can it not be the case that some things just happen for no reason whatsoever? That judgment goes to the heart of discussions in classical Jewish philosophy of divine providence.

If we assume, as they did, that God is not imperfect in any respect, then, given their Aristotelian standards for perfection, the following claims arise. First, any action of God is independent of anything other than God. However, "anything other than God" need not mean that God can do what is impossible. What is impossible would be contrary to the

---

[7] I take this to be the main claim that William Alston makes in his *Perceiving God* (Ithaca: Cornell University Press, 1991). If we were to judge scientific and philosophical claims by the same standards that we (philosophers) demand for traditional religious claims, then the latter, no less than the former, would be found intellectually wanting. In effect, we use a double standard for reasonableness – one for questions of religion and a very different one for questions of science. I will look in greater detail at Alston's claims at the end of this book.

will of God, since the laws of nature are an expression of God's will. Hence, God's perfection would not be compromised by self-limitation to the rules of logic.[8] Second, what God does will be "good," but the good involved here need not be a human good. As the creator deity of the world, it is clear that humans exist as part of the world, whose scope, even in the radically reduced scale of the classical Jewish philosophers, greatly exceeds the concerns of humanity as humanity. Hence, there is no reason to believe that just because something is not good for humans, it is not properly judged good, and this is possible even if we posit, as revelation requires, that God loves us.[9]

God and schemata

Does this mean, as many contemporary philosophers will claim, that statements about God are simply in no sense verifiable, and therefore they are empty of practical meaning for living in the world? I think we have already seen that this is not the case. A notable example of falsification is the universal rejection of accepting the Hebrew Scriptures on the basis of a literal interpretation of their meaning. The term "God" does not function in isolation. It functions as a part of a most general way of understanding reality, and that understanding affects how we live in the world. The life of Torah, which is a discipline that guides every aspect of human existence for committed Jews, is a practical consequence of a general view of absolutely everything in which God, as both the creator and the revealer of the Torah, plays a critical role. How we judge God rests on how we judge the worldview in which God functions, and that is judged epistemologically by how successful it is in making sense out of everything we know and ethically by how successful it is in making sense out of how we interact with other human beings. The answer, of course, is very vague. However, for the reasons suggested above, the vagueness here is not inappropriate to the subject.

Franz Rosenzweig

In this regard, what can be said about Rosenzweig's presentation of epistemic claims about God? Rosenzweig accepts on the authority of

---

[8] This, of course, does not settle the issue, and I will consider this line of argument further in connection with the atheological arguments.

[9] Once again, this does not settle the issue, and I will consider it further in connection with the atheological arguments.

Immanuel Kant[10] that no valid proof can be provided for the existence of God. With specific reference to the various forms of the cosmological argument, on his view particulars in the world are generated from nothing by sheer chance. Hence, at least with respect to origins, he rejects the principle of sufficient reason in any of the forms relevant to the cosmological argument. Furthermore, he agrees with Kant that they stand or fall on the validity of the ontological proof, and the ontological proof is not valid. Rosenzweig's affirmation of God's existence is closer in form to Isaiah and the Hebrew Scriptures than it is to the medieval philosophers. He presents a word picture of reality, and God functions as one of three critical elements within that picture. In other words, God exists because God is a critical element in his picture of reality. The claim of God's existence stands or falls, logically, on the acceptance of the picture itself.

In support of the picture Rosenzweig offers two lines of (implicit) argumentation. First, God is a critical element in his picture of reality. That picture is formed by reasoning beyond the skeptical conclusions of philosophy in order to offer a more adequate way than any other conceptual model to understand absolutely everything. Here "absolutely everything" includes religious life as well as physical nature and human society.

Second, the fact that God is an element is a consequence of his reading of the history of philosophy. That narrative, given in the introduction to *The Star*, determines three (and only three) general topical foci for human philosophical speculation – theology (about God), physics (about the world), and psychology (about the human, which includes both epistemology [human rationality] and ethics [human will]). God is an element because that is a critical focus of human speculation at its highest level.

ONTOLOGICAL ARGUMENTS

Background

I have already mentioned that Rosenzweig agrees with Kant's judgment that the cosmological argument is reducible to the ontological argument, and that the ontological argument is not valid. Most contemporary

[10] In *The Star*, Introduction, "For God: Metaphysics," with reference to Kant's *Critique of Pure Reason*, Transcendental Doctrine of Elements, second part: Transcendental Logic, book II: The Dialectical Inferences of Pure Reason, chapter III: "The Ideal of Pure Reason."

philosophers would agree with Kant, but not all. I turn now to what some of them say.[11]

This particular form of argument is distinctly Christian. It was first formulated by Anselm and has no precedent in any of the arguments for God's existence set forth by the Muslim and Jewish philosophers. Of all the classical attempts to prove God's existence, it has the least rhetorical value (it is the least likely to persuade anyone who is not a logician) and the most logical value (it is the most likely to persuade a logician). It is because of its logical force that I will consider it even though it has no precedent in any of our Jewish sources.

Anselm states the ontological argument in at least three forms. It appears in two versions in his *Proslogion*,[12] and it is stated again in his published correspondence as a reply to Gaunilo. How different these three statements are is still controversial. Norman Malcolm[13] considered them to be different and judged the second version that appears in the *Proslogion* to be the best.

I will not go here into the logical details of the argument. Its strategy is the following: God is defined as "a being no greater than which can be conceived." That definition constitutes a logical class. The argument is that this class, unlike other classes, cannot be null, that is, it necessarily has at least one member. It can also be argued that it has at most one member, but that is a different argument. The first constitutes a proof that God exists and the second that God is one. Medieval Jewish, Muslim, and Christian philosophers were concerned to establish the second part of the argument as well as the first, because polytheism was for them a real consideration. For modern thinkers, however, the real options seem limited to monotheism (that there exists one and only one God) and atheism (that there exist no gods, including God). Hence, the focus of attention in modern philosophy of religion stays solely on the evidence for the first claim, while the second is simply taken for granted.

---

[11] What follows in this section is drawn primarily from an article I published many years ago: "On Proving God's Existence," *Judaism* 16,1 (1967), 21–36. It is also based, as are the other arguments considered in this chapter, on Richard Gale's presentation in *On the Nature and Existence of God*. In this case, special attention is given to the interpretations of this argument by Norman Malcolm ("The Ontological Argument," *Philosophical Review* 69 (Jan., 1960), republished in Norman Malcolm, *Knowledge and Certainty* [Englewood Cliffs, NJ: Prentice-Hall, 1965]), James Ross (*Philosophical Theology* [New York: Bobbs-Merrill, 1969]), and Alvin Plantinga (*The Nature of Necessity* [Oxford: Oxford University Press, 1975]).

[12] *St. Anselm's Proslogion*. English translation by M. J. Charlesworth (Notre Dame, IN: Notre Dame University Press, 1979).

[13] In Malcolm, "The Ontological Argument," 141–162.

The class of "God"

The argument itself begins with a definition of the class of God, that is, the class to which God would belong in the statement "God (here functioning as a proper name) is God (here functioning as a predicate term)," where the sentence is understood to be an assertion of an individual (the subject term) exemplifying the general class (the object term). The argument focuses not on the proper name that is the subject term, but on the predication, which names a class.

What the argument leaves open is the ontological status of classes and individuals. Presumably that should not matter in the argument. Be that as it may, the argument is intended to show that this class (again, whatever is its ontological status as a class) has at least one member, and this state of affairs is necessarily the case. That argument, as we shall see, turns on the claim about the logical relationship between claiming that something is "great" and claiming that it has "limits." In general, it is assumed that to the extent that anything is limited by something else, it is less than it would be otherwise. In other words, "greatness" and "limitation" are inversely proportionate.

The argument proceeds in three steps.[14] First, it is argued that if a God exists, then he exists necessarily. Second, it is argued that if a God does not exist, then he does not exist necessarily. Hence, a God's existence is either necessary or impossible, but it cannot be contingent. The judgment about God's existence, therefore, is limited to two purely logical options. The existence or non-existence of God cannot be merely a contingent fact. Finally, third, it is argued that, given these options, it is more reasonable to affirm that God exists than that he does not exist, because there is nothing about the definition of God to suggest that his existence is impossible.

The argument

The first step (A) is a demonstration that God cannot come into existence. (A1) Given the definition of God, it is impossible for God to be limited. (A2) If something comes into existence, that state of affairs either is caused or merely happens. (A3) However, neither alternative is possible for something that is unlimited. Hence (from A3), something that is

---

[14] Here I am following Gale's summary of Malcolm's reformulation of Anselm's second argument in the *Proslogion*.

unlimited cannot come into existence. Therefore (from A1), God cannot come into existence.

The second step (B) is a demonstration that God cannot contingently not exist. (B1) It is necessarily the case that if the non-existence of something is a contingent fact (i.e., it does not exist but it is possible that it exists), its existence is also a contingent fact (i.e., it could exist). Hence, (B2) if God's non-existence were contingent, his existence would be contingent. However, we have already seen in step one that his existence cannot be contingent. Hence, his non-existence as well cannot be contingent. Therefore, if God does not exist, God's non-existence is necessarily the case.

The third step (C) concludes the argument to demonstrate that necessarily God exists. The conjunction of steps one and two establishes that (C1) either God necessarily exists or God necessarily does not exist. Hence, (C2) if it is conceivable from his definition that God exists, then he exists, and if it is inconceivable from his definition that he does not exist, then he does not exist. However, (C3) there is nothing about the definition to suggest that God's existence is impossible. Therefore, God necessarily exists.

Critique

At a more general level, the claimed validity of the ontological argument rests on what is argued in the first step, and it is here that there is room for objection. What it concludes is that if God exists he does so necessarily. What is not possible is for God's existence to be a contingent fact. If it were, there would have to be some cause for it other than God himself, and if that were the case, God would be limited in the sense that his being or not being would not be solely in his control, for it would depend on something other than himself. A deity so limited would not fit the definition given, because it is conceivable that there could be something else not so dependent, and that something else, at least in this respect, would be greater than (i.e., superior to, i.e., more independent than) God, which means that God would not be God.

What the argument so far assumes is the value of autonomy over dependence. In every respect, something that is independent is better than something that is dependent. "Better" here seems clearly to have a moral sense. Hence, the argument, at least so far, presupposes a certain understanding of ethics – one that was shared by at least one tradition of philosophy, namely that which runs from Aristotle through Spinoza. However, it is not, as we have seen, the only philosophical tradition. I have opted so far in this book for an alternate tradition that runs from the Hebrew Scriptures through Buber and Rosenzweig. Here relationality is judged superior (at least morally) to independence. Hence, at least on these grounds – the implicit moral judgment that correlates independence with greatness – the argument would be rejected, at least in the form so far considered.

It can also be argued, contrary to what is claimed in the third step (C3), that the definition of God is such that it is impossible for God to exist, which means that the class of beings no greater than which can be conceived is necessarily a null class. I will not argue that here. The purported proofs are included in the atheological arguments to be considered below. Here the only intent is to show a weakness in the ontological argument as stated. That the definition of God does not appear to be self-contradictory does not mean that it is not. It may be the case that I have not thought enough about it to see the inherent incoherence it entails. Hence, and this is no surprise, even if the argument is valid, it certainly is in no sense persuasive.

The non-perfect God of revelation

Just what is it that this argument purports to prove? It is not, contrary to the use of the term "God," anything of theological interest, for it says nothing about the individual whom Jews, Muslims, and Christians call by the name "God." Rather, it is an argument about a class, and what it asserts is not only that some classes are logically null sets (viz., those that name chimeras) but that there are other classes (or, at least one) that can be shown to be logically not null (i.e., that necessarily have at least one member). That is something of serious interest to logicians. It even has important implications for philosophers who are epistemologists, because it entails a denial of at least one foundational truth in Anglo-American circles of academic philosophy – that necessary truths are purely formal in nature and provide no information about the world. However, it says nothing of theological interest.

The ontological argument lacks theological value in at least two respects. First, the God of creation and revelation is not a class. He is an individual. Second, the God with whom we are concerned, namely the deity of both those who follow Maimonides and those who follow Rosenzweig, is "a being such that whatever is or is conceived to be is not God," and this entity is not "a being no greater than which can be conceived," or, more accurately, cannot be so defined as Anselm's definition functions in the ontological argument as it has been reconstructed above. I will explain what I mean.

As Anselm himself states his argument, the definition of God is purely negative. It does not say who or what God is; it says who or what he is not. As such it conforms to the standard of Maimonides' negative theology. No matter how great something is, that something is not God. However, it seems clear that as the definition is used in all of the modern revisions of it, Anselm's definition is transformed into a positive statement: God is a most perfect being. Yet, that is not what the Maimonidean and Rosenzweigian traditions claim.

Prima facie God is not a most perfect being, because we have no idea what such a being would be. A positive definition is intelligible only if we can understand what it says. However, we have no idea what it means to be most perfect. Hence, the definition is not intelligible. In fact, if this definition stands as it is, we should conclude the ontological argument with the judgment that necessarily God does not exist, because the definition of God is inherently and deeply unclear.

For example, we do not know that God is unlimited. In fact Jewish tradition suggests that he imposes all kinds of limits on himself. This imposition of limits in the Kabbalah is how God creates the world.[15] Furthermore, in Rosenzweig's case, each new creature in the world limits God, for it defines God. God can be anything that is not, until it comes to be, and then God cannot be it. Hence, it is not even clear that Rosenzweig's God can be called a "necessary being," since what he is not depends on what is and whatever comes to be is, as we have seen, a contingent fact.

The critical point is that God is not anything positive at all, and what the modern versions of the ontological argument do is transform Anselm's totally negative definition into a statement about positive being. What is, it is assumed, is better than what is not. That is more than Anselm says and it may be more than he intended. It is certainly more than Maimonides and Rosenzweig intended. For them the nothing is no less real than the something. For Maimonides the nothing (which he calls "privation") is not as valuable morally as the something, but that need not be the case for Rosenzweig.

---

[15] What I have in mind here is the concept of divine contraction (*tsimtsum*) in order to make room for the world to exist.

For Rosenzweig most of what is in creation is nothing and not something. Nothing is also the realm of interpersonal relationship, for it is things that are something, not wills. However, there is a sense that something is better than nothing, that the end-limit of every movement from nothing is a something. However, this something is an ideal and not actual. It would follow, then, given Rosenzweig's ontology, that if God is to be defined as what is most perfect in the sense of a mathematical limit, God necessarily does not exist, for God is the infinite ideal end towards which all that is is directed in its motion.

Hence, the ontological proof may be read as a kind of moral demonstration rather than an ontological one, one that asserts a moral end and not one that affirms an actual existent. Such an interpretation would transform Anselm's proof into the kind of moral argument that Kant gives for God's reality. In this (Kantian and Cohenian) sense, God is real even though he is not actual and will not be actual until the end of days. However, this is a deity of redemption, who is neither the God of creation nor the God of revelation, and the theme of this book is revelation.

My conclusion, therefore, is that whatever value the ontological proof of Christian philosophy has for logic and epistemology, it has limited value for Jewish philosophical theology. What it establishes may be the reality of the God of redemption who functions as an ideal end towards which both the world and the human are ultimately directed. However, it establishes nothing about the God of revelation. This God is the radical other who is present to us as the other in experience. The God considered in the ontological argument is in no sense personal, but the deity with whom we are concerned is radically personal. This deity is known through religious experience, and it is to arguments from religious experience that I will now turn.

MODERN ARGUMENTS

Review

So far I have examined two kinds of theological arguments. In both cases the proofs are modern reformulations of classical philosophical discussions. The first group, the cosmological arguments, turns on claims about the nature of the world, where that nature is determined by whatever the current state of the sciences was at the time that the arguments were composed. Here reformulations are a matter of updating the science and seeing how the changes introduced by the update changes the nature of the argument. As such, all cosmological arguments are inherently relativistic. It is not that they do not prove what they claim to prove. It is only that what they prove is conditional, for it depends on the truth of what science claims and those judgments are always subject to revision.

The second group, the ontological arguments, is independent of empirical facts and scientific judgments about the world. They are purely logical arguments and, as such, are of interest to logicians, but not to theologians. Theology deals with a God who functions in lived reality, and the deity of the ontological proofs has no lived reality, or at least none that is relevant to the proofs themselves. "None" however is perhaps too strong a claim.

At least on some interpretation, the God of the ontological argument is an ethical ideal, who, as an ideal, points the way towards redemption, and that ideal is relevant to understanding the God of revelation. The revealed deity is a presence in the present, and that present presence stands between an origin and an end. The origin is creation and the end is redemption. The present God of revelation is understood to be the originating God of creation as well as the ending ideal God of redemption. These aspects of God define the parameters for interpreting the God of the present who, as present, reveals only himself and nothing about himself. If there is anything in this case to know, it comes not from God but from our experience of God. Hence, to know what there is to know about the God of revelation, we must turn to an entirely different category of proofs of God's existence – those that rest not on the physical sciences and not on logic alone but on religious experience.

Some thirty years ago I published an article that explores theological doubts about whether or not the God of Judaism and the Hebrew Scriptures is the deity that is identified in western philosophical literature as "God."[16] In that article I proposed a form of argument from religious experience that predates the kind of contemporary proofs associated with William Alston and others.[17] Here I will focus on these more recent proofs and will integrate them into what I argued in my earlier essay.

[16] "That the God of the Philosophers is not the God of Abraham, Isaac, and Jacob," *Harvard Theological Review* 65,1 (1972), 1–27.
[17] The primary William Alston reference is *Perceiving God*. The "others" in this case include William Wainwright (especially in *Mysticism* [Madison: University of Wisconsin Press, 1981]), and Wayne Proudfoot (in *Religious Experience* [Berkeley: University of California Press, 1985]).

Arguments from religious experience

A number of contemporary philosophers of religion have advanced the claim that reports by religious people of experience of God constitute evidence for his existence. There are many people who make these personal claims, and a very large number of them can be considered reliable witnesses – that is, they are sane and honest. Hence, their testimonies constitute sound evidence to support the claim, on empirical grounds, that God exists. More specifically, I have argued that the fact that so many people in honesty claim religious experience of God at least requires an explanation. The structure of my argument runs as follows:

The logic of legal evidence and testimony

Given that reports of religious experience are analogous at least to other kinds of first-person accounts of experience, those reports constitute evidence for what they claim in much the same way as testimony in a court of law constitutes evidence. In fact, arguments based on religious experience are logically more like legal arguments than are the kinds of classical arguments so far considered. In a case to determine whether or not someone committed a crime, juries and judges cannot make this decision on their own. The question cannot be settled by pure logic, for what is judged are contingent truths of fact. Judgment requires experience, which neither the juries nor the judges have. In these cases they are dependent on the reports of witnesses, and witnesses are to be taken at their word unless there is good reason not to do so. Contrary evidence in these cases generally means to discredit the testimony, and discrediting the testimony requires discrediting the witnesses by showing them to be dishonest or not mentally competent. Both strategies have been used by committed atheists to discredit those who claim religious experience. However, the large number of people who claim such an experience, even when we limit ourselves to the present, is far too great to be reasonably discredited in this way. What, then, is needed, if the position of atheism is to be defended, is a way to account for dismissing the testimony of so many witnesses without dismissing their sanity or integrity.

(i) *Sigmund Freud: religious witness as natural illusion.* To my knowledge the only atheist who has provided such an argument is Sigmund Freud. The argument is presented in two of his works – *Totem and Taboo*[18] and

---

[18] James Strachey (ed.), *Standard Edition of the Complete Psychological Works of Sigmund Freud*, vol. xiii, translated into English by James Strachey with Anna Freud, Alix Strachey, and Alan Tyson (London: Hogarth Press and the Institute of Psycho-Analysis, 1912–13).

Moses and Monotheism.[19] There Freud argues that, having murdered Moses in a vain attempt to eliminate the guilt he placed on them in his effort to raise them from the slave people they were into a "mighty nation," the people Israel were faced with a new and far more grave guilt. Moses had come to be for them like a god. In his murder he is exalted from being *like* a god to being God, and from being empowered as a national leader to being worshiped as a deity. Israel's collective belief in having experienced God is simply a mass psychotic act of projection in order to overcome the guilt collectively felt for murdering its national father figure. In the course of time the fantasy is abstracted from its original setting, which, in its new more universal form, has appeal to all kinds of people, Israelite and gentile. The appeal is in the shared psychological desire of the human beings in general to murder their same-gender parent. Belief in God is a belief in a cosmic father figure, and the psychological value of this belief is that it provides a way to deal with the guilt of a natural but judged immoral fantasy about parents. The psychological need is so strong and so universal that it can produce collective fantasies of the sort that are reported in religious experience.

The strength of this Freudian tale is that it provides what atheists must but usually fail to provide, namely an explanation of why so many people can experience someone who does not exist. The explanation treats religious experience as a natural and widespread human illusion. However, many of us would contend that the explanation is less believable than what it is intended to explain away. Given a choice between accepting that there is a deity who is the object of much religious experience and accepting Freud's account of the Hebrew Scriptures, western religion, and the human psyche, affirming belief in God is the more reasonable choice.

(ii) *On the analogy between sense and religious experience.* The critical assumption in all of the arguments from religious experience, including mine, is that somehow reports of experiencing God should be treated in the same way as we treat all other first-person reports of sense experience: we should understand that prima facie what these people claim to have experienced is true, and that truth means that there is something in reality to which their experience corresponds.

There are two questions to be raised here about this argument. One has to do with the relationship between religious experience and other kinds of sensory experience. Are they the same or are they only analogous? Another has to do with how sense-experience reports function

---

[19] English translation by Katherine Jones (New York: Knopf, 1939).

logically for claims about reality. The first is the more difficult, so I will consider the second claim first.

(iii) *Is seeing believing?* It is not the case that we can say, so to speak, that "seeing is believing." As we saw above in the discussion of contemporary evolutionary psychology, what we sense of reality is not the same as reality. In chapter 6 I looked at this claim from the perspective of judgments about objects in space and time. That objects exist is a mental construct from data taken in by the senses and assimilated by our brains. Were our brains different than they are, they would construct different objects, if they constructed objects at all. The same applies to our judgments about space and time. What we do is simply assume, with relatively little reflection, that the way our brains construct reality corresponds in some sense at least to the way reality is. We make this assumption primarily for pragmatic reasons, but there are stronger reasons as well.

The pragmatic justification for the assumption – that how we see reality is the way reality is – is that this assumption enables us to survive. For example, we judge that there is some object in front of us that we identify as a door, and then we proceed to open it in order to pass through into a different space. When we pass through, we see other objects in a different space, which leads to further actions based on the same assumption that the way we construct reality is more or less the way it is.

If there were no real correspondence of any sort, then we should expect some discontinuity in our experience, and when in fact this is what we do experience, we reevaluate our judgments. For example, we see, while walking in a desert, a pond of water in the distance. If there really is a pond, we will see ourselves getting closer to it as we walk in that direction, and eventually we will reach it, where we will experience a cool refreshing series of sensations from drinking real water in the real pond. If we do not have these experiences – if we never seem to get closer to the pool or if, once there, we taste what seems to us to be sand rather than water – we reevaluate our original judgment about what it is that we have experienced. There was something real there, but that reality was not what we thought it was.

Such reevaluation is not uncommon. For example, from the fact that we see a stick being broken into two parts that constantly change in size as we pass the stick from the air into water does not lead us to conclude that the original stick is actually broken and that the relative sizes of the two parts are in fact changing. We judge this experience to be an illusion, and, when armed with an appropriate theory of optics, we are able to explain what we saw as the normal way one experiences a single unchanging visual object passing from one medium into another of different density. Hence, judgments of reality are not based solely on sensation. They are judgments about what is real, based not only on what is sensed and how the brain structures those sensations but also on what we believe about reality. Judgments of empirical reality are, therefore, as much philosophical judgments as they are empirical.

Are religious experiences like this? Some religious people claim that they are. Most, however, do not. They use the kind of example given above to argue that there is an analogy, but not an identity, between religious experience and other kinds of sense experience. The critical difference has to do with objectivity. The pond that I see in the distance in the desert will be visible not only to me, but to most human beings who stand where I stand, and the sense factors that will lead me to judge that there really is or there really is not a pool there will lead others to the same judgment. However, religious experience is more private. In fact, it is not inconceivable that in a group of people standing together at a single place, only some, possibly only one, of them will have the religious experience, and that experience could be judged to be veridical. The question that rightly should be asked is by what criteria this judgment can be made, since, in other kinds of sensory experience, its very private nature would constitute prima facie evidence that the experience is not veridical, that what I thought I experienced was illusory.

(iv) *On evidence for religious experience truth claims.* Richard Gale has argued, and I agree with him, that there must be tests to determine whether or not a religious experience is veridical, whether what is claimed to have been experienced in fact exists. It is no more intelligible to claim that religious experience is incorrigible than it is to claim that any other kind of experience is incorrigible. That, for example, I tell you in all honesty that I see pink elephants in my bathroom is certainly sufficient evidence for the truth of the fact that I am seeing pink elephants in my bathroom. However, that is not a statement about what is in fact in my bathroom; it is a statement about what I am seeing. Whether or not what I see is in fact there requires more rigorous standards of evidence. The same claim applies to truth judgments about religious experience. That I say that I have experienced God and I am both honest and sane is sufficient evidence for the claim about me, namely, that I do really experience what I say I experience. However, it is not sufficient evidence for the claim about the truth of what I experience. Hence, the claim that I experience it does not prove that it, whatever it is, exists. In this case the "it" is God.

What makes claims about experience of God problematic is that generally – at least in Judaism – the God experienced cannot be seen. There may be, as in Ezekiel chapter 1, visual experiences that accompany the encounter with God, but the experience of God himself is not visual, because there is nothing to see. Furthermore, there is nothing to sense in any other way. God can no more be touched, smelled, tasted, or even heard in any literal way than he can be seen. Rather, all that is experienced is a presence. To be sure, those who experience God's presence draw from that experience lessons that are associated with hearing God speak, but it is never claimed by the classical philosophers and modern theologians whom we have discussed that the term "speech" is used here in any literal way.

Speech is caused by sound waves that are assimilated into the brain as sounds that are further interpreted by the mind to be information. In the case of religious experience (i.e., experience of God, i.e., experience of divine revelation) the information is processed from the presence without any of the physical steps. Literally, for us speech consists of sound waves; it is not itself information. To use a computer analogy, the physical speech is the hardware through which the information is processed by the software of our minds. In the case of religious experience, there is no hardware.

The question, then, of veridical religious experience – religious experience in which the object of the experience can be expressed in language and that expression can be judged in some sense to be true or false – comes down to this: can the object of an experience be judged veridical if in principle that object, namely God, is not anything positive in the physical world of space and time? Certainly, in this respect, to experience God is not like experiencing anything else. Is the dissimilarity so great that no claimed experience of God can be judged to be reliable evidence for anything other than the mental state of the person who reports the experience?

Richard Gale, on the one hand, answers in the negative. The difference between religious experience and other kinds of direct experience is such that there are no valid grounds to grant to religious experience authority in cognitive claims. On the other hand, there are a number of philosophers who would answer in the affirmative and claim that the dissimilarity is not great enough to disqualify some cognitive claims based on religious experience.

Alston has argued for what he calls a "presumptive inference rule" – that religious experience, like all other experience, has prima facie epistemic justification. Its cognitive claims are to be judged veridical unless, and only unless, there are good reasons not to accept them. A "good reason" for rejecting such claims is that belief in them by religious people does not endure over the course of time. Another good reason is that the affirmation of these specific beliefs is incompatible with affirming other religious beliefs that are coherent and have persisted through time.

In a way that is not dissimilar to that of Alston, W. T. Stace[20] has argued that religious beliefs based on religious experience must be judged in the context of a community of religious believers. As this claim is formalized in the Roman Catholic Church, the community sets the standards by which religious experience is judged, and different communities may have different criteria.

Gale, for one, argues that additional criteria are necessary that are more universal, that are not restricted to judgments within specific religious communities. Certainly there are claims that are consistent within different religious communities that are inconsistent between the communities, for there are real, conceptually substantive differences between religious communities. There must be some way, he argues, to judge between these claims, just as there are ways to make these judgments within a community.

Wainwright also proposes that cognitive claims from religious experience must be tested by criteria established within specific religious communities. However, in addition he suggests a more universal test. What Wainwright proposes is an assessment of the predictive power of the belief. The truth of a religious belief, irrespective of its origin, is to be judged by its moral consequences, both for the person who holds the belief and for the behavior of the community of shared believers. Beliefs that make people better people than they would be otherwise are better beliefs.

Wainwright's predictive-power tests belong to another set of modern theological proofs that are associated primarily with William James.[21] I will consider them in a moment. First, however, I will look at how this argument about judging the veracity of claims based on religious experience applies to what has so far been determined to be a Jewish philosophy of revelation.

Religious experience in the context of Jewish philosophic theology
It is central to the theory of revelation that has been developed so far in this book that the Torah is a product of divine inspiration, and this

---

[20] In *Mysticism and Philosophy* (Philadelphia: Lippincott, 1960).
[21] In *The Varieties of Religious Experience* (New York: The Modern Library, 1902), as well as in *The Will to Believe and Other Essays* (New York: Longmans, Green, 1897).

inspiration is a kind of religious experience. The claim being put forward here is that at some more or less specific time at some more or less specific place the people Israel encountered the presence of God, and that encounter led the people to develop stories, beliefs, and laws that came to be expressed verbally in the words of the Hebrew Scriptures. Furthermore, the ongoing rabbinic tradition of interpreting those words and then interpreting the interpretations is also a consequence of divine inspiration, for the revelatory relationship between God and Israel is continuous through time. This claim for the believability of revelation presupposes that there is some analogy between experiencing God and other kinds of experience.

As we have seen, some philosophers of religion would argue against the above believability claim, because they discount any valid analogy between religious and sense experience. Gale, for example, presents a set of tests by which content claims from sense experience are to be judged, and he says that none of them are applicable to religious experience. Some of these tests are described above: logical and empirical consistency, the reliability of the experiencing subject, continuity between content claims, and what Wainwright called prediction. To this list Gale and others add that there must be reasonable independent evidence for the truth claim: to be veridical there must be a way to give a causal account of what was experienced.

Gale claims that the possibility of a causal account, prediction, and the agreement criteria do not apply to religious experience, but that is because he admits individual religious experience independent of any community of believers. It is this commitment to individual autonomous religious experience that leads him to reject all other claimed analogies between sense and religious experience as well. He argues, for example, that in sense experience the object perceived and the perceiver occupy the same time and place, but that is not the case in religious experience because the object, God, occupies neither. He makes this claim in part on the authority of Strawson who argued that empirical objects can be individuated only by location in space and time.[22]

However, with respect to Jewish philosophical theology, while God cannot be literally "in" a place and "at" a time, God is always associated with a time and a place, because the experience of revelation is always situated in the concrete and, as such, associated with what functions

---

[22] P. F. Strawson in *Individuals* (New York: Anchor Books, 1963). In making this claim Strawson says nothing that had not already been universally claimed by the Aristotelians. Individuation is a principle of matter, and matter is expressed in terms of spatial-temporal location.

as a body. An example would be the appearance of the fiery pillar that accompanies God's appearance at the Tent of Meeting in the story of Israel's exodus. Another example is Ezekiel's description of the chariot in his inaugural experience of divine revelation. The pillar and the chariot are not God, but they are the body of God in the sense that they locate the experience of the divine love at a specific time and place. As such, the experience of God is not dissimilar to the experience of what is called in religious language the "soul" of the lover by the beloved or the beloved by the lover.

Furthermore, contrary to Gale's account of religion in general, rabbinic thought does not treat individual experience of God as veridical. It does admit that such an encounter occurs. (It is what the Midrash associates with an individual receiving a *bat kol*, a divine voice.) However, any content associated with such an experience is discounted in rabbinic decisions.[23] What counts as authoritative content arising from revelation is always communal in nature. Saadia argued, for example, that an event can be called a "miracle" only if it is predicted by a prophet who also interprets the revelation as having cosmic significance. Note that to be a "miracle" has nothing to do with being contrary to the laws of nature, but it has everything to do with the event being situated in a larger community rather than just the life of the individual prophet.[24] The same is true of prophecy, and therefore of revelation, in general. The recipient of revelation from God is the prophet, and there is no individual prophecy in the sense that the meaning of the experience relates solely to the prophets. In general, prophets do not prophesy for themselves or even for their families. Rather, prophecy relates to nations (notably Israel) and its meaning relates to the meaning of everything – God, the world, and the human.

Against this background of Jewish philosophy, I would argue, contrary to Gale, that any claim for conceptual content inferences from religious experience can only be assessed within the context of a religious community. In effect it is this community that functions vis-à-vis the believer as the body of God,[25] for it defines the concrete ways and contexts in which the deity of the community is to be encountered. However, this judgment does not mean, as Gale seems to think, that truth judgments

---

[23] As in the oft-quoted case of Rabbi Joshua ben Hanania successfully overruling the appeal to a *bat kol* by Eliezer ben Hyrcanus in the Babylonian Talmud, Baba Metsia 59b and Hullin 44a.

[24] See N. Samuelson, "Halevi and Rosenzweig on Miracles," in David R. Blumenthal (ed.), *Approaches to Judaism in Medieval Times* (Brown Judaic Studies 54; Chico, CA: Scholars Press, 1984), pp. 157–172 and in *The Star*, part II, Introduction, "The Theology of the Miracle."

[25] See Michael Wyschogrod, *The Body of God* (San Francisco: Harper and Row, 1989).

cannot be made between such communities. This difference requires some explanation.

With Alston and Wainwright, I would agree that truth judgment about religious experience functions within a community. I would want to argue this claim in general, namely, that all assessments of truth occur within a more or less specific community of learners or seekers, and what count as criteria for assessment vary between communities.[26] However, that truth judgment is so situated within a community does not exclude judgments from one community to another. Judgments, however, cannot be made, as Gale seems to suggest, by standing outside any community. There is no way to stand nowhere, and there is no single favored place for judgment. Rather, what one must do is translate the statements from one community into statements within another community, which is very much like translating sentences from one language into another. There is no mechanical way to do this, and the art of judgment is largely an art of translation.[27] If a different truth assessment occurs in the two relevant faith communities after the translation, and it is a good translation, then, as Gale claims, we cannot assess the truth of the claim. However, we do learn something even then – we learn about the different natures of the two communities of seekers.

Note that this specific disagreement with Gale does not mean that I disagree in general with his assessment of arguments for God's existence from religious experience, namely, that religious experience as such is not cognitive, so that no truth-value judgments of any cognitive claims that arise through religious experience can be assessed on the basis of the experiences themselves. The reason for this judgment is not, as Gale claims, that there is no analogy between sense and religious experience, but because the nature of God is such that experience of him has no cognitive content. What is experienced in experiencing God is pure, personal presence. It is an experience at least analogous to love between persons, and in both kinds of love nothing cognitive can be inferred solely from the experience.

However, I do not mean to say that the experience does not have consequences through which cognitive content arises. That certainly is the case in what we have seen so far about revelation. What God reveals

---

[26] As I understand it, this argument for the communal nature of truth judgment comes from C. S. Peirce. See Peter Ochs, *Peirce, Pragmatism and the Logic of Scripture* (Cambridge: Cambridge University Press, 1998).

[27] I have written about this judgment with specific reference to interreligious dialogue in "The Logic of Interreligious Dialogue," in Thomas Dean (ed.), *Religious Pluralism and Truth: Essays on Cross-Cultural Philosophy of Religion* (Albany: State University of New York Press, 1995), pp. 133–149.

is himself and only himself, but, in response to that experience of divine love, the loved ones create both beliefs about what is true and pragmatic-ethical imperatives to behave in certain ways. These beliefs constitute Jewish religious doctrine, and this prescribed behavior constitutes Jewish law. Their authority is ultimately the experience of God, but their veracity and moral value is not dependent on the experience *per se*. There is no difference in logically assessing the claims of such a religious belief rather than any other belief that has, independent of the originating experience, a comparable level of probability. This is precisely what I have been involved in doing in this book – examining the believability of one central religious doctrine. Among those claims is the judgment that the God of revelation exists.

Pragmatic arguments

So far, attention has been given to theological arguments, that is, philo-sophic arguments that claim to demonstrate that God exists. I have looked at the two forms of classic demonstrations – the cosmological and the ontological arguments – and one form of modern argument based on religious experience. Concerning the cosmological arguments, I concluded that they have a restricted kind of validity, that what these arguments conclude about God is dependent on what they presuppose from science about the world.

The ontological arguments suffer under no such restriction. To the extent that they are valid, what they prove is true in all possible worlds. However, I argued that what they conclude has little, if any, bearing on this theological discussion, and especially on Judaism.

Finally, concerning the modern arguments from religious experience, they justify the claim that there is some form of valid analogy between religious and other kinds of sense experience, and they justify making cognitive claims on the basis of religious experience no less than on the basis of other kinds of experience. However, they do not justify concluding solely on the basis of the experience that the cognitive products from the experiences are true. With specific reference to God, while encounter with God does provide a reasonable ground for affirming that the other that is encountered is real, it gives in principle no knowledge in any way of this other that is encountered.

There is one other kind of modern theological philosophical argument that I should consider before moving on to the philosophers' atheolo-gical arguments. There are what can be called "pragmatic arguments,"

arguments based in one form or another on the claim that a reasonable person ought to believe in God. I considered above one such argument from Kant and Cohen, namely, that belief in God is a necessity of moral thinking. Another argument of this form was offered by William James in *The Will to Believe*. However, most philosophers today discount such an argument, at least in the form that James presents it, as irrelevant to the question. Whether or not it is useful, even morally, to believe that God exists is not in itself a sufficient reason to hold this belief. In fact it can be argued that to believe something that you know to be unjustified solely because you believe it to be morally useful is itself immoral, since it is morally wrong to claim to believe what you know that you do not believe.

Another form of pragmatic (i.e., useful) argument for God's existence is Blaise Pascal's famous wager.[28] Here it is argued that, based solely on probabilities, it is more reasonable to believe in God than not to. Since reason cannot settle the issue one way or the other, both options of belief are equally probable; hence the bet either way is an even bet (i.e., each affirmation has a 0.5 probability). However, there is a radical difference in the payoff for belief in these two cases. If you believe that God exists and he does not, you lose nothing. On the other hand, if God does exist, then you gain all the promised rewards of heaven. Conversely, if you believe that God does not exist and he does not, you gain nothing, whereas, on the other hand, if God does exist, you suffer all the promised punishments of hell. Hence, any reasonable person will choose to believe in God.

The objections to this argument are innumerable, so many and so obvious in fact that it is hard to believe that Pascal intended it to be a serious argument. In any case, the argument presupposes a certain Christian notion of divine providence, which is not necessarily shared by all Christians and certainly is not widely accepted by Jews. Furthermore, even if we grant this notion of divine reward and punishment, belief on this basis would not be sincere belief and therefore would not count as a qualification for receiving the presumed promised rewards of heaven. Furthermore, such belief would be, as we saw in the previous case, immoral, and, as such, would qualify the believer for damnation. Again, it is difficult to imagine how anyone would take this kind of argument seriously, which is certainly not the case with the other theological arguments examined above.

---

[28] See Blaise Pascal, *Pensées and Other Writings*, English translation by Honor Levi (Oxford and New York: Oxford University Press, 1995).

The question now remains whether the arguments for not believing in God's existence are as good as, if not better than, the theological arguments. If they are as good but not better, I will conclude that modern philosophy has little if anything to contribute to this discussion of the believability of revelation. However, if they are better, philosophy will provide serious reasons for not believing in revelation in the way that I have presented it, and that will require a radical reconsideration of what I have claimed to be a believable concept of revelation based on a reasonable conception of what the human and the divine poles are that define the relationship.

PROOFS THAT GOD DOES NOT EXIST

OVERVIEW

All of the versions of the ontological theological argument concluded that a God defined as "a being no greater than which can be conceived" cannot merely happen to exist or not to exist. Such an entity either exists necessarily or its existence is impossible. The determination between these options depends on the intelligibility of the concept of a being no greater than which can be conceived. The final step, that God is a necessary being, is based solely on the intuition that the definition is intelligible. However, that intuition need not be true. The conception of God on these terms may seem to be intelligible, but with deeper reflection it could turn out not to be.

For those readers who may have some difficulty understanding this last point, let me give an example. The notion of a centaur – a creature that is human from the waist up and a horse from the neck down – seems to be intelligible. As far as we know there are no such creatures, but that does not mean that there could not be, for there seems to be nothing incoherent about the assumption. However, on deeper reflection it turns out that a centaur, at least as I defined it here, is a chimera. It seems to be possible for there to be a centaur, because we only consider the external form of a human and a horse body, but we do not think about what it really means for a single entity to combine both in the way suggested.

What the human body cavity contains above the waist is a human digestive system. If the upper body is really human, the centaur takes in food through its human mouth that is digested in the human body and then passed on as human waste into the body of the horse where, presumably, it is again digested. However, no horse body cavity, which contains the horse's digestive system, can digest human waste. Hence, if what a centaur appears to be externally is what it really is, then necessarily there are no centaurs.

It could be argued that all we need to do is redefine what we mean by a centaur and then, given its reconstructed definition, we can admit the possibility at least of centaurs. We could say, for example, that centaurs have human heads mounted on top of very long necks that have only the external appearance of a human body. Or, we could say that centaurs are humans with six legs, the fore-two functioning as hands, and the external shape of the lower part of this human body, below the human digestive system, is that of a horse. At least prima facie it seems that such a creature, although not actual, is possible.

We would proceed in the same way to redefine what we mean by the term "God" if it were to turn out that the concept of an unlimited being is not intelligible. A being no greater than which can be conceived would not be a perfect being if the notion of a perfect being is unintelligible. If the notion of a perfect being is unintelligible, then it is not a being no greater than which can be conceived, for anything that could exist would be greater than it. In truth, the only proper way to understand Anselm's definition of God is negatively, devoid of any positive content.

In effect, one way to understand medieval Muslim, Jewish, and Christian theology is as a working out of what it would mean to conceive of a deity who is greater than anything else. These philosophers attributed to God every perfection that they could, because prima facie what is perfect is greater than what is imperfect. However, not every perfection fits, and those that do not cannot be attributed to the deity.

What the modern atheological proofs – the demonstrations that God does not exist – do is focus on this classical debate. From what I can tell, they raise no concerns about theology that had not already been raised in classical Abrahamic religious philosophy. Rather, they give these discussions a different emphasis, one that removes them from their original context.

The general form of the atheological proofs is as follows: to define God in the way that he is defined entails a specific pair of attributions that are mutually exclusive, which means that God does not exist. The specific sets of pairs raised are the following: (1) God's perfection means that he is perfectly good and perfectly powerful, but the world that he created is imperfect. Similarly, God is immutable and eternal, but the world he creates is in time and continuously changing. The underlying problem it highlights is how we are to understand the relationship between an eternal God and a temporal world. I will call this line of argument "the creation paradox."[29] (2) God's perfection means that he always knows everything so that what he knows cannot change, but in the world things change all the time and most of these generated events could not have been known before they occurred, because they are contingent. I will call this line of argument "the contingency paradox."[30] (3) God is perfectly good and powerful, but human beings are free to make bad decisions. I will call this line of argument "the human volition paradox."[31] I will now look at each of these paradoxes more closely.[32]

THE CREATION PARADOX

It is a consequence of God's radical simplicity that God is what he does and that act cannot change. Hence, if God creates the world, creating-the-world is what God is and his act is continuous through all time. However, prima facie the creation of the world seems to be a temporal event. At a particular time God did something he had never done before, namely, he created the world, and that particular act ends once the world is created. The solution to the problem proposed by all the classical philosophers – Jews (notably Maimonides and Gersonides), Muslims, and Christians (notably Augustine) – is to affirm creation as an atemporal event.

---

[29] Gale calls it the "creation-immutability argument" in chapter 2 of *On the Nature and Existence of God*.

[30] Gale calls it the "omniscience-immutability argument" in chapter 3 of *On the Nature and Existence of God*.

[31] Gale calls it the "deductive argument from evil" in chapter 4 of *On the Nature and Existence of God*.

[32] In Gale's first chapter he mentions another paradox – that God is omnipotent but limited by the rules of logic, for he cannot do what is logically impossible – but he does not devote any significant amount of analysis to it. It bears some relationship to another proposed paradox that he discusses at length (in chapter 5 of *On the Nature and Existence of God*), but I will not consider it here. The issue raised about logic in general, like the other issues, was considered by medieval western philosophers and dismissed with relative ease. The laws of logic, like the laws of nature, are expressions of the will of God. For God to violate them would mean that God not be God, for it would mean that he could change his mind. God is not limited by this restriction, because the limitation is an exclusive result of his will. The source of the paradox is confusing divine will (which is unrestricted) and human will (which is inherently restricted, viz., what a human wills need not happen).

The issue raised in chapter 5 also has to do with logic. In this case the argument focuses on David Lewis's account of what it means to say that something is "actual" (in *On the Plurality of Worlds* [Oxford: Blackwell, 1986] and in *Counterfactuals* [Boston: Harvard University Press, 1973]). In the concrete, Lewis's discussion and Gale's response are interesting and definitely worth reading, but at the more general level at which the present discussion is proceeding it adds nothing that is not already part of the discussion of the first three paradoxes, especially the second on contingency.

Gale argues that this position means that time is not real, which denies an essential tenet of theism. It seems to me that Gale is wrong on both claims. First, the claim that creation is an atemporal act is standard, at least in classical Jewish philosophy as well as in Christian and Muslim medieval philosophy.[33] Second, this view in itself entails nothing about the reality of time. That all events within the universe are subject to time does not mean that the universe as a whole is in time. What is true of the parts need not be true of the whole. For classical Jewish philosophy at least, that God creates the universe out of nothing means that everything, including time, is created; but if time itself is a product of the act of creation, the act cannot itself take place in time.

Furthermore, to claim that time is real does not say in itself anything about how it is real. As we saw above, evolutionary psychology describes the human sense of time and space as a product of how the brain developed in response to environmental needs. These scientists tend to be realists about this claim, and argue that although the time and space external to the human mind need not be exactly the way the mind constructs it, the fact that this is a successful survival mechanism is sufficient reason to assume that the mental construction reflects reality.

Furthermore, to say that something is real need not be the same as saying that it exists. Still, even if we claim that it does exist, in what way does it exist? Certainly no one says that time and space exist in the same way that objects in time and space exist. For the Aristotelians, time and space were measures of motion; for modern physicists they are the dimensions in which vectors are described. Certainly for both kinds of science they are real, but that does not say either that they exist or, if they do, how they exist.

For the classical Jewish philosophers, out of their Aristotelian sources, the physical universe is a spatial-temporal world different from the absolute reality of God. However, what makes it different is matter, and matter is nothing. The nothing is itself real, and that, I am sure, runs counter to what Gale would call "common-sense," but much of the common-sense view of reality has very little to do with how scientists, past and present, have constructed reality. Certainly a world modeled on quantum mechanics, where nothing really has a definite location simultaneously in both time and space, is radically different from the common-sense

---

[33] See N. Samuelson, *Judaism and the Doctrine of Creation* (Cambridge: Cambridge University Press, 1994).

view that to be a particular entity entails being at a definite time in a definite place.

Similarly, the classical Jewish philosophers granted reality to our physical world, as they did to our mental world, but believed that world to be significantly less real than the radically different world of God. In these respects the modern Jewish theology of Franz Rosenzweig is no different than classical Aristotelian Jewish philosophy.

Gale claims that such a view of an eternal God means that God is not a person, which contradicts a basic tenet of theism. However, we have seen, in the above discussion of the human in Jewish philosophy and theology, that to be a person need have nothing to do with temporal-spatial location. As Rosenzweig uses the term, a human is a "person" in the way that they are situated in the world, and that involves time and space as well as a body. Certainly no such claim is to be made about God in a monotheistic tradition that is seriously committed to God's incorporeality. However, in the sense of the term "person" as I used it, as that non-material aspect of the human that is conscious of another person, God also can be called a person. This sense of the term has nothing to do with a body as such, although it does require something to be identified as a body. In our human case interpersonal relations are always in the present, but they are located vis-à-vis a body, our own body. In God's case there need not be a body. That is certainly the position of the classical Jewish philosophers, as it is the position of Buber. It is a consequence of understanding God to be the eternal-thou that God cannot in any sense be objectified, which further means that God cannot have a body. However, in Rosenzweig's case, there is something like a body. God is defined by not being anything that is. In this sense all that is objectively in the world is the body of God; but God is his body by not being it.

The term "body" is being used here in a semi-technical way that requires a word of explanation. In general a body situates us as human beings in a world among objects, but insofar as we have souls, insofar as we are the object of the kind of relationship with others out of which at least moral duties arise, we are beyond our bodies, and are, in Gale's sense of the term, "persons."

A person, according to Gale, "must be an agent that performs intentional actions so as to bring about some goal and end."[34] In the world of Jewish theology everything has at least this potential, including God.

---

[34] Gale, *On the Nature and Existence of God*, p. 92.

THE CONTINGENCY PARADOX

What it means to say that God is perfect can be analyzed as follows:[35] Single-term predicates are either graded or ungraded. By graded predicates I mean a class of predications, A, such that any two members of this class are so related that if something, a, is f, and something else, b, is g, and f and g both belong to A, then in this respect a is better than b because f is better than g. An example of a class of graded predicates are bowling score averages. (If a has a 250 bowling average and b has a 200 bowling average, then a is a better bowler than b.) In such cases, if for independent reasons the class of predicates is admissible of God (bowling is not), only one member of that class can be affirmed of God, namely the highest grade. (Hence, if God could bowl, which he cannot, his average could only be 300.) In the case of all other classes of predicates, either every member of the class can be affirmed of God or no member can.

In general, the contingency argument depends on knowledge being a non-graded predicate. Knowing anything is good; not knowing anything is bad; and one kind of knowing is not better than any other. Hence, if God knows anything, he knows everything. However, there is at least one kind of knowledge God cannot have, and that is of future contingents, events that have not as yet occurred that need not occur. God cannot know them, because, if he did, their occurrence would not be contingent. Yet, almost everything of religious interest belongs to the class of contingencies. Hence, if God cannot know contingencies once they are actual, God cannot be a God in whom there would be any human interest.

This is an old problem that goes back to Aristotle himself.[36] There are possible, classical solutions to it, most of which seem to be unfamiliar to the modern philosophers that Gale cites.[37] For Maimonides, the problem of God knowing future contingents simply points to the fact that God's knowledge is radically different from human knowledge. We have no

---

[35] See Samuelson, "That the God of the Philosophers is not the God of Abraham, Isaac, and Jacob."

[36] See the following publications by N. Samuelson: "The Problem of Future Contingents in Medieval Jewish Philosophy," John R. Sommerfeldt and E. Rozanne Elder (eds.), in *Studies in Medieval Culture*, vol. VI (Kalamazoo: The Medieval Institute, Western Michigan University, 1976), pp. 71–82; "Gersonides' Account of God's Knowledge of Particulars," *Journal of the History of Philosophy* 10 (Oct., 1972), 399–416; *Gersonides on God's Knowledge of Particulars* (Toronto: Pontifical Institute of Mediaeval Studies, 1977). In Aristotle's original version, which is independent of a theological context, the problem is called "the once and future sea-battle."

[37] I have in mind here A. N. Prior (in "Thank Goodness That's Over," *Philosophy* 34 [1959], 12ff.), Robert Coburn (in "Professor Malcolm on God," *Australasian Journal of Philosophy* 41 [1963], 143–162), and John Perry (in "Frege on Demonstratives," *Philosophical Review* 86 [1977], 474–497 and "The Problem of Essential Indexicals," *Nous* 13 [1979], 3–22).

idea how God knows anything, and our problem with this category of knowledge is that we erroneously assume that how God knows is somehow like the way that we know.

For Gersonides, the point is the same, but not as radically made. God knows what he knows in a single act of knowledge, and he knows what he knows as its cause. In contrast, humans know what they know in multiple acts, and they know them as effects. This means that God does not know contingents at all. This lack, however, is not a lack, and that is because, on Gersonides' understanding, knowledge is a graded predicate. The highest knowledge is knowledge of God. To know anything else is to know something less worthy of knowledge. Hence, what God knows is himself and only himself. However, this knowledge entails knowledge of everything else. Furthermore, what makes "everything else" different from God is matter, which is nothing and is the source of contingency. Hence, what God knows of everything else is its form, which ultimately is God. Everything else there is to know about reality is its matter, which is not to know anything. Such knowledge is not knowledge; it is only (reasoned) opinion, and, because of its inherent inferiority, God is better for not knowing it than knowing.

It may well be objected, as Gale does, that a God so limited is a deity of no religious interest, for what would be the point of praying to a deity who thinks that we humans and everything that matters to us as humans are only nothing, and, as such, are not worthy of attention. Rosenzweig would agree. To be the God of revelation God must know us. However, "knowing" here is not the same kind of knowing as the classical Jewish philosophers spoke of, and it is not the kind of knowledge of which this paradox speaks.

God, who is wholly other (or, in Buber's language, "eternally thou"), knows us as a lover knows a beloved, in intimate, personal relationship. It is the same way that we know him. Such knowledge may have cognitive consequences for human belief and ethics, but those are human consequences not attributable to God. Of God we know only that he is present to us in revelation and this presence both is in him and provokes in us an act of love.

THE HUMAN VOLITION PARADOX

Last of all for consideration here is the paradox of human volition. Divine perfection entails in God perfect power and perfect goodness, both of which are inconsistent with the appearance of evil in the world. Evil is of two kinds – natural and volitional. Natural evils are disasters in nature. These are handled by a best-of-all-possible-worlds scenario. What seems evil to us may be evil from a human perspective, but that need not be evil from a divine perspective. After all, the world does not exist for the sake of human beings. On the contrary, we exist for the sake of God's world.

The more serious problem is the evil we ourselves will. That these acts are really evil, here meaning contrary to what God wills, is accepted, at least, on the testimony of the Hebrew Scriptures. We are told certain divine commandments, and we are to believe that God really wants us to obey. However, clearly we do not obey them, at least not most (let alone all) of the time. How are we to explain this discrepancy between divine will and what exists in God's world, given that he is perfect? There are several possible responses that have emerged in the tradition of Jewish philosophy, some of which are included in the positions of the modern philosophers that Gale considers on this question.

The key rabbinic pronouncement in this case is *ha-kol tsafui ve-ha-reshut netunah livnei-adam*. This expression is often translated to mean that there is free will and determinism, but that is not correct. What it says is "Everything is foreseen and permission is given to human beings." Just what this saying means is not clear, and that is why there is room for interpretation.

The biblical text itself is no less perplexing. For example, God "hardens" Pharaoh's heart to not let the children of Israel leave Egypt, despite the fact that all of Pharaoh's court urges him to do so, since to do so is in his best interest. The hardening is not for the sake of Pharaoh or even for Egypt, but for the sake of God who wants to use this event to make a point about his greatness to the nations of the world. Still, even though Pharaoh's decision is forced and against the will of all of his people, the people and Pharaoh are punished for not obeying God.

That commands have rewards for obedience and punishment for disobedience suggests that humans have choice over whether or not to obey. On the other hand, heart hardening suggests that people can be forced to choose, and the rewards or punishments for their choices seem to be independent of the intent of the actors. On this literal rendering of the Exodus narrative, the text raises serious problems about divine justice. We deserve neither rewards nor punishments for what we choose to do if God forces us to choose the way that we choose.

Ha-kol tsafui suggests that nothing happens in the world of which God is not aware. The question is whether this means that everything is predetermined to happen as it does. Otherwise, how could God know that it will happen? On the other hand, *ha-reshut netunah livnei-adam* suggests that humans are able to decide for themselves what they will do. However, if that is the case, do not the actions chosen have to be indeterminate?

One option is to adopt what is called "soft determinism." It is a favored implicit position of many of the Jewish Aristotelians. The judgment, even when held, seems not to be said in a straightforward way, but sometimes it is.

The clearest example is the words of the first Jewish Aristotelian, Maimonides' immediate intellectual predecessor, Abraham ibn Daud.[38] He argues that God's perfection does not mean that his creation is perfect. If it were, there would be no world at all. Rather, it means that it is as perfect as a world could be and still be a world, that is, still not be God. Its imperfections are, by comparison with God, evils, but only by comparison with God. With reference to the world as a whole, everything is as it should be, including human volition. Human obedience leads to predetermined benefit and human disobedience leads to predetermined harm, both of which are in the service of God's intention for his created world. However, human beings do not know this, and they should not. If humans believed that everything was determined, they would not be able to act, but their actions are part of the predetermination. Hence, what they decide to do does have causal impact on the world, but what they decide is predetermined. It is part of this predetermination that they do not believe that their choices are predetermined. Hence, the appearance of human choice is itself a feature of this being the best of all possible worlds.

In general, the Jewish philosophers favor this kind of soft determinism. God, but only God, can be said to have "free will" (*ratson chofshi*),[39] where human beings are said, instead, merely to have "choice" (*bechirah*). None of this is seen to be a compromise of divine power and goodness.

Where the real problem arises, at least for the Aristotelian Jewish philosophers, is with matter. Matter is the principle of individuation and indeterminacy. To the extent that what is is material it is unknowable, even by God, and to that extent the world is individuated. Without matter

---

[38] Abraham ibn Daud, *The Exalted Faith.* English translation and commentary by N. Samuelson (Rutherford, Madison, et al.: Fairleigh Dickinson University Press, and London and Toronto: Associated University Presses, 1986).

[39] It is not even clear that God's will is "free" in the sense that he can will other than he wills, for it can be argued that God necessarily wills only what is best. His will is free only in the sense that it is not subject to external-to-God determination.

there are no individuals – only forms or classes or ideas. With matter there is indeterminacy, even for God. Hence, to the extent, but only to the extent, that there is material there is room for human freedom, but this freedom is at the cost of divine power.

It is with this last sentence that the so-called "free will defense" arises. In Christian terms, God allows free will, and therefore indeterminacy, because a world in which some agents can freely choose to obey God's commandments is a better world than one in which they are forced to obey. Gale considers a number of versions of this argument, the most important of which is Plantinga's,[40] which Gale rejects, primarily on the grounds that it takes the Bible too literally. The proposed solutions to the problem are all too anthropomorphic. I agree completely with Gale.

What is wrong, at least from the perspective of Jewish philosophy and theology, with all of these arguments is twofold. First, they are based on the presumption of some positive knowledge, namely, of what it means to say that God is perfect. This in fact claims too much. What we know about God is that whatever it is that we know, it is not God. For Buber, this definition is what it means to call God "the eternal thou." For Rosenzweig's student, Emmanuel Levinas, it is what it means to call God "the wholly other."

Second, the kind of knowledge involved here is the wrong kind of knowledge. God reveals himself through prophecy, but what is revealed cannot be described in positive, literally interpreted, propositions. It is a knowledge of a different kind, an awareness of the presence of an other in the present. From this awareness, which is revelation, arises content – the kind of claims that can be judged in what Rosenzweig called the "unspoken language" of the logic of positivist philosophy and science. However, these propositions are human responses to the revelation, and not the revelation itself.

In this respect revelation is like creation. We can know about creation, from science and from the Scriptures, but what we know is what follows from creation; not creation itself. In terms of modern astrophysics, we have some knowledge of the first few moments after creation through to the present, but not the moment of creation itself. It is an end-limit on what we know. That knowledge that we cannot know is what it means for scientists to call the moment of creation a "singularity." The same is the case with revelation. What we can know from revelation is the Torah that is produced in response to the encounter, but the encounter itself

---

[40] In *God and Other Minds* (Ithaca: Cornell University Press, 1967) and *The Nature of Necessity* (Oxford: Oxford University Press, 1975).

cannot be known. What is for creation a "singularity" is for revelation a pure "presence of the presence (*shechinah*)." It is what Levinas interprets Scripture to mean by Moses knowing God "face to face," that is, as pure presence in the presence of the other pure presence.

CONCLUSION

I have now dealt with the last external authority that could raise questions or issues to challenge the formulated belief in revelation – contemporary philosophy of religion. Of all the authorities surveyed, it has been the least rewarding. Unlike the others it has offered nothing new to enlighten the task.

Physics provides information that enriches our understanding of God's revelation of the created world, and evolutionary psychology enriches our understanding of what it means for the human to be the recipient of divine revelation. However, modern analytic philosophy of religion has told us very little that can inform our understanding of what it means for God to be the transmitter of revelation. If anything, in this case the influence ought to be reversed, for a knowledge of Jewish sources can significantly inform (and, I think, improve) the general philosophic discussion of who and what is God.

The critical failing of all of the proofs considered above is that they do not give sufficient credence to the judgment that there is no positive knowledge of God. They move too easily from Anselm's proper definition of God as "a being no greater than which can be conceived" to the improper definition of God as a most perfect being. This weakness was especially apparent in the above consideration of the so-called atheological proofs.

The modern philosophers of religion considered in the final section of this chapter all assumed that their task was to decide, relatively independently of any data from actual religions, what can be said about God and what is the truth value of these claims. This way of proceeding is radically different than the way philosophers work in most other areas. When philosophers practice philosophy of science, for example, their speculation presupposes specific bodies of scientific statements. Philosophers of religion presuppose no such relevant data, and it is in this (erroneous) assumption that most of the problems with modern philosophy of religion arise. If we presume no data, there are no limits on what can be said, and it is very unlikely that anything intelligible can be said without limits, without rules beyond mere logic to direct the speculation.

We have seen the modern philosophers of religion generate paradoxes out of an assumed positive definition of God, and these paradoxes have been used to deny God's existence. The paradoxes themselves are not new. As we have seen, all of them have been discussed, centuries ago, in the texts of classical Jewish philosophy. Those discussions are subsumed in the presentations in the first part of this book.

Richard Gale's solution to all of the stated paradoxes in the atheological proofs was to limit God's perfection. However, such a limitation is not really a limitation. It only seems to be, and the source of the illusion is the belief that God can be conceived of in positive terms. This is certainly how these discussions were treated in classical Jewish philosophy. Its issue was how to best understand what the Hebrew Scriptures say about God, where "best" means "most believable." In forming their conclusions these philosophers used for a schema a mixture of Platonic and Aristotelian natural philosophy. They were committed to the philosophy only as a best available way to interpret Scripture. However, the real, or primary, commitment was not to this particular kind of philosophy. Rather, it was to the truth of the Hebrew Scriptures and the usefulness of philosophy in discovering that truth.

These philosophers held up perfect knowledge as a personal ideal, but they did not believe that they or anyone else had attained it. They turned to the published thought of Plato and Aristotle for a schema not because it was perfect but because it was better than any other alternative available to them. That at least in principle other alternatives existed was what they learned from discovering the limitations of their accounts of God.

Therefore, the claimed paradoxes of the atheological arguments do not function as disproofs of God's existence; rather they highlight what the classical Jewish philosophers and modern Jewish theologians basically took for granted – that no philosophical worldview can be completely adequate in explaining the truth of the revealed text of the Hebrew Scriptures.

Gale grants that these paradoxes do not constitute valid disproofs of God's existence. For him too, what they do is highlight the need to reconstruct our understanding of God. He takes the right direction for such a reconstruction to lie in abandoning the claim of divine perfection in favor of a more finite view of God in line with the theological proposals of American Pragmatists like William James. For the immediate concern here – to see what philosophers like Gale say about God that would raise issues about our understanding of the God of revelation out of the sources of Judaism – Gale's formulation of the problem and his suggested solution are not relevant.

I am not claiming that God is either perfect or imperfect, limited or unlimited, because I am not claiming that God is anything at all. Rather, I affirm, in keeping with the Maimonidean tradition of negative theology, that God can only be defined by not being anything that is. Furthermore, this understanding of God functions – with respect to interpreting the biblical and rabbinic tradition of divine revelation through the ever expanding Torah – in the way that Rosenzweig described what it means for God to reveal himself to the human. Revelation is not content; it is rather the pure presence of God in love; the claimed content is only the human response to that love, and, in the case of the people Israel, the Hebrew Scriptures are the record of that response.

As such, the Hebrew Scriptures are authoritative for belief and behavior – "authoritative" but not determinative. We are to decide for ourselves what is right to believe as well as what is right to do, but decisions are not made in psychological vacuums. They are made in societies, out of inherited sources of authority.

For religious Jews the Torah is such an authority. Hence, thinking about what is true and what is good – what is right – begins with thinking about what these sacred texts say, and thinking about them seriously. "Seriously" here means that we favor them in our deliberations, but to favor them does not mean that they have the final say. We first decide what they mean, guided by our literary tradition of commentary, and then, having made this determination, consider if what they say is right. If it is not, then we do not abandon our authorities; rather, we reconstruct them so that what we say becomes part of the continuous tradition of commentary from the past and into the future. The process never ends, at least not until the end of days.

What we have seen in this section on God and modern philosophy is that philosophy as a discipline raises no real reasons for me to reconstruct what I have to say about my understanding, from Maimonides and Rosenzweig, of God as the revealer of Torah. The theological proofs considered above do not prove that God exists in the way that they were intended to do. They fail, first, because the God of whom they speak is not our God. They speak of a perfect being, but for us such a deity, even if it does exist, is an idol, that is, it is not our God of revelation (or of creation for that matter). Second, they fail because they cannot demonstrate that their deity necessarily exists in all possible worlds. At best they only demonstrate that this God exists in the kinds of worlds that their philosophy presupposes, and these are in the end only some of the possible worlds, whether or not they are the actual one, which cannot in itself be known, at least not with the desired certainty.

The atheological proofs accomplish even less. They purport to be proofs that God does not exist, whereas in fact all they do is highlight inadequacies in the philosophical language used to interpret who or what God is. One would think that by highlighting these inadequacies they would be informative, and therefore useful to this theological enterprise, but, alas, they are not even that, for the issues they raise are not new. The classical Jewish philosophers dealt with them, and their solutions became part of the intellectual inheritance that informs this Maimonidean/Rosenzweigian understanding of God as the revealer of the Hebrew Scriptures.

What philosophy cannot do, biblical scholarship may do. Even on the weak understanding of revelation, it is assumed that the Hebrew Scriptures are in some sense divine, a human response to their authors' encounter with the divine presence. They are, as such, a testimony to that revelatory encounter. However, as a testimony, as we have seen above, they are as valid as the bearers of the testimony can be judged to be honest, and there is reason to believe that they are not men of integrity. This final challenge arises from the academic field of biblical criticism. It offers the most difficult questions that have to be faced about the believability of the revelation, which is why they were put off to the end of the book. It is now time to face them.

CHAPTER 8

Are the Hebrew Scriptures revealed?

REVIEW

In the first part of this book I developed a conception of revelation as a relationship between God and the people Israel out of which arises a form of content-information (i.e., of communication) called "Torah." This view was developed out of Jewish sources, namely, the Hebrew Scriptures, classical Jewish philosophy, and modern Jewish theology. Several individual voices were involved in forming this conception, but the dominant ones were those of Maimonides in philosophy and Rosenzweig in theology.

The second part of the book has been an examination of how believable this conception of revelation is. With this chapter that discussion will be concluded. Here I have been looking at sources of authority outside Judaism in order to see if they raise issues that can undermine a reasonable belief in the doctrine of revelation as here presented. Those sources have been both philosophical and scientific.

In chapter 5 I considered philosophical issues from contemporary ethics that forced me to reformulate what I took from Rosenzweig as a general concept of revelation. I had to remove the implicit racism in the conception of Israel that he absorbed from Jewish philosophy, primarily from Judah Halevi,[1] and I had to disavow the irrationalism in

---

[1] Both Judah Halevi and his remote disciple, Franz Rosenzweig, had important sources for their racial readings of the chosenness of Israel. As we have seen (in chapter 1), the biblical text, when taken literally, defines a hierarchy of species of creatures based on the commandments given to them – inanimate creations have none, animate creatures have one, humans have seven, Semites (i.e., those whom the Hebrew Scriptures identify as the descendants of Abraham) have eight, and Israel (i.e., the descendants of Abraham's grandson, Jacob) have six hundred and thirteen. Rosenzweig in particular bases his judgment on the grounds that Christians are pagans who become Christians through choice (viz., to be baptized), whereas Jews become Jews by birth (viz., in virtue of their natural mothers, whether or not they are circumcised or named through a Jewish ceremony of initiation). However, this is no simple racist picture, and it should not be read as if it were. The biblical distinction between species is a legal and social distinction, not a biological

his conception of religious belief that he accepted from his European romantic literary tradition. Jews may be born Jews, but the Jewish people are chosen, not because of their blood but because of their Torah. Furthermore, there is no sharp line between rational knowledge and religious belief; rather, the two are part of a single spectrum, differing only in the range of probability assignments to the claims of each.

Next, in chapter 6, I considered challenges from modern science and the analytic philosophy of religion. In this case the adaptations were less problematic. Philosophy of religion added little if anything to the understanding of revelation and God as a revealer, primarily because the very skilled logical exercises of these Anglo-American philosophers – given their apparent unfamiliarity with (at least) serious Jewish philosophical theology – are irrelevant. They deal with a conception of God that has little similarity to our self-revealing deity. What they say about their God is an interesting exercise in logic, of undoubted value for logicians, but (once again) it says hardly anything that is relevant to the discussions in this book.

The case with the sciences is significantly different. What they say is relevant. Still, again, in this case the adaptations required are less dramatic than they are in the challenges from ethics. Both the view of the world from modern physics and the view of the human from modern evolutionary psychology proved to be most compatible with the worldview of Franz Rosenzweig. However, I dissociated myself markedly from the claims of the classical Jewish philosophers. The restructuring of the beliefs here constituted a rejection of their use of the Aristotelian sciences in order to provide a schema for understanding revelation. What resulted is a new interpretation based on modern science that is actually closer to the literal sense of the Hebrew Scriptures than is the classical Jewish philosophical view. There is little difference in the view of the world, but significant difference in the view of the human.

The most important changes involved expanding the conception of the dimensions of the universe while reducing the difference between

one. From the perspective of the biblical text, read literally, at the level of physical nature, all creatures – animate and inanimate, Israelite and non-Israelite – are the same, viz. compounds of the four elements, generated through the activity of earth. Similarly, for the rabbis, human beings of non-Jewish parentage may become Jewish through an act of choice, and there is no legitimate difference between these kinds of Jews. Jews by birth and Jews by choice are subject to all the same communal rules and privileges, without distinction. Even Halevi cannot be read on a simplistic racist interpretation. For him the main difference between Jews and other human beings is that only Jews have the power of prophecy (i.e., the potential to receive divine revelation). For him this is the only difference. However, the children of converts have this power, which would not be possible if the potential for prophecy was to be understood in purely racial terms.

human beings and other creatures. Humans do not differ in kind from other animals. Rather, they occupy one end of a spectrum of ways of consciousness and knowing, biologically driven for the sake of species survival, that are shared by all life forms. Human beings certainly seem to be more intelligent than other animals, but that does not make humans radically different from animals. Rather, what most marks humans as human is their awareness of the other as a radical other whose presence generates moral obligations. It is morality, not cognition, that distinguishes humanity most, and this morality is rooted in revelation.

Underlying the discussion throughout this book is the assumption that it is reasonable to treat the Hebrew Scriptures as they have come down to us through rabbinic tradition as authoritative. I have assumed that they must in some sense be treated as revealed. The question has not been whether they are revealed, but what sense we can make out of believing in them. However, there is good reason to question this most fundamental assumption, and that reason for doubt comes from the modern academic study of the Bible. This discipline is the source of the most serious challenge to the claim that revelation is believable and it is to this challenge I will now turn.

THE BIBLE AS A PIOUS FRAUD

Historical background

Late in the nineteenth century the Christian German Bible scholar, Julius Wellhausen, put forth a thesis, known as the "Documentary Hypothesis," that the five books of Moses (i.e., the Torah) are a composite work of no single authorship, put together from previously existing materials that themselves are composite works of no single author. In making this claim he identified four basic layers – (1) a source called "J" that consists primarily of narratives in which God is called by the proper name of *yhvh*; (2) a parallel source called "E" that consists primarily of narratives in which God is called by the general term *el* or *elohim*; (3) a source called "D" that constitutes primarily the Book of Deuteronomy, namely, the text of what is prima facie Moses' discourses to the new generation of Israelites after forty years in Sinai, immediately before Moses' death and the initiation of Israel's conquest of the land of Canaan; and (4) a source called "P" that is made up of priestly laws dispersed through the entire Pentateuch.

Wellhausen's work was not entirely original. As we shall see below, it is a modern reconstruction of ancient challenges, by non-Jewish religious communities, to the authenticity of rabbinic Judaism. Also, Wellhausen's thesis builds upon the work of earlier German academic Bible scholars, notably Karl Heinrich Graf and Wilhelm Vatke. However, it is Wellhausen's synthesis of these earlier positions that becomes, in a sense, a foundational text for the modern academic field of biblical studies.

Since Wellhausen first published his *Prolegomena zur Geschichte Israels* in 1885 the hypothesis has undergone substantial change, and, undoubtedly, will continue to do so into the future. However, the essential claims remain the same: (1) the Hebrew Scriptures in general, and the Pentateuch in particular, are a composite work from earlier, equally composite layers; (2) modern academic studies in fields such as linguistics, literature, and archeology can help the historian to identify the layers; and (3) the task of the historian of the biblical period is to identify the human author or authors of each source.

Again, the narrative that results from these studies undergoes significant change in each generation of biblical scholarship, and there are important disagreements between these scholars in any particular generation, including the present one. This scholarly non-consensus itself is for present purposes an important consideration, because it affects the logical weight that must be given to scholarly claims in this field vis-à-vis judgments about the believability of the Jewish doctrine of revelation.

For now, however, I will set aside the question of how to assess the relevance of modern academic biblical studies to my interest in Jewish philosophical theology. I will first present a summary of what may count as a reasonable contemporary consensus about the narrative of the history of the text of the Hebrew Scriptures.

The story I will summarize is the one presented by Richard Elliott Friedman in *Who Wrote the Bible?* [2] Friedman is a professor of biblical studies at the University of California, San Diego and a student of Harvard University's Frank Moore Cross. Cross's version of the Documentary Hypothesis constitutes a kind of "orthodoxy" in this ever evolving field of scholarship, and Friedman is one of his more prominent disciples. What recommends his *Who Wrote the Bible?* as a focus text, besides the credentials of its author within the field, is its comprehensiveness and clarity. The picture of the history of the Bible that emerges can be summarized as follows.

---

[2] San Francisco: HarperCollins, 1989.

The Israelites emerge as the dominant people in the geographic region of the contemporary state of Israel around 1200 BCE. Politically they are ruled by interrelated but distinct groups of priests and military leaders. Out of the military leaders (called "judges") emerges a united monarchy – the first king being Saul, the second David, and the third Solomon. During the reign of David the city of Jerusalem is conquered and made the political capital. At these times there are different groups of priests who administer different sanctuaries throughout the Israelite state. Among the priesthood three groups in particular are to be distinguished: (1) "Aaronide" priests, a clan of priests who trace their descent back to Aaron; (2) "Mushite" priests, a clan of priests who trace their descent back to Moses; and (3) other clans of priests of less distinguished pedigree who function throughout the land in a diversity of locations. Interest here is solely in the Aaronide and Mushite clans.

When David becomes king and establishes Jerusalem as his capital, he brings to the city two governing priests – Zadok and Abiathar. Zadok is an Aaronide, whose clan, until then, functioned out of the southern city of Hebron, located within David's familial tribe of Judah. Abiathar is a Mushite, whose clan, until then, functioned out of the northern city of Shilo. By bringing both to the capital David responded to the political reality of the power rivalries between the different tribes under the newly created monarchy. This compromise lasted only one generation. Solomon felt sufficiently strong that he could turn the power over exclusively to his Judean priesthood. Hence, while Zadok remains, Abiathar is expelled, thereby disenfranchising the northern tribes and its dominant Mushite priesthood.

Following the death of Solomon, a civil war breaks out between the north and the south, and in this case, unlike the American experience, the northern rebels are successful and establish an independent state of their own. The civil war occurred in the year 922 BCE. The northern kingdom of Israel experiences a series of subsequent rebellions and is ruled by a variety of different royal dynasties. However, the Mushite priesthood centered in Shilo remains stable, giving the nation whatever degree of political stability it had. The southern kingdom of Judah remains relatively stable as well, in both monarchy and priesthood. All kings are members of the Davidic dynasty, all governing priests are Aaronides, and all of them govern together from the city of Jerusalem.

The northern kingdom of Israel survives for two hundred years, until, in the year 722 BCE, it is conquered and destroyed by the Assyrians. Assyria also invades the southern monarchy of Judah, but (for whatever reason) it fails to conquer it. Judah continues to exist for more than one hundred and thirty-five years. Notable for present purposes during this period are the reigns of two kings – Hezekiah (715–687 BCE) and his great-grandson Josiah (641–609 BCE). It is Hezekiah who centralizes all worship in the Temple of Jerusalem. However, the unification lasts only for his reign. His son, Manasseh, reestablishes the local sanctuaries, governed by clans of local (non-Aaronide and non-Mushite) priests.

Hezekiah's theocratic centralization is reinstituted by his great-grandson, Josiah. Josiah was only three years old when he became king. Clearly at that age he could not himself govern, so the real power lay in the hands of his guardians. It is reasonable to speculate that those guardians came from the Aaronide priesthood of Jerusalem. It is in this context that we should interpret the statements in the Bible[3] that in the year 622 BCE Josiah (then twenty-two years old) was informed by the scribe Shaphan that the priest Hilkiah found a "scroll of the Torah" in the Jerusalem Temple. It is this scroll that provided both the legitimization of and blueprint for the cultic reforms of Josiah's reign.

The "discovery" of this scroll of Torah is for present purposes one of the two most critical events in biblical history. I will return to examine it in more detail after I have concluded my historical narrative with the second most critical event.

In the year 587 BCE, Nebuchadnezzar of Babylonia (the conqueror of the Assyrians and their replacement as the dominant empire in the Near East) burns down the city of Jerusalem with its palaces and Temple. He exiles a significant portion of Judah's population to Babylonia and sets up a governor, Gedaliah, to rule the subject nation. Gedaliah is murdered, which brings reprisals from Babylonia, with the result that the remaining Judean leadership flees for refuge to Egypt. Among those who join the exiles in Egypt is the prophet Jeremiah. Notable among the refugees in Babylonia are the prophets Isaiah and Ezekiel.

The exile lasts for about fifty years. Babylonia, the conqueror of Assyria, is itself conquered. The replacement empire is Persian and its ruler is Cyrus. In 538 BCE Persia authorizes the reestablishment of a Jewish state in Judah, and a second Temple is completed just twenty-three years later, in 515 BCE. However, it is a Temple that lacks the ark, cherubim, and Urim and Thummim of the first Temple, and the new state lacks prophets and (most notably) kings. While there are allusions to a Davidic descendant (Zerubbabel) at the beginning of the state,

---

3 2 Kings 22:8 and 2 Chron. 34:14–15.

references to him disappear by the time that Ezra is appointed the city-state's civil governor, with authority over its exclusively Aaronide priesthood, and Nehemiah is named the city-state's military governor. Ezra introduces a series of political and cultic reforms that include cultic centralization with an exclusively Aaronide (Zadokite) priesthood.

Ezra is not only a priest; he is also a "scribe," and, as a scribe, he is associated with a "Torah" (Neh. 8:13). The book of Ezra refers to cultic regulations "written in the Torah of Moses, the man of God" (Ezra 3:2), and Nehemiah says that Ezra, the "priest" and "scribe," read its words to all of the people in the seventh month of his rule (Neh. ch. 8). The reading of this Torah of Moses is the second critical event.

So far I have not said anything that is not explicitly stated in the biblical text. As yet what I have said is only the background for the Documentary Hypothesis. It is not the Hypothesis itself that describes a certain way to understand the historical events described above.

The Documentary Hypothesis

In the version of the Documentary Hypothesis presented by Friedman, the above historical narrative is interpreted as follows: our story begins with two separate narratives of the entire history of the first Jewish polity that are presently situated both in the Torah proper (the Pentateuch) and in what rabbinic Judaism calls the "early prophets" (viz., Joshua, Judges, 1 and 2 Samuel, and 1 and 2 Kings).

One narrative is called the "J" source, because the predominant reference to God is by the name *yhvh*. This source is an oral tradition known to the Aaronide priesthood centered in Hebron. It reflects the understanding of the nation's history from the perspective of the southern territory. Its notable features are that it presents a relatively anthropomorphic conception of a merciful deity, and that it either de-emphasizes the importance of the tribal founders (i.e., the sons of Jacob) or presents them in a negative light, with the lone exception of Judah. The other is called the "E" source, because the predominant reference to God is by the general terms *el* and *elohim*. This source is an oral tradition known to the Mushite priesthood centered in Shilo. It reflects the understanding of the nation's history from the perspective of the northern territory. Its notable features are that it presents a relatively transcendent conception of a deity of justice, locates Jacob at Peni-El in places where J locates him at Hebron, and gives all of Jacob's sons considerably more attention than does J.

J and E were composed sometime after the civil war (in 922 BCE) and before Israel's demise at the hands of the Assyrians (in 722 BCE). We do not know when they reached the form in which we find them in the Hebrew Scriptures. We do know (at least according to the Hypothesis), however, who unified them. It was the priests of Shilo.

The author of the "D" source also comes from the class of Shilo priests. As noted above, D is primarily the main part of our present book of Deuteronomy as well as the books of the "early prophets" in the Hebrew Scriptures. Its signature feature is that it calls for the centralization of all cultic activities in Jerusalem. The composer (of original material) and editor (who adapted earlier materials to fit his creative plan) of D is identified by Friedman as either the prophet Jeremiah and/or his scribe Baruch ben Neriyah.[4]

D is not our first written text. Predating it was at least the so-called "Covenant Code" – Exod. 21:1–27; 22:1–30; 23:1–33, whose source is also attributed to the Shilo priesthood who wrote E. However, the Covenant Code is only a priestly law code. It is not a sacred narrative, and therefore significantly different from what we would recognize as a "Torah from Moses." It is D that is our first "Torah" so understood. Note further that D is not intended to include the Covenant Code, but to replace it. As such, D is a politically radical document that, while appearing to be conservative (i.e., to conserve what had always been the nation's laws), is in fact a revolutionary displacement of the existing order.[5]

D is our first written Torah and, if the Documentary Hypothesis is correct, it is what W. M. L. De Wette in 1805 called a "pious fraud."[6] At least on the interpretation considered here, the D document was composed by a single individual (or, a small group of individuals) with the conscious intent of passing his/their creation off to a general public as an authentic copy of the original constitution between God and the

---

[4] The Babylonian Talmud (Baba Batra 15a) identifies Jeremiah as the author of 1 and 2 Kings, as it identifies Moses as the author of the Pentateuch, and Joshua as the author of Joshua.

[5] Actually this statement is more radical than anything that Friedman himself explicitly says. As we shall see below, Friedman's intent is to play down the radicalness of the reforming nature of each emerging written document in order to avoid the charge of their being "pious frauds." Other Bible scholars are less discreet. For example, Bernard M. Levinson, near the conclusion of his study of the laws of Deuteronomy, says that "Deuteronomy's polemic, although it does not name its object, rewrites literary history. By circumscribing Sinai and silencing the Covenant Code, the redactors of Deuteronomy sought to clear a textual space for Moab as the authentic – and exclusive – supplement to the original revelation (Deut 28:69)"; *Deuteronomy and the Hermeneutics of Legal Innovation* (New York and Oxford: Oxford University Press, 1997), p. 153.

[6] See Friedman, *Who Wrote the Bible?*, p. 102.

nation of Israel centuries before. That makes it clearly a fraud, something that intentionally claims to be what it is known by its author(s) not to be. Whether or not the lie was "pious" depends on the intention of the liars. That, for now at least, remains an open question. In any case, it is sufficient to note that, if it is a fraud, it is not the last one in this story of the composition of the Bible. As D was written in the guise of a conservative work whose real intention was revolutionary, so other frauds were composed that do to D what D did to his/its predecessors (at least to the Covenant Code).

I mentioned before that Jeremiah, together with Baruch, wrote two versions of D. A first (Dtr^1) was composed during the reign of Josiah, which is to say, no later than 609 BCE. In this original version the narrative of our first Torah concludes with the glorification of this monarch's reign. As such, the tale it tells has a happy ending. It begins with greatness (with Moses and the theophany at Sinai) and ends with greatness (with Josiah and his cultic restoration). However, the story does not have a happy ending. A still fairly young Josiah (thirty-five years old) is killed in battle, his successors decentralize (again) the cult, and the nation is destroyed by Babylonia in 587 BCE. The happy ending turns out not to be true, so our author reconstructs his narrative with a new, truer, account (Dtr^2).

What was written as a, so to speak, "comedy" (i.e., not a funny book, but a book that has a happy ending) is transformed into a "tragedy" (i.e., a book that has an unhappy ending). The nation returns to its former sinful ways, and that turn leads to its destruction. Hence, D establishes a tragic view of history as its model for the nation's self-understanding.

It is not a picture without hope, for there is hope of restoration. But the restoration itself is not part of the narrative. If there is hope, as there seems to be, that hope lies beyond the world that the narrative presents. Within the world of the story, life ends in death, not in rebirth. As such, D pioneers the way the Jewish people will continue to understand their world and their lives. It is not a picture of the world as they would want it to be. Whatever the intention of the author of the Hebrew Scriptures, it was not to create a fantasy. Rather, it is a model for understanding the world as it is. Whatever the quality of fraud in its authorship, it does not intend to present a view of reality that is not true. In this sense it is not a fraud, and perhaps that is what it means to call the lie "pious." It is a question to which I will return shortly, but I have not yet finished my summary of the Documentary Hypothesis.

At some time after the destruction of the northern kingdom (722 BCE), during the reign of Hezekiah (715–687 BCE) an Aaronide priest(s) composes and edits his/their own distinctive sacred history of Israel, comparable in form to Jeremiah's, that focuses its happy ending on the reign of Hezekiah rather than on the reign of Josiah. The name scholars have given to this fourth source is "P."[7] If this thesis is correct, it is P that incorporates more ancient legal material such as the Holiness Code. On this reading, Jeremiah's D was written to supplant P as well as J and E.[8] The combined JE favored Moses over Aaron. P was composed by an Aaronide priest whose intent was to rewrite history in a way that would favor his ancestry and, consequently, his clan. Hence, what P did to JE – rewrite sacred history and law, effecting a revolution in conception and politics under the guise of preserving both – D does to P. However, what D does to P and P does to JE, the final redactor of the Pentateuch (called "R") does to D.[9] This final redactor is Ezra.

In the end, Friedman reaches the same conclusion that most of those biblical scholars before him had reached – the Torah that we possess was a "pious fraud" perpetrated on subsequent centuries of Jewish people by the fifth-century-BCE priest and scribe, Ezra, and his authority came not from God and from revelation and not even from previous tradition but from the power of the Persian empire. The Torah that defines Judaism and (subsequently) Christianity and that deeply influenced the third Abrahamic faith, Islam, is the creation of the power of a pagan nation, Persia, by Judeans who served in its employ and by its authority.

Historic precedence for the charge of falsification

The claim that the Torah upon which the Jewish people base their faith was a fraudulent creation by Ezra is an ancient charge. I cannot say what its origin is, but no Jewish philosopher deals with it more extensively than does Abraham ibn Daud in his *Exalted Faith*.[10] In this case the charge – raised by twelfth-century-CE Christians, Karaites, and Muslims, but most

---

[7] The earlier accepted scholarly view was that P was later than D and in fact P is the work of the final redactor (R).

[8] Jeremiah 8:8 reads, "How do you say, 'We are wise, and Yahweh's Torah is with us'? In fact, here, it was made for a lie, the lying pen of scribes." On Friedman's reading, (*Who Wrote the Bible?*, p. 209), the scribes are the authors of P and their "Torah" is the P source.

[9] Friedman calls this "The Great Irony" (ibid., p. 217). His phrase expresses an image of a trickster deity. This God of humor uses irony in order (paraphrasing Gilbert and Sullivan) to make the punishment fit the crime, so that (paraphrasing the rabbis) those who live by the word die by the word.

[10] See Abraham ibn Daud, *The Exalted Faith*. Edited Hebrew translation by Gershon Weiss, and translated into English with commentary by N. Samuelson (Rutherford, Madison, et al.: Fairleigh Dickinson University Press, and London and Toronto: Associated University Presses, 1986), Book II, Basic Principle 5, pp. 184–216.

forcefully argued by Muslims – is against the authenticity of the standard rabbinic text of the Hebrew Scriptures. That text rests for its authority on a tradition of transmission, and a tradition has no greater epistemic authority than its weakest link. If the tradition is not continuous and/or if one link in that tradition is not reliable, the tradition itself is not reliable. The weak link is Ezra.

First, it is discontinuous with its sources, because from the beginning of the Babylonian exile (587 BCE) until Ezra reads his copy of the law of Moses (458 BCE) there is no record of a copy of this text. There is an "ancient tradition," noted in the first–second-century-CE pseudepigraphic *Fourth Book of Ezra*, that the original scroll of the Torah was burned in the first Temple, and that Ezra, under the guidance of divine revelation, restored it.[11] Perhaps that is what Ezra (at least) believed he was doing when he redacted the Torah. However, that assumes that he was a man of good character, and there are reasons to doubt it, not the least of which are the reasons alluded above, namely, that he was a representative of a foreign and pagan government whose ultimate authority to rule over Judah was force of arms.

Ibn Daud does his best to respond to this line of argument against the reliability of Israel's Torah, but it is his most difficult challenge, and it may be argued that his efforts did not succeed. In his attempt to construct a theological history of ancient Israel that demonstrates the continuity of a general consensus about its central text, Ibn Daud is forced to distort Jewish history in a way that anyone familiar with its history would recognize as a distortion.[12]

This weakness may be one reason why Ibn Daud's initiation of Jewish Aristotelianism did not have the impact on subsequent generations of Jewish philosophers that the later *Guide of the Perplexed* by Maimonides had. It may also explain why the citation of biblical texts ceased to function in logical arguments in the way they had functioned in earlier works of Jewish philosophy. In a deductive argument, the conclusions are as strong as the premises. Hence, a philosopher will look for premises that are as indubitable as possible. Earlier philosophers, such as Saadia, draw the premises of their arguments from common-sense consensus, foundational principles of contemporary science, and biblical texts. Later philosophers, Jewish philosophers after Ibn Daud, cease to use biblical

---

[11] Friedman, *Who Wrote the Bible?*, p. 224.
[12] See Abraham ibn Daud, *The Exalted Faith*. English translation and commentary by Samuelson, pp. 203–204. Also see the introduction to Gershom Cohen's translation of Ibn Daud's *The Book of Tradition* (Philadelphia: Jewish Publication Society, 1967).

texts as premises. Hence, for example, a late Jewish Aristotelian such as Gersonides constructs arguments based on the interpretation of biblical texts, but he makes those arguments strictly separate from his philosophical demonstrations. No biblical text is ever cited by him for authority in a strictly philosophical argument.

What was a critical line of challenge in classical Jewish philosophy is no less a challenge today. My interpretation of revelation as a believable doctrine is based on the assumption that in some significant way the existent Hebrew Scriptures testify to encounters with God and the Jewish people. How can they be treated with such authority if they are the product of a series of frauds?

IS THE BIBLE BELIEVABLE?

If the Torah is a fraud, can it be believed? Certainly the answer must be negative if we accept a strong interpretation of revelation, for, without a doubt, if we accept as plausible the account of modern academic Bible scholars about the evolution of the Hebrew Scriptures – that they emerged through a process of redaction of independently edited sources from even earlier independent oral and written materials, all of human origin – then we cannot with consistency claim that the Torah is revealed, where "revelation" means a content that is transmitted directly from God to human beings. The claims of modern Bible scholarship and a strong belief in *Torah mi-sinai* simply are incompatible. The affirmation of one as true entails a denial of the truth of the other.

What if the Torah is an "impious fraud," that is, what if its different authors not only said what they knew was not true, but had motives for saying it that were purely self-serving? Can we still say that the Torah was revealed even in the professed weak sense of revelation as divine inspiration?

Consider, for example, the recent study of the Book of Deuteronomy by the well-recognized, contemporary academic Bible scholar, Bernard Levinson.[13] Although Levinson's presentation of the origin of the legal content of the Book of Deuteronomy does not say so explicitly,[14] Levinson's editors of D are not only frauds, they are impious frauds, for

---

[13] *Deuteronomy and the Hermeneutics of Legal Innovation* (1997).

[14] His interests are exclusively those of a modern Bible scholar who, at least in his academic life, seems to make a sharp separation between what falls within his mind's eye as a scholar and what he may care about beyond that relatively narrow focus – "relatively narrow," that is, from the perspective of philosophy and theology.

the motive guiding all of their legal innovations seems to be power. D priests disenfranchise the priestly authors of the Covenant Code, and, as part of their political coup, they substitute their own account of history and law for their predecessors, all cynically in the name of their predecessors. Then later, post-exilic editors do to D what D had done to P, for the same cynical, impious reasons.[15] If Levinson is right – and certainly Bible scholars should decide this question solely on the basis of the evidence relevant to the text, independent of any consideration of philosophy and theology – then it is difficult to imagine how one can continue to credit the Hebrew Scriptures as a revealed text, even on the weak sense of revelation. This claim of biblical scholarship does seem to qualify as a possible falsification instance of the central thesis of this book, that my reconstructed explanation of the doctrine of revelation, with specific relationship to Judaism, is believable.

However, is the Torah really a fraud at all? Friedman claims that it is not. Specifically with relationship to the laws of P, including the Holiness Code, he argues that D's author "embedded the law code in the P stories. This gave it historical authority. No one had to ask from where these laws came. The text was explicit: they came from God through Moses – and Aaron."[16] What Friedman says here could be said for P (vis-à-vis JE) and R (vis-à-vis D) as well. The author(s) presented what they believed to be the law that constituted the covenant between God and the nation Israel. He/they further believed that competing claims – from JE (i.e., the combined tradition of J and E) and/or from P against the author of D, and from D against the author of R – were in truth not the word of the living God of Israel. Jeremiah, for example, was a prophet who honestly saw his pro-Babylonian pronouncements in truth to be God's words, and interpreted the pronouncements of his rival pro-Assyrian and/or pro-Egyptian prophets to be false testimony, for it did not occur to him that contrary content could be attributed to an encounter with the same deity. The same can be said for all of the prophets, and it could also be said for the authors of the various sources of the Hebrew Scriptures. They stated what they believed God's word to be and located that word within a historical context, the details of which were drawn from their own oral and literary national traditions. When they composed their texts, they believed their creations to be the word of God, which, as such, was a true presentation of the Torah of Moses. However, that does not mean that they believed they were forming a document that would be treated, as it

---

[15] See Levinson, *Deuteronomy*, pp. 152–157.   [16] Friedman, *Who Wrote the Bible?*, p. 215.

came to be at some time during the second commonwealth, as a literal copy of the manuscript that Moses received directly from the hand of God on Mt. Sinai.

On this interpretation I can affirm without an accusation of fraud, pious or impious, a doctrine of sources produced by different people at different times that come together into a single edited text that eventually comes to be understood literally as what God dictated to Moses. Furthermore, such an interpretation would support, even add verification to, my proposed weak theory of revelation as divine inspiration. Furthermore, it is, so understood, evidence of the wonderful way that God's presence motivates human beings who are open to it to produce creations far beyond anything they could have independently devised themselves.

Implied by this final examination of Friedman's thesis is also an (at least potentially) different perspective on my earlier answer to the challenge raised by Levinson's scholarship. D and P need not be revealed, but that does not mean that the Hebrew Scriptures are not revealed. Not even Ezra is the final redactor. His work – the Pentateuch and the early prophets – is combined with later works called "prophets" as well as still-later works called "writings" to form what we call the Hebrew Scriptures or "Tanakh."

None of these Bible scholars discussed here have dealt with the identity of the final editor. I have no idea who it (they) is (are). The final redactor, be it an individual or a committee, lived some time after Ezra and some time before Judah Ha-Nasi compiled the Mishnah (viz., in 200 CE),[17] most likely after the destruction of the second Jewish state and Temple.

Certainly this final editor bears some resemblance to the earlier editors whom I have considered here, but he (or she or it or they) is not the same, and there is no reason (at least not yet) to think that he was a fraud, even if the sources were fraudulent. Whatever the origins of the materials, this last editor had to struggle with the reality of a destroyed Temple and Jewish state, and somehow he put together the texts in such a way that they would make sense out of all of Jewish history up to that point in time.

Perhaps it should have done so, but, at least understood literally (as we saw in part I), it did not. The destruction of the second Temple could not be handled in the way that the destruction of the first Temple was handled. No rewriting of the history and the laws of Scripture would work. Instead, what was needed was a non-literal way to read the already

---

[17] I believe this is a very highly conservative dating range of time. A more precise dating is not relevant to present purposes.

existing Scriptures that the final redactor(s) assembled, and that "way" was provided by the development of a rabbinic tradition of textual interpretation – first in the Midrash, then in the work of the classical Jewish philosophers, and finally in the writings of the modern Jewish theologians considered in this book. It is their work that is in the final analysis the believable response of the Jewish people to the continuous presence of the divine.

Friedman himself acknowledges in his concluding chapter that the unified Bible is a far richer work than any of the sources from which it was composed. A God who is both a creator deity guided by uncompromising universal justice (which is to say the laws of nature apply equally to all beings without qualification, including their moral or spiritual character) and a revealer deity guided by his concrete love for a particular people (which is to say that God reveals himself to individual prophets who have no special entitlement in virtue of family background or even in virtue of talent to be prophets) in specific places at specific times is a far richer deity than either a mere creator deity of nature (such as the God of Spinoza and, for that matter, of Einstein) or a mere merciful deity of revelation whose professed unlimited loving nature is contradicted by the hard reality of most of our lived lives. A mere deity of science is not rich enough to capture reality, while a mere deity of loving self-revelation is simply not real at all. Only through the combination of the two source concepts (if at least this moderate version of the Documentary Hypothesis is accepted) do we uncover a text that is rich enough (as the Bible is) to capture our experience of reality as we truly experience it.

My weak interpretation of the Documentary Hypothesis also seems to agree with Friedman, who says that the "mixing of the sources into one text enriched the interpretive possibilities of the Bible for all time."[18] In other words, our Torah, no matter what the origins of its sources and even independent of the original intent of its various editors and redactors, is a product of encounter with the divine that, as such, transcends mere human creativity.

---

[18] Friedman, *Who Wrote the Bible?*, p. 236

Conclusion

I have now concluded my philosophical-theological study of the concept of revelation from a Jewish perspective. Revelation is one of three
foundational beliefs of Judaism. Together with the doctrines of creation
and redemption, these three constitute dogmas of Jewish religious faith –
dogmas in the sense that without them the only rationally viable interpretation of Jews choosing to be Jewish would be as an accidental fact
of birth.

The first part of the book examined Jewish sources of philosophy and
theology in order to formulate a best possible interpretation of what the
concept of revelation means, where "best" means both (1) consistent with
the totality of historical Jewish sources as well as contemporary Jewish
religious life and practice, and (2) most worthy of assent by reasonable
human beings who care that what they believe should be true, that is,
be consistent with how they experience the world, other human beings,
and God.

I looked at the Hebrew Scriptures themselves, classical Jewish philosophy, and modern Jewish theology. A full range of all of these sources
was considered. However, the focus was more on some texts than others.
Here the choices were made primarily on grounds that the texts chosen
are "best" in the sense stated above, that is, most believable. In the case
of the Hebrew Scriptures the focus was on the Pentateuch; in the case
of classical Jewish philosophy the focus was on Maimonides' *Guide of the
Perplexed*; and in the case of modern Jewish theology the focus was on
Rosenzweig's *The Star of Redemption*.

I then settled on a single general interpretation of revelation, and
began to explore whether or not there are good reasons, external to
the internal logic of these Jewish texts themselves, not to believe what
was otherwise concluded to be reasonable. Part I of this book was the
study of the internal Jewish sources; part II examined challenges from
external texts to the conclusions of part I. In this case the challenges came

from political ethics, modern physics, evolutionary psychology, analytic philosophy, and source-critical Bible studies.

Can we now say that we, as reasonable people, can believe in revelation? I would say yes, but not in just any conception of it. I distinguished two senses of the term "revelation" as it applies to the traditional rabbinic affirmation of *torah mi-sinai*, that is, of the claim that God gave the Torah to Moses at Sinai. I isolated a strong sense of the term that claims that God in fact speaks words to people, and those words are the content of revelation. On this strong interpretation, the words written in at least the Pentateuch are words literally spoken by God, as are the words attributed to God in the biblical books of the prophets. Furthermore, the rabbinic determinations of what those words mean also have the status of revelation, that is, of the words that God speaks through the rabbis to the nation Israel.

My conclusion has been that revelation, so understood, is not a reasonable belief, and I arrived at this judgment primarily through closely and carefully reading traditional Jewish sources. First, a literal interpretation of the Hebrew Scriptures, especially in the light of Jewish history, cannot be true. Furthermore, rabbinic Judaism has never taken the literal meaning of the words of the Bible to be what the Bible really means.

Second, based on the philosophy of Maimonides, what we know about God is that we know nothing about him, and this lack of positive knowledge of God defines him. Furthermore, any positive attribution of anything humanly knowable to God is not only wrong; it is blasphemous. Hence, on the authority of Maimonides at least (but not only Maimonides), to take the words of the Scriptures, let alone the pronouncements of the rabbinic interpreters of those words, as literally constituting the word and will of God is to be guilty of what both the Bible and rabbinic Judaism consider to be the gravest of all sins, the sin of idolatry.

Third, based on the theology of Rosenzweig, what we learn about God from Maimonides' negative theology is that to know God is to encounter a presence so radically other from ourselves that the experience can have no humanly expressible content whatsoever. However, the intensity of the divine presence is such that a human response to it is inescapable, and that response gives revelation the content that it, in itself, necessarily lacks.

To understand revelation as a pure experience that inspires human response with content constitutes what was at the beginning specified as the second, weaker sense of the term "revelation." The notion of revelation as divine inspiration has been associated primarily with modern liberal interpretations of Judaism in opposition to modern Orthodoxy. I have argued here that this so-called "liberal" understanding reflects far better than its alternatives an authentic understanding of how the term revelation functioned in all of the pre-modern Jewish religious texts, from the Hebrew Scriptures throughout the evolving history of written commentaries on these texts by our rabbis. Furthermore, not only is the belief in revelation as divine inspiration the most authentically Jewish interpretation of the concept; it is also its most believable interpretation.

Let me, in conclusion, present a final word on what I at least mean when I affirm my belief in revelation. At some time in our pre-national past a group of Israelites, under a leadership whom our textual tradition has called "Moses," encountered God. That encounter produced a response, and that response is the defining covenant between God and the Jewish people. At first the terms of the covenant were undefined. They were no more than a pledge of love between the newly formed human collective and God. It merely said that God would be a deity for Israel and Israel would be a nation for God. In more specific terms what this pledge meant was that God would protect his people, and the people would obey its deity. At first the people as a collective would go before their deity to learn his will. In time, representatives of the people replaced the people as a whole in these encounters. Later, the place and the means by which these encounters were to take place became increasingly defined until a specific place (a Temple in Jerusalem) was designated with a specific class of people (a Jerusalem priesthood) to represent the people in their attempt to keep faith with their loving pledge to obey their deity's will. Later still, the place is replaced by a text, the Hebrew Scriptures, the priests are replaced by a class of scribes, and this Israelite understanding of relationship with God as defined by text and scribes evolves into a chain of rabbinic tradition, where written rabbinic discussions of the original written texts become themselves revealed texts, devices through which a nation responds to its continuous encounter with its deity.

Do I know that what I have said is true? No. It is a belief, not knowledge. However, it is a reasonable belief, and that is what I have argued for in this book. To believe in revelation as it has been characterized here is more reasonable than any other alternative.

The immediate consequence of this last answer is that I believe, although I do not know, that all Jews ought to accept the interpretation of revelation presented in this book (as well as the interpretation of creation presented in *Judaism and the Doctrine of Creation*) precisely because it is the best (i.e. most consistent with Judaism's literary past and most reasonable) currently available interpretation of the fundamental beliefs that underlie adherence to Judaism. What are the consequences for Jews who do not share this interpretation? If the above argument is correct, they are wrong – wrong that is, only if I am right.

The probability that I am right about revelation may be (as argued here) higher than for any alternative interpretation, but it is relatively low compared with the probability of other religious beliefs such as the doctrine of creation. First, what the tradition of Jewish philosophy says about revelation is less consistent and coherent than what it says about creation, primarily because there is no single foundational text for interpreting revelation as compact yet as clear and detailed as are the opening chapters of the Book of Genesis. Second, there is a significant difference between how our sacred tradition can be related to contemporary science on these two theological issues. Modern science can in fact tell us a great deal about creation – the origin of the universe – independent of a revealed tradition, and that independence is in itself useful, for it enables science to inform (rather than to merely interpret) our understanding of the revealed tradition about creation. Furthermore, the relevant scientific claims in this case, mostly from astrophysics and cosmology, have a reasonably high degree of probability in themselves. The situation, as we have seen, is radically different when we turn to revelation. Here the relevant sciences about the origin of humanity, the ways that humans relate to themselves and others, and the nature of moral judgments – the different disciplines that fall under the generic title of evolutionary psychology – make claims that, in comparison with other disciplines (especially physics), have relatively low degrees of both clarity and probability.

The problem is not with these sciences as such. Rather, the problem is with the subject matter. The world of the human is vastly more complex than is the physical universe, and this difference in complexity affects the clarity and certainty of claims made about both subject matters. In this case, while useful, the sciences in no way inform a religious understanding of revelation at all comparable to their value for the study of creation. The same can be said about the usefulness of the academic humanities, including the field of history, and including the study of the Hebrew Scriptures as history.

Are the claims about truth in this book limited solely to truths for Jews, or are they the kinds of claims that should be affirmed by all people? The question is not clear. It presupposes an understanding of understanding that is, in my judgment, far too simplistic. Language is used in the context of a community of meaning; change the community and what the shared language means changes. Words like "revelation" and sentences like "God revealed the Torah to Moses at Sinai" have one range of meanings in the context of Jewish texts that is shared and not shared more or less in different religious traditions.[1] Nor are facts merely facts. How we know whatever is external to our brains is dependent on how our brains function, and how our brains function is intimately connected with how we use language. Consequently, what is and is not a fact cannot be discussed independently of our language for discussing it. Hence, the "fact" of Moses receiving or not receiving the Torah from God at Sinai is not independent of what it means to assert (or to deny) the related proposition.

If, for example, Christians and Jews mean the same thing when they speak about the revealed status of the Hebrew Scriptures, they should, as reasonable people, make the same affirmations and negations about it, but religious language is simply too rich within different traditions to assume uncritically an identity of meaning. The issue is important. I certainly would welcome Christian philosophical theologians translating what I have said about Jewish philosophy into a language in which what I say can be compared with or studied in terms of Christian philosophical and theological traditions. I would welcome the same in the case of Islam, Hinduism, Buddhism, and the other world religions. I think the more such translations are made between major religious traditions the richer the academic discipline of religious studies would be. However, there is no way to predict without this work of translation the extent to which the truth claims I have deduced here about Jewish religious belief are universal.[2]

Will what I have said here about revelation always be believable? That is unlikely. It is the most reasonable way to understand the doctrine of revelation now, based on the present available data – from both lived experience and from Jewish texts. However, the data change. In the course of time we will have experiences, individually and collectively,

---

[1] I think the closest sharing is with Islam and Roman Catholicism, and with Abrahamic religions in general far more than with Asian religions, including Buddhism.

[2] The conditionality of truth judgment affirmed here is certainly an expression of epistemological contextualism, but it is in no way an affirmation of epistemological subjectivism. For example, "$1 + 1 = 0$" in the context of base two, but not in the context of base ten where "$1 + 1 = 10$." Word and sentence meanings are context dependent even when their veracity is determined by correspondence to an external state of affairs. In my example, different bases are different languages, much as the doctrinal claims of different religions are different languages even when the linguistic tokens used are the same.

sufficiently unique that our perspectives on life will change. There are no substances; only processes. The world does not stand still, and neither does our human experience of it.

Change is continuous and that change will itself change our perspectives on what we think, even about change. There will always arise new texts to guide Jewish religious life, and these new texts will change the way we read past Jewish texts. As the world continually changes, so does the written record of our encounter as a people with God, and that change should change what we think about every Jewish dogma, including revelation. What astrophysics tells us about the world and its origin changes how we read what our tradition says about creation. Similarly, what psychology and cognitive sciences tell us about being human and what theology tells us about being God change how we read what our tradition says about revelation.

By embracing this notion of change, unquestionably we side with a liberal rather than an orthodox understanding of what it means to be spiritually Jewish. However, there is no opposition intended here to a traditional understanding of Judaism. On the contrary, this book is first and foremost an exercise in religious traditionalism.

In this sense also this book is a work in Jewish conservatism – not in any parochial sense that it expresses anything about a conservative movement in opposition to a reform or a reconstructionist movement. All of these movements are institutions in Jewish communal life that are expressions of religious liberalism. With respect to Jewish philosophy and theology the separation between them has no importance. What this book does say, however, that is relevant to all of them, is the following. A Judaism without commitment to taking seriously the entirety of the Jewish past is not a viable Judaism. A Judaism that only takes seriously what that past says about practice but ignores what that past says about belief is also not a viable Judaism. Finally, a Judaism that dismisses reason is also not a viable Judaism. A Judaism that is not reasonable is unbelievable, and a Judaism that is not believable is no real Judaism at all.

> come, gaze with me upon this dome
> of many colored glass, and see
> his mother's pride, his father's joy,
> unto whom duty whispers low
>
> "thou must!" and who replies "I can!"
> (E. E. Cummings)

Works cited

Abraham Ben David Ha-Levi (ibn Daud). *Sefer qabbalah*. English translation by Gershom Cohen. *The Book of Tradition*. Philadelphia: Jewish Publication Society, 1967.

Al-ʿaqida al-rafiʿa. Edited Hebrew translation by Gershon Weiss. English translation by Norbert M. Samuelson. *The Exalted Faith*. Rutherford, Madison, et al.: Fairleigh Dickinson University Press, and London and Toronto: Associated University Presses, 1986.

Allen, Reginald E. (ed.). *Studies in Plato's Metaphysics*. New York: The Humanities Press, 1965.

Alston, William. *Perceiving God*. Ithaca: Cornell University Press, 1991.

Anselm. *St. Anselm's Proslogion*. English translation by M. J. Charlesworth. Notre Dame, IN: Notre Dame University Press, 1979.

Babylonian Talmud. Hebrew–English edition. London: Soncino Press, 1990. Translated into English by Maurice Simon under the editorship of I. Epstein.

Batnitzky, Leora. *Idolatry and Representation: The Philosophy of Franz Rosenzweig Reconsidered*. Princeton: Princeton University Press, 2000.

Bland, Kalman. *The Artless Jew: Medieval and Modern Affirmations of the Visual*. Princeton: Princeton University Press, 2000.

Borowitz, Eugene. *Renewing the Covenant: A Theology for the Postmodern Jew*. Philadelphia: Jewish Publication Society, 1991.

Buber, Martin. *Ich und Du*. Heidelberg: Lambert Schneider, 1958. English translation by Walter Kaufmann. *I and Thou*. New York: Scribner, 1970.

Cassirer, Ernst. *Der Mythus des Staates*. Frankfurt a.M.: Fischer Wissenschaft, 1985. English translation, *The Myth of the State*. New Haven: Yale University Press, 1946.

Chayevsky, Paddy. "Gideon." New York: Dramatist's Play Service, 1998.

Coburn, Robert. "Professor Malcolm on God." *Australasian Journal of Philosophy* 41 (1963), 143–162.

Cohen, Hermann. *Religion der Vernunft aus den Quellen des Judentums*. Wiesbaden: Fourier, 1978. English translation (of 1918 edition) by Simon Kaplan. *The Religion of Reason out of the Sources of Judaism*. New York: Frederick Ungar, 1972.

Copleston, F. C. *Aquinas*, Baltimore: Penguin Books, 1955.

Dawkins, Richard. *The Selfish Gene*. New York and London: Granada Publishing Co., 1978.

Dennett, Daniel. *Darwin's Dangerous Idea: Evolution and the Meanings of Life*. London: Penguin Books, 1995.

Eilberg-Schwartz, Howard. *The Human Will in Judaism: The Mishnah's Philosophy of Intention*. Brown Judaic Studies 103. Atlanta: Scholars Press, 1986.

Frank, Daniel H. and Leaman, Oliver (eds.), *History of Jewish Philosophy*. Routledge History of World Philosophies 2. London and New York: Routledge, 1997.

Freud, Sigmund. *Totem and Taboo*. In the *Standard Edition of the Complete Psychological Works of Sigmund Freud*, vol. XIII. Edited and translated into English by James Strachey with Anna Freud, Alix Strachey, and Alan Tyson. London: Hogarth Press and the Institute of Psycho-Analysis, 1912–13.

Moses and Monotheism. English translation by Katherine Jones. New York: Knopf, 1939.

Friedman, Richard Elliott. *Who Wrote the Bible?* San Francisco: HarperCollins, 1989.

Gale, Richard. *On the Nature and Existence of God*. Cambridge: Cambridge University Press, 1991.

Geach, P. T. "The Third Man Again," in R. E. Allen (ed.), *Studies in Plato's Metaphysics*. New York: The Humanities Press, 1965. Pp. 265–278.

Gibbs, Robert. *Correlations in Rosenzweig and Levinas*. Princeton: Princeton University Press, 1992.

Why Ethics? Signs of Responsibility. Princeton: Princeton University Press, 2000.

Goodenough, Ursula. *The Sacred Depths of Nature*. New York and Oxford: Oxford University Press, 1998.

Guttman, Julius. *Philosophies of Judaism*. English translation by David W. Silverman. Philadelphia: Jewish Publication Society of America, 1964.

Hefner, Philip. *The Human Factor*. Minneapolis: Fortress Press, 1993.

James, William. *The Will to Believe and Other Essays*. New York: Longmans, Green, 1897.

The Varieties of Religious Experience. New York: The Modern Library, 1902.

Kant, Immanuel. *Kritik der Reinen Vernunft*. English translation by N. Kemp Smith. *The Critique of Pure Reason*. London: Macmillan, 1929.

Kellner, Menachem Marc. *Maimonides on Human Perfection*. Atlanta: Scholars Press, 1990.

Must a Jew Believe Anything? London and Portland: Vallentine Mitchell and Co., 1999.

Kellner, Menachem Marc (ed.). *The Pursuit of the Ideal: Jewish Writings of Steven Schwarzschild*. Albany: SUNY Press, 1990.

Kenny, Anthony. *The Five Ways*. New York: Schocken Books, 1969.

Kochen, Lionel. *Jews, Idols and Messiahs: The Challenge from History*. Oxford and Cambridge, MA: Basil Blackwell, 1990.

Kreisel, Howard. *Maimonides' Political Thought: Studies in Ethics, Law, and the Human Ideal.* Albany: State University of New York Press, 1999.

Leakey Richard. *The Origin of Humankind.* New York: Basic Books, 1994.

Levi Ben Gershon (Gersonides). *Milhamot adonai.* English translation by Seymour Feldman. *The Wars of the Lord.* Philadelphia: Jewish Publication Society of America, 1985.

Levinas, Emmanuel. *Totality and Infinity: An Essay on Exteriority.* English translation by Alphonso Lingis. Pittsburgh: Duquesne University Press, 1961.

Ethics and Infinity. English translation by Richard A. Cohen. Pittsburgh: Duquesne University Press, 1985.

Time and the Other. English translation by Richard A. Cohen. Pittsburgh: Duquesne University Press, 1987.

Nine Talmudic Readings. English translation by Annette Aronowicz. Blooming-ton: Indiana University Press, 1990.

Levinson, Bernard M. *Deuteronomy and the Hermeneutics of Legal Innovation.* New York and Oxford: Oxford University Press, 1997.

Lewis, David. *Counterfactuals.* Boston: Harvard University Press, 1973.

On the Plurality of Worlds. Oxford: Blackwell, 1986.

Maimonides, Moses. *Dalalah al-chairin.* Hebrew translation by Joseph Bahir David Kapach. Jerusalem: Mosad ha-rav kook, 1072. English translation by Shlomo Pines. *The Guide of the Perplexed.* Chicago: University of Chicago Press, 1963. (Referred to as *Guide.*)

Mishneh Torah, hilchot yesodei hatorah. Brooklyn, NY: Moznaim, 1989.

Malcolm, Norman. "The Ontological Argument." *Philosophical Review* 69 (Jan., 1960). (Republished in *Knowledge and Certainty.* Englewood Cliffs, NJ: Prentice-Hall, 1965. Pp. 141–162.)

Knowledge and Certainty. Englewood Cliffs, NJ: Prentice-Hall, 1965.

Midrash rabbah. Translated into English under the editorship of H. Freedman and Maurice Simon. London and New York: Soncino Press, 1983.

Mikraot gedolot. New York: Pardes Publishing House, 1951.

Newton, Isaac. *Philosophice Naturalis Principia Mathematica.* English translation by I. Bernard Cohen and Ane Whitman. Berkeley: University of California Press, 1999.

Novak, David. *The Election of Israel: The Idea of the Chosen People.* Cambridge: Cambridge University Press, 1995.

Ochs, Peter. *Peirce, Pragmatism and the Logic of Scripture.* Cambridge: Cambridge University Press, 1998.

Pascal, Blaise. *Pensées and Other Writings.* English translation by Honor Levi. Oxford and New York: Oxford University Press, 1995.

Perry, John. "Frege on Demonstratives." *Philosophical Review* 86 (1977), 474–497. "The Problem of Essential Indexicals" *Nous* 13 (1979), 3–22.

Peters, Ted. *Genetics: Issues of Social Justice.* Cleveland: Pilgrim, 1998.

Pinker, Steven. *How the Mind Works.* New York: W. W. Norton & Co., 1997.

Plantinga, Alvin. *God and Other Minds.* Ithaca: Cornell University Press, 1967.

The Nature of Necessity. Oxford: Oxford University Press, 1975.

Plato. *Parmenides*. English translation by Francis M. Cornford in *Plato and Parmenides: Parmenides' Way of Truth and Plato's Parmenides*. Indianapolis and New York: Bobbs-Merrill, 1939.

The Republic of Plato. English translation by Francis M. Cornford. New York: Oxford University Press, 1945.

Timaeus. English translation by Francis M. Cornford in *Plato's Cosmology*. London: Routledge and Kegan Paul, 1966. (First published by Kegan Paul, Trench, Trubner and Co., 1937.)

Poma, Andrea. *The Critical Philosophy of Hermann Cohen*. English translation by John Denton. Albany: SUNY Press, 1997.

Prior, A. N. "Thank Goodness That's Over." *Philosophy* 34 (1959), 12ff.

Proudfoot, Wayne. *Religious Experience*. Berkeley: University of California Press, 1985.

Rawls, John. *A Theory of Justice*. Cambridge, MA: Harvard University Press, 1971.

Rolston, Holmes. *Genes, Genesis, and God: Beyond Selfishness to Shared Values*. New York: Columbia University Press, 1997.

Rosenzweig, Franz. *Der Stern der Erlösung*. Frankfurt a.M.: J. Kaufmann, 1921. English translation by William Hallo. *The Star of Redemption*. Boston: Beacon Press, 1971, and Notre Dame, IN: Notre Dame Press, 1985.

Der Stern der Erlösung, in *Franz Rosenzweig: Der Mensch und sein Werk, Gesammelte Schriften*. Vol. II. Haag: Martinus Nijhoff, 1976. (Referred to as *The Star*.)

Ross, James. *Philosophical Theology*. New York: Bobbs-Merrill, 1969.

Rowe, William L. *The Cosmological Argument*. New York: Fortress Press, 1975.

Saadia Ben Joseph. *Sefer emunot ve-de'ot* English translation by Samuel Rosenblatt. *The Book of Beliefs and Opinions*. New Haven: Yale University Press, 1948.

Samuelson, Norbert. "On Proving God's Existence." *Judaism* 16,1 (1967), 21–36.

"That the God of the Philosophers is not the God of Abraham, Isaac, and Jacob." *Harvard Theological Review* 65,1 (1972), 1–27.

"Gersonides' Account of God's Knowledge of Particulars." *Journal of the History of Philosophy* 10 (Oct., 1972), 399–416.

"The Problem of Future Contingents in Medieval Jewish Philosophy," John R. Sommerfeldt and E. Rozanne Elder (eds.), *Studies in Medieval Culture*, vol. VI. Kalamazoo: The Medieval Institute, Western Michigan University, 1976. Pp. 71–82.

Gersonides on God's Knowledge of Particulars. Toronto: Pontifical Institute of Mediaeval Studies, 1977.

"Halevi and Rosenzweig on Miracles," in David R. Blumenthal (ed.), *Approaches to Judaism in Medieval Times*. Brown Judaic Studies 54. Chico, CA: Scholars Press, 1984. Pp. 157–172.

An Introduction to Modern Jewish Philosophy. Albany: State University Press of New York, 1989.

"Divine Attributes as Moral Ideals in Maimonides' Theology," in Ira Robinson, Lawrence Kaplan, and Julien Bauer (eds.), *The Theology of*

Maimonides: Philosophical and Legal Studies. Studies in the History of Philosophy 17. Lewiston, Queenston and Lampeter: Edwin Mellen Press, 1991. Pp. 69–76.

"Maimonides' Doctrine of Creation." in *Harvard Theological Review* 84,3 (1991), 249–271.

"God: The Present Status of the Discussion," in Steven T. Katz (ed.), *Frontiers of Jewish Thought.* Jerusalem, London, Paris, Buenos Aires and East Sydney: B'nai B'rith Books, 1992. Pp. 43–59.

The First Seven Days: A Philosophical Commentary on the Creation of Genesis. Atlanta: Scholars Press, 1993.

Judaism and the Doctrine of Creation. Cambridge: Cambridge University Press, 1994.

"The Logic of Interreligious Dialogue," in Thomas Dean (ed.), *Religious Pluralism and Truth: Essays on Cross-Cultural Philosophy of Religion.* Albany: State University of New York Press, 1995. Pp. 133–149.

"A Case Study in Jewish Ethics – Three Jewish Strategies for Solving Theodicy." in *Journal of Jewish Thought and Philosophy* 5 (1996), 177–190.

A User's Guide to Franz Rosenzweig's Star of Redemption. Richmond: Curzon Press, 1999.

Seeskin, Kenneth. *Searching for a Distant God: The Legacy of Maimonides.* New York and Oxford: Oxford University Press, 2000.

Sefer ha-aggadah. Edited by Ch. N. Bialik and Y. Ch. Rabinitzki. Tel Aviv: Dvir, 1956.

Smith, Brian Cantwell. *On the Origin of Objects.* Cambridge, MA: The MIT Press, 1996.

Spinoza, Baruch. *Tractatus Theologico-Politicus.* English translation by A. G. Wernham. Oxford: Oxford University Press, 1965.

Stace, W. T. *Mysticism and Philosophy.* Philadelphia: Lippincott, 1960.

Strawson, Peter F. *Individuals.* New York: Anchor Books, 1963.

Swinburne, Richard. *The Existence of God.* Oxford: Clarendon Press, 1979.

Tattersall, Ian. *The Fossil Trail: How We Know What We Think We Know about Human Evolution.* New York and Oxford: Oxford University Press, 1995.

Tirosh-Rothschild (Samuelson), Hava. "Jewish Philosophy on the Eve of Modernity," in Daniel H. Frank and Oliver Leaman (eds.), *History of Jewish Philosophy.* Routledge History of World Philosophies 2. London and New York: Routledge, 1997. Pp. 499–573.

Vlastos, Gregory. "Postscript to the Third Man: A Reply to Mr. Geach," in R. E. Allen (ed.), *Studies in Plato's Metaphysics.* New York: The Humanities Press, 1965. Pp. 279–292.

"The Third Man Argument in the Parmenides," in R. E. Allen (ed.), *Studies in Plato's Metaphysics.* New York: The Humanities Press, 1965. Pp. 231–265.

Vonnegut, Kurt. *Cat's Cradle.* New York: Dell Publishing, 1998.

Wainwright, William. *Mysticism.* Madison: University of Wisconsin Press, 1981.

Weinberg, Steven. *The First Three Minutes.* New York: Bantam, 1977.

Westfall, Richard S. *Never at Rest.* Cambridge: Cambridge University Press, 1980.

Wilson, Edward O. *On Human Nature*. Cambridge: Harvard University Press, 1978.

Wolfson, Elliot R. *Through A Speculum That Shines: Vision and Imagination in Medieval Jewish Mysticism*. Princeton: Princeton University Press, 1994.

"Jewish Mysticism: A Philosophical Overview," in Daniel H. Frank and Oliver Leaman (eds.), *History of Jewish Philosophy*. Routledge History of World Philosophies 2. London and New York: Routledge, 1997. Pp. 450–498.

Wyschogrod, Edith. *Saints and Postmodernism: Revising Moral Philosophy*. Chicago and London: University of Chicago Press, 1990.

Wyschogrod, Michael. *The Body of God*. San Francisco: Harper and Row, 1989.

Index of names

Index of subjects